FLAUBERT AND HENRY JAMES

FLAUBERT AND HENRY JAMES

A Study in Contrasts

by

DAVID GERVAIS

First published 1978 by
THE MACMILLAN PRESS LTD
London and Basingstoke
Associated companies in Delhi
Dublin, Hong Kong, Johannesburg, Lagos
Melbourne, New York, Singapore, Tokyo

Typeset in Great Britain by
R & R CLARK LTD
Edinburgh

British Library Cataloguing in Publication Data

Gervais, David
Flaubert and Henry James
1. James, Henry – Criticism and interpretation
2. Flaubert, Gustave – Criticism and interpretation
I. Title
813′.4   PS2124
ISBN 0-333-23668-8

Printed in Hong Kong

Pour Marie-Marthe

CONTENTS

Preface

An interest in a foreign literature may begin from an interest in the literature written in one's own language. We sometimes travel to understand our native land better, how its culture has strengthened or curtailed the way we look at things. Readers of foreign literature, like travellers, never quite detach themselves from their own national cast of mind; it is a glass through which everything they see is subtly coloured. Yet, like the Claude glass of the eighteenth-century connoisseurs, it can shed a light on things which makes them give up previously unnoticed aspects of themselves. We expect an Anglo-Saxon reader of French literature, like Henry James, to be often mistaken simply because he is not French, but we also hope that he will put us on to things that most French readers would miss.

In James's *Portraits of Places*, there is a fine account of the effect of comparing one country to another. It can serve as well as a shrewd counsel to the literary *comparatiste*:

> It is hard to say exactly what is the profit of comparing one race with another, and weighing in opposed groups the manners and customs of neighbouring countries; but it is certain that as we move about the world we constantly indulge in this exercise. This is essentially the case if we happen to be infected with the baleful spirit of the cosmopolite – that uncomfortable consequence of seeing many lands and feeling at home in none. To be a cosmopolite is not, I think, an ideal; the ideal should be to be a concentrated patriot. Being a cosmopolite is an accident, but one must make the best of it. If you have lived about, as the phrase is, you have lost that sense of the absoluteness and the sanctity of the habits of your fellow-patriots which once made you so happy in the midst of them. You have seen that there are a great many *patriae* in the world, and that each of these is filled with excellent people for whom the local idiosyncrasies are the only thing that is not rather barbarous. There comes a time when one set of customs, wherever it may be found, grows to seem to you about as provincial as another; and then I suppose it may be said of you that you have become a cosmopolite.[1]

James wears his own cosmopolitanism urbanely but not lightly. The 'cosmopolite' is both attractive and frightening to him. The attraction comes out in the knowing tone of phrases like, 'You have seen that there are a great many *patriae* in the world . . .' but he also

senses that such knowingness can lead to a spirit of arid detachment.
He is clearly struck by the danger of his judgements of foreign
countries acquiring an empty complacency, should he lose his
American viewpoint for judging them from. Like some kinds of
literary traveller, the 'cosmopolite' can easily slip into the illusion
that he is surveying the whole field from above. There are parts of
T. S. Eliot's *Selected Essays* that give an idea of what this 'baleful
spirit' can do. James, who was less given to wearing his reading on
his sleeve, seems always to have approached French literature in full
awareness that he himself was an Anglo-Saxon, with his heritage
from the novel in English right at his fingertips. His criticism of
Flaubert is that of a novelist engaged in learning about his own
art, always eager to take a new and foreign lesson or to profit from
his subject's mistakes, always conscious that he has to apply what
he learns, just as he judges it, in terms of a different tradition. It
is for this reason that he was able to offer so formidable a challenge
to the Anglo-Saxon admirer of Flaubert, and that one only gets
the full benefit of his criticism of Flaubert's novels by turning too
to what he did in his own. It is in this way, and not to track down
Flaubert's 'influence' on James, that this book needs to be com-
parative.

There is a subtle account of creative learning in one of Proust's
essays on Ruskin, a writer to whom he felt deeply indebted:

> Mediocre minds generally imagine that to let one's self be guided
> in this way by the books one admires is to rob one's judgement
> of a portion of its independence. 'What does it matter to you
> what Ruskin felt: you must feel for yourself.' Such an opinion is
> founded on a psychological error which will be apparent to
> anyone who, having undertaken this spiritual discipline, feels its
> effect in an infinite enlargement of his powers of understanding
> and feeling which yet never paralyses his critical sense. . . . For
> such voluntary servitude is itself the beginning of liberty. There
> is no better way of discovering what one's own feelings are than
> to try to recreate in one's self what has already been felt by a
> master. It is in this searching effort that we bring our own thought
> to light along with his.[2]

James's relation to Flaubert, like Proust's to Ruskin, can only be
understood if we leave each writer free to confront the other,
undistorted by the links which the literary historian makes between
them. It is a relation made up of things James developed and things
he reacted against, of lessons learnt and lessons skipped. In it we
see the two novelists facing each other across time like two mirrors,
each reflecting things in the other and receiving a reflection back

from it. To think of them together is a way of understanding them
both, as long as we first take both separately. Thus, a direct comparison of their work is left to my last chapter, when it can be
grounded in independent readings of each of them. The advantage
of such comparison is that it gives a critic something against which
to measure his sense of a writer's greatness, rather than just pro-
moting him to some individual eminence, somewhere between
Valhalla and limbo. The comparison also has the merit of putting
the reader, whose taste will be different, on guard.

Flaubert and James are too different for there to be any point in
making them out to be less unlike each other than they really are.
That spoils one's chance of seeing their relation as a way of getting
clearer what the assumptions of one's own cultural tradition are. A
French writer would write a very different book on the subject from
this one. My title does not propose yet another factitious hybrid – a
Flaubert/James to put beside Dickens/Kafka or Hardy/Lawrence
or Ibsen/Shaw – since its stress is on 'contrast', not assimilation.
The notion of 'influence' too often makes art out to be an imitation
of earlier art with 'genius' stirred in, like pectin in jam, to make it
set. It also tends to put too much emphasis on the influenced writer
so that the influencer's work gets inertly left as a known quantity.
Great writers are great because they are unlike previous great
writers. Blake wrote that:

> I do not believe that Rafael taught Mich. Angelo, or that Mich.
> Angelo taught Rafael, any more than I believe that the Rose
> teaches the Lilly how to grow, or the Apple tree teaches the Pear
> tree how to bear fruit.[3]

It follows that only when we have tried to let a writer breathe in
his own air can comparison begin.

A writer is not, of course, simply a supernatural apparition.
Proust did not read Ruskin, or James Flaubert, just to find out
how different they were themselves. They wanted to transform
another vision into a vision of their own. Roland Barthes, attacking
the notion of 'influence' while also casting a doubtful eye over the
notion of 'genius', maintains that 'a work of art begins precisely at
the point where it deforms its model'.[4] It is in this deforming, or
transforming, in James's own novels, that my subject comes together.
James never depended on Flaubert as, for a short time in his earliest
work, he depended on Balzac. In the preface to *Roderick Hudson*
he recalled that, 'one nestled, technically, in those days, and with
yearning, in the great shadow of Balzac'.[5] He never saw Flaubert
as a 'shadow' to nestle in: he was sometimes more like an enemy.
The critical interest of their relation is therefore undiminished by

the objection that, 'to focus James's art against a background of continental writers is not to focus it at all.' I do not want to 'focus
James's art' *against* any source or to see Flaubert's, which I take to
be greater, as a mere 'background' to James.

In an essay on Turgenev in *French Poets and Novelists*, James
says that, 'The great question as to a poet or novelist is, How does
he feel about life? What, in the last analysis, is his philosophy?' It
is a question which James would not, perhaps, have relished answering himself. A riposte he wrote about the reception of one of his
early tales is typical of how he feels 'about life':

> Nothing is my last word about anything – I am interminably
> super-subtle and analytic – and with the blessing of heaven, I shall
> live to make all sorts of representations of all sorts of things. It
> will take a much cleverer person than myself to discover my last
> impression – among all these things – of anything.'

As well as suggesting the intelligence and elasticity of imagination
which are James's strengths, this immodest piece of modesty prompts
an interesting question about his art: Did he ever go to the bottom
of his 'philosophy'? (One might argue that it was a failure to do so
which kept him so prolific.) My discussion of *The Portrait of a Lady*
tries to argue that his art holds back from the brink of its own
deepest insights. In some ways, if we read between the lines of his
brilliantly tentative essays on Flaubert, we can get an idea of what
those insights were. For James confronted Flaubert essentially on
the ground of the difference in their philosophies. This book will
try to analyse that difference in terms which will not, perhaps, win
a ready assent. I believe that James's 1902 essay on Flaubert shows
a novelist whose own art is untragic failing to respond fully to a
novelist whose art, at its best, can be tragic. 'At its best' because,
like so many nineteenth-century novelists, Flaubert often fell just
short of the tragic utterance he was sometimes capable of.' The
same thing might, with more reservations, be said of James too, for
there are more obvious bids at tragedy in his novels than in Flaubert's. I myself think he is strongest as a writer of comedy though.

This 'study in contrasts', then, has as its final purpose to begin
a discussion of the possibility of tragic art in the novels of the
nineteenth century. This theme is the occasion of an on-going
meditation which runs right through my book. Some readers of
Flaubert and James may have less interest in it and it is not something about which I have a definite line to argue for. It is central
because of the questions it enables the book to raise.

1977   D. G.

Acknowledgements

In this, the last and pleasantest page of a book to write, I want to express my thanks to all those people who have helped me to develop my thoughts about Flaubert and James. A full list – of colleagues, students, post-graduates and so on – would be too long. I can only thank by name the following people, who have read parts of this book as they were written and with whom I have enjoyed many conversations on Flaubert and James: Professor K. J. Fielding, Dr A. D. Hook, Professor D. W. Jefferson, H. A. Mason, Dr K. M. Newton, Dr J. P. Parrinder, Professor A. J. Steele, Dr T. J. Worthen. Two debts must be singled out. Geoffrey Strickland read the whole manuscript at an earlier stage and his criticisms, both written and in talk, have been invaluable. I would like to thank J. M. Newton for his talk, criticism, encouragement and, even more than these, for his own work, not only on James, which has been a constant source of suggestion. It ought to be more widely known than it is. Needless to say, the book has many faults, despite the help it has had, and the faults are my own. I don't know how to put into acknowledger's prose what I owe to my wife who, for a long time, has been saddled with the burden of an author's company and yet managed to encourage him. All the translations in the book, by the way, are my own, done with her help.

The publishers and I are grateful to Laurence Pollinger Ltd and the Estate of the late Mrs Frieda Lawrence for permission to quote the extracts from *Phoenix I* and *Phoenix II* by D. H. Lawrence; also to the editors of *The Cambridge Quarterly* for permission to use as Chapter 2 a slightly altered version of an article originally published by me in their journal.

1 Two Versions of Tragedy

I

James's essays on the French novelists are not just literary criticism but a kind of travel writing. Nowhere is this more apparent than in his approach to Balzac, where he is exploring not simply *La Comédie Humaine* but the nature of French society and the French imagination. His response to French novels is open and flexible but free of suggestibility; to every accommodation he makes towards them he brings reservations which are the upshot of his pondered sense of his own Americanness. Pound observed that, 'The essence of James is that he is always "settling-in", it is the ground-tone of his genius.'[1] With Flaubert he is always trying to 'settle in' and never quite managing to. To see why this is one has to look at what it meant to be a young American in Europe in the decade after the Civil War.

The expatriate often leaves his native land in the hope that away from it he will be more free to grow in his own way. Abroad, the fancy is less bound by norms; one feels detached from the tight-knit web of customs and institutions in which the natives are caught. The experience is one of constantly discovering what those customs and institutions actually are without the attendant obligation to conform to them, save in a nominally polite way. This discovering always includes a large element of guess-work and even invention, which compounds the freedom of being abroad with a freer play of the mind. Observation may be heightened but so too is the instinct to play with reality. James had few prejudices but, the more he lived abroad, the more his imagination embroidered what he found there. Europe gave him not only a greater scope for his acute sense of manners but the constant opportunity to invent a Europe of his own. Nothing could have been less pseudo-European, and his novels are full of pictures of Europe which could never have been written by a European. It is possible to speculate that if James had stayed in America he would have taken longer to liberate his novels from caricatures like Miss Birdseye, in *The Bostonians*, who is always just failing to come to life because she represents some-thing too *known* for him to work at creating. A later comic American like Waymarsh, in *The Ambassadors*, shares some of that aura of mystery possessed by the European characters; James invents him as he goes along.

When a pre-Civil War writer like Hawthorne visited Europe he was able to remain far more comfortably ensconced in his viewpoint

as an American. James's review of the *French and Italian Journals*
describes him as 'the last pure American – attesting by his simple
responses to dark canvas and cold marble his loyalty to a simpler
and less encumbered civilisation'.[2] By James's generation such
assurance was gone. 'An American as cultivated as Hawthorne is
now almost inevitably more cultivated, and, as a matter of course,
more Europeanised, more cosmopolitan.'[3] One of the main elements
of this new cultivation was the reading of the European novelists
in preference to the authors favoured at Concord. Brooks describes
this change in *New England: Indian Summer*:

> . . . the younger men no longer read the Greek and Roman
> authors, who had once afforded the models that stirred the young.
> They read, along with works of science, the new French novelists
> and playwrights, who pictured city life as the only life for
> ambitious men and described the life of the province as dull
> and silly. This change in reading habits was decisive; for, while
> those who had known their Plutarch and Virgil had grown up to
> spacious lives in villages, in hamlets and on farms, as the older
> statesmen and writers abundantly proved, the young men, steeped
> in modern books, were almost all uprooted before they read them.
> This reading confirmed their habits as *déracinés* . . . and Emerson's
> noble saying, 'Make much of your own place', became for them
> a menace and a byword.[4]

Much, though not all, of this applies to the young James. But if his
condition was 'uprooted' it also opened up a new avenue for finding
out what it meant to be an American. He might have argued that
to be American on Hawthorne's provincial terms was to be un-
conscious of half one's Americanness. His own sense of nationality
was sharpened as he came to know better what was meant by Frenchness or Englishness.

Travel must have nurtured James's gift for that ambiguity of
response which makes it so tantalisingly difficult to know quite
where he stands at any given moment. Comparing countries and
literatures reinforced his delicate distaste for drawing conclusions.
In the words of one of his critics, 'if the side he presents to the
English seems "very artistic" and French, his attitude toward the
French themselves is consistently that of the "English-speaking
consciousness".'[5] He epitomised Pater's 'relative spirit', yet without
succumbing to Pater's feline passivity. Whatever he saw or read in
Europe he not only registered but criticised and re-made in his own
imagination, just as, at the end of his life, whenever he read a new
novel, he began re-writing it in his own mind before he had read
it through. The central interest of his biography of the American

sculptor William Wetmore Story, whom he had known in Rome in the early 1870s, is its record of this transfiguring of the Europe of fact. As he reminisces about his Roman past, drawing out its evocations with fond, leisurely nostalgia, James braves 'even the imputation of making a mere Rome of words, talking of a Rome of my own which was no Rome of reality. That comes up as exactly the point – that no Rome of reality was concerned in our experience, that the whole thing was a rare state of the imagination. . . .'[6] All this hardly suggests a *déraciné* weaned away from the culture of his ancestors by modern French fiction. Yet it is quite consonant with James's criticism of French fiction, where he is always wondering how his reading might be transmuted into something new and American. A famous letter written in 1867 to his friend T. S. Perry might serve as an epigraph to this criticism:

> I feel that my only chance for success as a critic is to let all the breezes of the West blow through me at their will. We are Americans born – *il faut en prendre son parti*. I look upon it as a great blessing; and I think that to be an American is an excellent preparation for culture. We have exquisite qualities as a race, and it seems to me that we are ahead of the European races in the fact that more than either of them we can deal freely with forms of civilisation not our own, can pick and choose and assimilate and in short (aesthetically etc.) claim our property wherever we find it. To have no national stamp has hitherto been a regret and a drawback, but I think it not unlikely that American writers may yet indicate that a vast intellectual fusion and synthesis of the various National tendencies of the world is the condition of more important achievements than any we have seen. We must of course have something of our own – something distinctive and homogeneous – and I take it that we shall find it in our moral consciousness, our unprecedented spiritual lightness and vigour.[7]

This 'moral consciousness' determines the tone of his essays on the French novel; everything he wrote about *Madame Bovary* and *L'Education Sentimentale* is pervaded by a regret for the 'spiritual lightness and vigour' he failed to find in them. As he remarked in his essay on Maupassant, 'The feeling of life is evidently, *de part et d'autre*, a very different thing.'[8]

This sense of the relativeness of 'the feeling of life' occupies James's essays on the French novelists quite as much as does the study of 'form', which is sometimes thought to be all that interested him in their work. An early book like *French Poets and Novelists* (1878) records his search for a way of making the French clarity of form compatible with the less clear-cut perceptions of the Anglo-Saxon moral sense. There is a quick reaction to what is taken to be the simple aestheticism of Baudelaire:

> The crudity of sentiment of the advocates of 'art for art' is often a striking example of the fact that a great deal of what is called culture may fail to dissipate a well-seated provincialism of spirit. They talk of morality as Miss Edgeworth's infantile heroes and heroines talk of 'physic' – they allude to its being put into and kept out of a work of art, put into and kept out of one's appreciation of the same, as if it were a coloured fluid kept in a big-labelled bottle in some mysterious intellectual closet. It is in reality simply a part of the essential richness of inspiration. . . .[9]

James is more selective in adopting a French aesthetic than a George Moore, who swallows his francophilia in such deep draughts that he seems at times a mere fan of French literature. The English novelists repay as much study as the French. 'They are inferior in audacity, in neatness, in acuteness, in intellectual vivacity, in the arrangement of material, in the art of characterising visible things. But they have been more at home in the moral world; as people say today they know their way about the conscience.'[10] Perhaps it is smug to treat the 'conscience' so confidently but is is a more serious smugness than that behind Moore's contempt for the way the English novelist sacrificed to the proverbial Young Person. James poked fun at the Young Person himself, in his review of Zola's *Nana*, but he also chose to emphasise the 'humour' of the English novel. Zola, he felt, 'would probably disapprove of humour if he *knew* what it is'.[11] 'Humour' is closely related to the freer moral explorativeness he finds in the English novel. The review of *Nana* stresses 'what saves us in England, in spite of our artistic levity and the presence of the young ladies – this fact that we are by disposition better psychologists, that we have, as a general thing, a deeper, more delicate perception of the play of character and the state of the soul.' (Ibid., p. 280.) Balzac, we are told in *French Poets and Novelists*, 'was neither a poet nor a moralist, though the latter title in France is often bestowed upon him – a fact which strikingly illustrates the Gallic lightness of soil in the moral region.' (p. 138.) In the same vein Flaubert is rebuked for failing to listen at 'the chamber of the soul'.[12] What such judgements reveal is perhaps an impatience with the inheritance of the French novelists from their own moralists, the aphoristic definiteness of perception we associate with a La Rochefoucauld. James crystallises his reservations in a letter he wrote in 1898 to Paul Bourget, after reading one of his novels:

Your love of intellectual daylight, absolutely your pursuit of complexities, is an injury to the patches of ambiguity and the abysses of shadow which really are the clothing – or much of it – of the *effects* that constitute the material of our trade.[13]

Something in a novel should always be withheld to stimulate relative judgements and exercise the faculty of wonder.

James's spirit of relative inquiry and his instinct to play imaginatively with reality combine to create the form of his novels, a form which composes social observation into often slightly fantastic situations which the novelist has the power and freedom to arrange as he wishes. This is particularly so in his work during the 1890s where, in some of the tales involving ghosts or writers, he treads a tight-rope between the realistic and the far-fetched and seems to arrogate realism to the projection of personal myths. The most extreme example is *The Sacred Fount*, where everything is built around the whimsical idea, shared by James and the narrator, that in all marriages one partner grows younger by drawing life from the other, who grows visibly older. The narrator of the novel is a kind of Jamesian novelist, eagerly seeking to dominate reality by structuring it to accord with his own fancy. Were it not for James's irony at his expense one might almost say that the novel was written by a more intelligent Emma Bovary. James constructs his novels on very different principles from those of the French novelists. In *Le Père Goriot* or *Madame Bovary* the rigorous concatenation of events is essentially a mirror of the pressure of social forces on the leading characters. This pressure is more a function of the author's realism than of his fancy and Balzac and Flaubert do not sponsor the dreams of Goriot and Emma as James sponsors the fancies of the narrator of *The Sacred Fount*. This helps to explain some of James's discomfort with the novels of Balzac, Flaubert and Zola. His admiration for their social documentation always contains a lurking doubt that fidelity to the real may inhibit the imagination. In the 1902 essay of Zola, *L'Assommoir* is described as giving the reader 'almost insupportably the sense of life' and Balzac is thought of as being 'personally overtaken by life, as fairly hunted and run to earth by it'.[14] However tragic the plots of James's own novels he always accords his characters a last refuge in pyrrhic moral heroism, a let-out through renunciation that is closed to Goriot or Emma Bovary or Zola's Gervaise. It is perhaps a refuge which his imagination also accords to himself and his readers.

To think of the refuges found by Isabel Archer or Fleda Vetch or Milly Theale is to come back to the 'humour' James missed in Zola and, more precisely, to the 'good-humour' which he felt so many of the French novelists lacked. In his review of Flaubert's letters his sympathy goes more naturally to George Sand's consoling replies to Flaubert's bitter outbursts than to Flaubert himself:

> Their letters are a striking lesson in the difference between good-humour and bad, and seem to point the moral that either form has only to be cultivated to become our particular kind of intelligence.[15]

The cheerful complacency of 'only to be cultivated' is characteristic. The same point is made about Maupassant too:

> Even those of our novelists whose manner is most ironic pity life more and hate it less than M. de Maupassant and his great initiator Flaubert. It comes back to our good-humour (which may apparently also be an artistic force). . . . (*Partial Portraits*, p. 273.)

How far did this belief in 'good-humour' issue from a real gaiety and how far was it a kind of insurance against the tragic sense of life? James himself was often ironic or evasive about it. There is a revealing letter written to Grace Norton, who often evoked his most personal statements, in which he tells her that, 'You really take too melancholy a view of human life, and I can't afford – literally haven't the moral means – to hold intercourse with you on that basis. I am never in high spirits myself, and I can only get on by pretending that I am. But alas you won't pretend – that you are; and scarcely even that I am.' [16] It would be difficult to say whether the tone of this is deeply serious or jocular.

This brief account of James's response to the French novelists can be brought to a point by quoting another letter to Grace Norton, in which he is again trying to comfort her melancholy. It gives eloquent expression to all those things in James which make his 'philosophy' so radically different from Flaubert's:

> You are not isolated, verily, in such states of feeling as this – that is, in the sense that you appear to make all the misery of all mankind your own; only I have a terrible sense that you give all and receive nothing – that there is no reciprocity in your sympathy – that you have all the affliction of it and none of the returns. However – I am determined not to speak to you except with the voice of stoicism. I don't know *why* we live – the gift of life comes to us from I don't know what source or for what purpose; but I believe we can go on living for the reason that (always of course up to a certain point) life is the most valuable thing we know anything about, and it is therefore presumptively a great mistake to surrender it while there is any yet left in the

cup. In other words consciousness is an illimitable power, and though at times it may seem to be all consciousness of misery, yet in the way it propagates itself from wave to wave, so that we never cease to feel, and though at moments we appear to, try to, pray to, there is something that holds one in one's place, makes it a standpoint in the universe which it is probably good not to forsake. You are right in your consciousness that we are all echoes and reverberations of the *same*, and you are noble when your interest and pity as to everything that surrounds you, appears to have a sustaining and harmonising power. Only don't, I beseech you, *generalise* too much in these sympathies and tendernesses – remember that every life is a special problem which is not your's but another's, and content yourself with the terrible algebra of your own. Don't melt too much into the universe, but be as solid and dense and fixed as you can. We all live together, and those of us who love and know, live so most. We help each other – even unconsciously, each in our own effort, we lighten the effort of others, we contribute to the sum of success, make it possible for others to live. Sorrow comes in great waves – no one can know that better than you – but it rolls over us, and though it may almost smother us it leaves us on the spot, and we know that if it is strong we are stronger, inasmuch as it passes and we remain. It wears us, uses us, but we wear it and use it in return; and it is blind, whereas we after a manner see. My dear Grace, you are passing through a darkness in which I myself in my ignorance see nothing but that you have been made wretchedly ill by it; but it is only a darkness, it is not an end, or *the* end. Don't think, don't feel, any more than you can help, don't con-clude or decide, don't do anything but *wait*. Everything will pass, and serenity and *accepted* mysteries and disillusionments, and the tenderness of a few good people, will remain. You will do all sorts of things yet, and I will help you. The only thing is not to *melt* in the meanwhile. I insist upon the necessity of a sort of mechanical condensation – so that however fast the horse may run away there will, when he pulls you up, be a somewhat agitated but perfectly identical G. N. left in the saddle.[17]

James seems to feed off his own emotionality, to be moved by his own sense of pathos. The bid for transcendence is a characteristically un-tragic way of dealing with tragic experience. He is reluctant to conceive of an 'end' to 'consciousness' or to consider whether the recognition of such an 'end' might entail a chastening spiritual growth rather than simply a feeling of being nullified. All his intelligence and persuasiveness is devoted to convincing Grace Norton that her anguish is private. What she needs is a 'standpoint in the universe', not her knowledge that 'no man is an island'. The reliance on self that James argues for, even in his 'voice of stoicism', is less tragic than it seems. The job of the self is to wait until the 'universe' changes again and the self is 'left in the saddle'. Beneath the gentleness of the letter is an intense faith in will, an unbounded sense of the power of 'consciousness'. The prose vibrates with a beautiful illusion of tragedy, not a staring into the tragic core of the real.

James's letter provides a pertinent contrast to Flaubert's thought about death and the power of consciousness. Here is part of a letter he wrote in 1846, just after the death of his sister Caroline and only a few months after his father's death:

> . . . you must have told yourself . . . that in time I would console myself for my father's death and at last end up by returning to the calmness of which I have been deprived for so long. Oh yes! calmness! Is there any for the paving stones of the high road, pounded by the waggon-wheels? Is there any for the anvil?
>
> In placing my life beyond the common sphere, in withdrawing myself from vulgar ambitions and vanities in order to exist in some more solid element, I had imagined that I would obtain, if not happiness, at least repose. What a mistake! Man is always there inside us, with all his bowels and the powerful links which bind him to humanity. Nobody can escape from suffering.[18]

This letter gives an effective reply to James but it is also interesting because it finishes by contradicting itself; Flaubert urges his correspondent never to marry or have children, so as to give as few hostages to evil fortune as possible. There is no point in courting suffering but this attitude merely throws away what spiritual maturity suffering has brought him. The 'atrocious injustice' of death makes him reject the pursuit of 'happiness' out of hand. Flaubert's thought is characterised by a constant struggle between two kinds of impersonality; the first is authentic and helps him to see life and death (especially death) with real clarity; the second is spurious and, like the end of this letter, tries to evade suffering by cancelling the human bonds which his true impersonality reveals to him. In the first kind a sense of commonalty is liberating; in the second it is a bondage which has to be overcome by pride and fantasy. At different moments, he conceived of the art he aspired to create in either way. Although he came to see the spurious impersonality of his juvenilia as expressing something unresolved in his non-artist self, that self went on re-surfacing in his mature work, jarring disconcertingly with his true impersonality. The manipulation of the blind beggar at the end of *Madame Bovary*, for instance, is one place where his art did not transcend personal emotion and will. It is, I suggest, precisely when art is only imperfectly impersonal that the critic has to turn to an artist's biography and this is why, to understand the mind behind both Flaubert's true and his false impersonality, one needs to turn to his marvellous *Correspondence*. Did the impersonality of his best work spring from the constant meditation on the ideal of *impassibilité* in his letters or, as one sometimes suspects, was it achieved in spite of it? For his thought about the artist's impersonality was closely bound-up with his thought about the artist's power and these two concerns, though different, both contributed to the feeling for form in his novels. The letters do not always give us the essential Flaubert, though they give us an essential part of him. In the earlier ones one often has the impression of a beach on which the flotsam and jetsam of European Romanticism has been washed up, and those he wrote to Louise Colet, during the composition of *Madame Bovary,* sometimes bring out the *cabotin* in him as much as the truth-teller. Yet the best letters also reveal more of his anger, his lyricism and his joviality than he cared to divulge in his finished work. They suggest, above all, the 'philosophy' behind the novels, what James called the 'great question' that has to be asked about any artist.

II

The cadence of lament at the passage of time pervades Flaubert's letters from beginning to end. 'How depleted everything becomes, how transitory, what a continuous melting-away life is!' (*Corr.,* II, p. 10.) This is from 1847 but its mood is almost that of his laments for Gautier and George Sand over twenty years later. They are less lyrical and more bitter, but they express essentially the same feeling. Flaubert's sense of mortality seems almost to have pre-dated his real experience of life. When the hero of *Mémoires d'un Fou* (1838) wonders whether it is his destiny to go through life feeling 'worn-out before bearing the burden and out-of-breath before beginning to run', he does so because his sense of death makes human effort seem unreal to him.[19] This *ennui* is more than a Romantic state of being 'half in love with easeful death': the young Flaubert carries on a positive love affair with the next world. In the *Mémoires* he adopts the mask of an old man through which to recount his experience and elsewhere he explains (or romanticises) his sense of death by playing with the ideas of metempsychosis and re-incarnation. He liked to think that he was conscious of his previous existences, as a boatman on the Nile and suchlike. They helped rationalise his feeling of being able to see through life before actually living it. The hero of *Novembre* (1842) claims that, 'it sometimes seems to me as if I have existed for centuries and that my being contains the débris of a thousand past existences'. (*OJI*, II, pp. 163–4.) An exceptional knowledge of the nature of things compensates him for his *ennui*. This myth of past experience is taken as absolving him from any commitment to live in the future. In more histrionic moments Flaubert regards his sense of death as a motive for pride, as when he tells Louise Colet, 'I have never seen a child without thinking that he will become an old man, nor a cradle without musing about a grave. The contemplation of naked woman makes me dream of her skeleton.' (*Corr.*, I, p. 221.) Such statements betray a relish of the grotesque which is too boyishly solemn to give expression to the tragic feeling beneath at which Flaubert is still only groping and gesturing. He is too intrigued by his own feelings to say much to ours. Much of the talk about death in the early writings makes us think of Flaubert more as a Peter Pan than as a precocious Tiresias. As Sartre says, 'A person who writes: "I was born with the desire to die", is making an observation about his own particular conditioning and not the human condition.'[20] Yet *Madame Bovary*, as Sartre would admit, does speak to 'la condition humaine' and we have to look first to Flaubert's own conditioning to see how it came to do so.

Still a child, Flaubert would often peep and pry into his father's dissection theatre in the Hôtel-Dieu in Rouen where the family lived. Things which repelled him fascinated him too and he was as fascinated by corpses as he was by the *bourgeois*. This fascination with death fuelled his appetite for making generalisations about life. In *Art et Progrès*, the newspaper he and his friend Ernest Chevalier wrote together at the start of their schooldays at the Collège de Rouen, he announced that this world and hell were one and the same place. If the world was hell to him it must be for everybody else too. The few extant sheets of the paper show him as an endearingly naïf child gleefully spouting the *vanitas vanitatum* of the prophet. Why did the young Flaubert feel on such easy terms with death before he knew any more of life than school came to? An awareness of death ordinarily depends on an awareness of what is precious in the life which death threatens, but the young Flaubert is always saying that life is not precious or that one must be careful not to let it become so. His own explanation is that what other people think of as life really boils down to the same thing as he means by death. His whole fantasy of being on the side of death is a stategy to make himself think just that: he wants to eradicate the quality of surprise from the future and he can do so only by seeing nothing but death in it. In other words, the fixation with death came not from his feeling reconciled to it but from a fear of it which forced him to find a way of getting round the need of reconciling himself to it. By pretending to speak from the realm of death he had the illusion of protecting himself from any death that lay beyond his own ego, in wait for it. Hence the usefulness of his past existences. They put death in the past and took it out of the future where it really belonged: stoicism was a kind of buffer against potential suffering.

In the passage where T. S. Eliot writes of *Othello*, which he sees as Shakespeare's analysis of *bovarysme*, comes this comment which applies very well to the young Flaubert: 'Stoicism is the refuge for the individual in an indifferent or hostile world too big for him; it is the permanent substratum of a number of versions of cheering oneself up. Nietzsche is the most conspicuous modern instance of cheering oneself up.'[21] Flaubert's more mature sense of the slow attrition of time – which Middleton Murry thought his most original contribution to the novel – undercut this kind of evasion. Nonetheless, in 1847, well after the death of Caroline Flaubert, we find him writing, 'All those people who feel a lot, who admit it and weep, are worth more than I am, for I console myself for everything because nothing diverts me and I can give everything up because nothing is necessary to me.' He goes on to recall watching over the body of his dead sister; 'I read Montaigne and my eyes strayed from the book to the corpse; her husband was asleep, groaning, the priest was snoring. I said to myself as I contemplated this scene that forms pass away and only the idea remains, and I shuddered with enthusiasm at the nuances of the writer's style.'[22] Flaubert goes on to say that, turning to look at the stars, he saw that Montaigne himself would eventually pass away too: the stars console him for everything. This is what they do for Othello too, when he blames his tragedy on the 'error of the moon'.

In his early, more personal writings Flaubert often uses the idea of death as the springboard of a desire for the absolute rather than as a *momento mori*: 'Oh! I would willingly give all the women in the world to possess the mummy of Cleopatra!'[23] The mummy is beauty which is dead. To call it up from the past would be to possess an experience which has already been lived before, thus by-passing the succession of partial deaths which constitutes experience in time. Flaubert wishes to transcend his sexuality by projecting it beyond the only sphere in which it can function. (Emma does the same thing at the end of *Madame Bovary* when she kisses the crucifix with virtually sexual passion.) Imagination transforms passion into a fiction of immortality. Yet Flaubert's scepticism is in proportion to his desire; his feeling that the Balzacian energy of his elders is bankrupt in his own generation makes him doubt the power of the imagination too. The Balzac novel which spoke most deeply to his own experience was *Louis Lambert*, in which the hero's flight into mysticism leaves him in an ambiguous state of premature agedness, either mad or in a state of permanent vision, married to the beautiful heroine whom he has never possessed. For the young man who longed for the mummy of Cleopatra, writing in *Novembre* of his hero's egocentric love for a prostitute, mysticism became one with doubt: 'I am afraid of loving only a conception of my mind and of cherishing in her only the love which she has made me dream of.' (*OJI*, II, p. 238.) Because the desire is infinite and its object finite the hero aspires to a love without an object, a kind of spiritual masturbation: 'Oh! if one could extract from one's self everything that is there and make a being out of thought alone!' (*OJI*, II, p. 237.) Life is too elusive and mobile to be caught in an act of possession. Marie, who initiates the hero into love, feels conversely. No man has ever possessed her as she has dreamt of being possessed: 'I'm a virgin! does that make you laugh? But don't I feel all the vague presentiments and the ardent languours of one? I have them all, except for virginity itself.' (*OJI*, II p. 227.) Either way, the self looks in vain for objects to confirm its desires. Its only hope of permanence lies in its own conceptions; the non-self promises nothing but a frustration which constantly subtracts from the freedom of the self. Both Marie and the hero refuse to acknowledge in the non-self an equivalent reality to their own. This marks a stage towards the idea of the artist as a creator without a self, distanced from the world he represents.

The objects of desire necessarily lie in the future; that is, their attainment lies in the desirer's future. Yet in Flaubert the future is unreal except for the premonition of death it brings. Only the old man can be seen through the child, the man in his prime doesn't count. The hero of the early tale *Quidquid Volueris* (1837), the outcast, misunderstood Djalioh who 'seemed born for the tomb' (*OJI*, I, p. 211), helps us explore this strange idea further. Hamlet-like he looks at a skull and exclaims: 'Oh! a death's head! with its hollow, staring eyes, the yellow hue of its surface, its chipped jaw-bone; mightn't reality be there, and truth be nothingness?' (*OJI*, I, p. 217.) If reality is the extinction of the self, then the life in which the self operates must be unreal. Therefore desire is unreal too. So thinks Smarh, the hero of a 'vieux mystère' Flaubert wrote in 1839, after he has been shown a vision of the world by the satanic genius who rules it: 'Farewell then, all those fine dreams and beautiful days which the lying dawn heralded to me, so glorious and so pure. I will thus have glimpsed a world of enthusiasm and transports, and the lightning will have shone before my eyes only to leave me in a gloom, beneath this paradise of thoughts from which the great cold blade of reality separates me for eternity.' (*OJI*, II, pp. 115–6.) The feeling depends on the vestiges of an exultant idea of the self's transcendence but the romantic sense of the self is stifled by a sense of the self's smallness. Man has no hand in making his destiny and no knowledge of its meaning. All that remains to do is to contemplate life from outside the arena of the self. Flaubert rationalises his view of his own destiny into a view of human life as a whole subject as to an inscrutably malignant 'fatalité'; his in fact rather robust sense of gloom and helplessness becomes a way of shirking responsibility for his own life. Let me turn from *Smarh* to a rather later work, *Par les Champs et les Grèves* (1847), the record of his tour of Brittany with Maxime Du Camp. Here is part of a meditation on a telegraph operator, aloft and alone in his cabin, seen during their visit to Nantes:

> The purpose, the aim, the sense of it? Who knows what it is? Does the sailor trouble his head about the land which the sail he guides carries him towards, the postman for the letters he bears, the printer for the book he prints or the soldier for the cause for which he kills and gets himself killed? Aren't we all more or less like this fine fellow, speaking the words we have been taught and have learnt without understanding. Spaced out in a line, looking at each other across the abysses which separate them, the centuries too transmit from one to another the eternal enigma which came to them from afar to go on far beyond them; they gesticulate and stir in the fog, while those who are posted on the mountain tops and make them move forward know no more of things than the poor devils below, who lift their heads to try to guess something of their meaning.[24]

This feeling is less deterministic than it may seem. The tone comes from the prospect of life's mystery and is very much more wondering and perplexed than the confident assertiveness of the passage from *Smarh*. Flaubert is only claiming to have seen through his and everyone else's inevitable ignorance of the meaning of life, he isn't pretending to have seen through life by casting off illusions which most people live by. There is still some posing in the prose but there is now a thought which a reader can identify with too. The passage marks a step towards the more detached irony of *Madame Bovary* by bringing under control the notion of 'fatalité' which Flaubert purloined from the Marquis de Sade. He no longer attributes the mystery of existence to some principle of Evil. What *Smarh* does help us to realise is that this new feeling about fate originated as much in dreams of a resistance to it as in a passive and self-destructive acquiescence.

Quidquid Volueris, which is sometimes seen as an early version of *Madame Bovary*, is a fantasy about resisting fate. It seems at first such a trumped-up performance that one refuses to take it seriously at all. Then it becomes clear that it is its very absurdity which demands to be taken seriously. It is the history of the luckless Djalioh, the offspring of a negro slave and an ape who had been coupled in a prank of his bourgeois master's: he is an outcast, a monster and a wishfully Byronic surrogate for the young author, scorned by people too base to perceive his inner richness and jokily paraded by his master and inventor as a pet. We meet him at the home of his master's *fiancée* Adèle, with whom he promptly falls in love. In loving her, his monstrosity comes home to him because he is sensitive to the fact that he repels her. With human feelings and an animal physique he is doomed to frustration. A victim of the sport of fate, the human (and bourgeois) world has nothing to offer him. Cut off from the immediate non-self in the society of other people, he projects his feelings onto nature. But unlike Emma Bovary, except at rare moments, his Rousseauesque feeling for nature soon turns into a variation on Sade's. He decides that the trick his master played on him in causing his birth was really perpetrated by the universe. If nature is therefore evil he cannot communicate with it either. Instead, his only means of proving the meaningfulness of his feelings is to emulate the persecutions of nature. Only by taking the side of death can he affirm the life inside him. Djalioh's sophistry is ingenious: if nature could echo his feelings, he can echo what he assumes from the joke of his birth to be nature's feelings. This is rather hard on Adèle. When his master marries her and she has a child by him, Djalioh decides that the only way of expressing his love for her is to murder her, then her child and then kill himself. Nature's cruelty to him vindicates his own cruelty to Adèle.

Put like that, the emotional syllogism of Djalioh's actions is just an absurd fantasy about the young Flaubert's desire to write demoralising masterpieces against his fellow-men, as he thought Byron and Rabelais had. But there is a missing link in the equation, a feeling that prompts Djalioh's actions which he shares with his fellows, despite being a monster. This is his sense of the passing of time. To kill himself is the only way he can triumph over time. Again, death is seen not as a symbol of temporality but as its conqueror. This desire to rival time is, I think, the deepest Flaubertian wish in the story and the description of Djalioh's feelings before the murder strikes its most authentic note:

What did the lost past matter to him, or the future which was summed-up by one insignificant word: death? It was the present which he did have, that minute, that instant which obsessed him; it was this same present which he wanted to annihilate, to tread under-foot and slaughter with his own hands. (*OJI*, I, p. 228.)

Forty years later, Flaubert wrote to George Sand: 'one doesn't make one's destiny, one undergoes it. I was a coward in my youth, I was afraid of life!' (*Corr.*, VII, p. 122.) The violence of *Quidquid Volueris*, which is essentially sado-masochistic, is an expression of this *lâcheté* because it is an attempt to sublimate his horror of time passing, which later he was to expend all his art on evoking. This is made clear by a passage in *Novembre* where the hero, as usual, is indulging in his habit of blaming his unhappiness on 'la fatalité':

. . . fate, which had weighed me down from youth on, seemed to me to extend over the entire world, and I watched it manifesting itself in all the doings of men, as universally as the sun shines on the surface of the earth. It became for me an appalling divinity which I worshipped as the Indians worship the walking colossus which marches over their bellies. I took pleasure in my pain and made no effort to get out of it; I even savoured it, with the desperate joy of a sick person who scratches his wound and starts laughing when blood appears on his nails. (*OJI*, II, pp. 184-5.)

Suffering can be embraced with laughter and appetite as long as one is doomed to it. But, as we know from the mature novels, it was not fate which Flaubert was really worried about but time. He didn't want time to pass or to grow older so he wanted to destroy the present moment like Djalioh and be suddenly old like the hero of *Mémoires d'un Fou*. A cult of fate made a better temporary solution to his problem than did the violence of *Quidquid Volueris*.

This analysis has perhaps given too many hostages to the common view that Flaubert was afraid of life and stood away from it. That is not a view to encourage, except, up to a point, in the case of the young Flaubert. It is easy to read the early works too seriously. The most interesting things in them were not written in any critical spirit, and their author clearly enjoyed cultivating a certain rather conventional pose. In *Quidquid Volueris* there is an element of near-farce and one suspects Flaubert of having more sympathy with the prank of Djalioh's master than his sentimental investment in the hero leads one to suppose. There are, in fact, some quite early letters which speak more seriously about the feelings Flaubert projected into his early fiction than the fiction does itself. In one of them, to Louise Colet, he considers his coldness as an 'infirmity, a shameful inner sickness, which I contracted through spending too much time with unhealthy things'. (*Corr.*, II, p. 12.) He is aware

that his ideas about death and fate have been a mask for feelings
he has so far been unable to give expression to. In a letter from
1847, in which he is complaining of his new difficulty in writing –
the early works were written too easily – he confesses this failure:
'It's strange how all my channels of feeling get blocked, how all my
wounds close and make a dyke against the floods of tears within.
The pus falls back inside me. As long as nobody can smell it, that's
all I ask.' (*Corr.*, II, pp. 5–6.) This kind of stern self-examination
would be inconceivable in a man who was simply afraid of life.

The sadistic streak which Flaubert expressed through Djalioh
persisted in his thought about art after he had begun *Madame
Bovary*, though by then it was taking the form of satire rather than
fantasy, exposing the reader and not just his own neuroses: 'It's
a fine thing to be a great writer and hold men in the frying pan
of one's phrases, making them jump in it like chestnuts.' (*Corr.*, II,
p. 329.) Yet satire laid bare the artist's as well as the reader's self,
and Flaubert translated his sense of suffering into art by deeper
means than this:

> No, we are not good, but our faculty of entering into all woes
> and supposing ourselves in their grip is perhaps true human
> charity. Isn't it the effort both of the greatest and the best of
> men to become in this way the centre of humanity, to try, in
> short, to be the general heart where all its diverse veins come
> together? (*Corr.*, III, p. 225.)

A proud spirit of mockery would inevitably cause friction within
the work of an artist who aspired to be a 'cœur général' in this
sense. Yet both satire and sympathy in Flaubert share the same
desire to view life from a more general viewpoint than that of one
individual suffering self. If there is pride in the wish to represent
the 'centre de l'humanité', there is humility and self-abnegation
too. When Flaubert told a prospective biographer that, as an artist,
he had no biography, he was not simply posing. It was what was
most humane in the Artist that dictated his attempt to transcend
self. If James could criticise Flaubert for his coldness in *Madame
Bovary*, it has to be remembered that he did so from the viewpoint
of a belief in the 'finer consciousness' and that, perhaps, he himself
always regarded his own imagination much more as an inseparable
part of his daily self than did Flaubert.

III

In his effort to become a 'cœur général' Flaubert sought more
elaborate ways of universalising his common *mal de siècle*, seeing

his own 'shameful inner sickness' as something attributable, not just to the nineteenth century, but to the timeless anguish of living under the aegis of some meaningless fate. To blame the *bêtise* of the times became for him a way of exonerating history itself, thus effecting a kind of divorce of convenience from the actual society in which he suffered his 'sickness'. This let him off committing himself to any contemporary ideal of human community, making it easier for him to commune with the greater past. It is the rôle of Vigny's Chatterton, the 'paria intelligent'.[25] Though the self can make no relation with other selves, as Emma Bovary finds out, Emma's plight can be duplicated under the sun of ancient Carthage in the operatic person of Salammbô. As Sartre says of *Smarh*, 'the process of disillusion is construed as an objective character of experience'.[26] It is this aspect of the 'cœur général' that I want to get out of the way first, its aspiration not so much to a general feeling of humanity as to a generalisation of humanity's *condition*. It is especially in writing about the past that Flaubert's need to take the other side against man comes out. It needs to be understood without self-righteousness if one is to appreciate the peculiar pathos it generated from his long flirtation with Romantic determinism. We do not need *Un Cœur Simple* to tell us that a lack of sympathy for those who try to change the world may have its roots in tenderness as well as in 'reactionary' politics. 'I'm a catholic and in my heart there is something of the green oozings of Norman cathedrals. My tendernesses of spirit are for the inactive, the ascetics, the dreamers.' (*Corr.*, III, p. 398.) The belief that one's own psyche could not be changed save at the cost of ignoring that it was bounded by death was paralleled by disbelief in social change. Since life repeated death politics must be a repetition of history.

When he describes the dinners he and Flaubert and Le Poittevin had as students Maxime Du Camp recalls that, 'I don't think we talked politics a single time'.[27] In *Par les Champs et par les Grèves* we find Flaubert musing about the dumb portraits and desolate tombs in the Château de Blois: 'History is like the sea, beautiful through what it effaces: the incoming wave removes from the sand all traces of the wave which has gone. One simply tells one's self that there has been a wave and there will be others yet. There lies all its poetry and perhaps all its morality too?' (P. 35.) There is a projected scenario for a novel about the orient in which 'the principal hero should be a barbarian who becomes civilised in contact with a civilised man who becomes a barbarian'.[28] The moral stance behind such comic denials that the world can change is a lofty one. It would presumably have been unnecessary to explore the civilised man and the barbarian from within. Flaubert could have regarded them as a headmaster regards schoolboys brought up on the carpet.

The implication of this parade of moral neutrality is disturbing; it permits an unfettered freedom to judge in which the last contempt is not to exploit this freedom at all. The real freedom is not to stoop to actual freedom. It allowed the young Flaubert some histrionic gestures, like this epigram in *Agonies, Pensées Sceptiques* (1838): 'After all, what is a revolution? a breath of wind which wrinkles the ocean, blows away and leaves the sea agitated.' (*OJI*, I, p. 417.) The apolitical young romantic watches the proceedings from the shore.

The drift of this is made clear by an amusing diary entry about Flaubert made by the Goncourts in 1879. He described to them his long-cherished plan for a novel about the battle of Thermopylae: 'I see in these warriors a troop of devotees of death, marching towards it with gaiety and irony. . . . This book must be for the nations a Marseillaise of a more sublime character.'[29] It was naïve to imagine devotion to death as summoning the energies of revolution, but not defeatist. For even if such devotion is *to* death it must come *from* life: from a conquest of the fear of death. Like the soldiers at Thermopylae, Flaubert was exalted by the contemplation of what he knew would destroy him. Life may be no more than a wind ruffling the sea but, pitted against its adversary, the breath becomes a passion. We are nearer than we thought to the Nietzsche of *The Birth of Tragedy* or the gay, glittering eyes of Yeats's old chinamen in *Lapis Lazuli*, which are equally derisive of modern humanitarian sentiment. Flaubert's fear of death went beyond the effete passivity of *Novembre* to a vitality found in the unblinking welcoming of the tragic. He too transcended *ennui* and depression, although we should not confound his exhilaration with that of Nietzsche and Yeats who both vaunt their sense of tragic joy without undercutting it by comedy as he did.

The revolutionary might not deny this Flaubertian vitality but he would say that it came from dwelling not on the acts of man but on the acts of God. He might describe Flaubert's death-glorifying view of history as mere metaphysical compensation for the depressions left by actual, unfinished history. To reject progress was to accept, if not to exonerate, the régime of the Second Empire, and Flaubert's hatred of the *bourgeois* became compatible with his social success in Imperial circles. Because he had no belief in the future, the present seemed too hollow for it to be other than futile either to attack or defend the régime which incarnated it. All the artist had to do was represent it.[30] Such a politics was hardly new. The seeds of it are there in Edgar Quinet's *Ahasvérus* of 1833, which was one of the young Flaubert's *livres de chevet*:

A strange sickness torments us nowadays. What shall I call it? It is not only yours, Réné, the love of ruins. Ours is more alive and more cutting. It is the sickness of the future. What kills us is more than the feebleness of our thought, it is having to support the weight of the future in the emptiness of the present.[31]

This 'weight' could only be lightened by turning back towards the past. So Flaubert imagined his own previous incarnations, and turned antiquity into a kind of nostalgic utopia. Paradoxically, this provided an escape from determinism.

This paradox goes back to Rousseau, for whom the young Flaubert had had immense admiration. One myth which he enjoyed as much as any of the many myths in the early part of the correspondence is the vision of himself as a kind of lugubrious, latter-day Emile: 'It's hardly money that I want (though I shouldn't object to having some) but liberty, not political liberty but the real kind, that of the wild bird or the savage.' (Corr. Supp., I, pp. 71–2). A strange sentiment for the autumn of 1848. He always drew a contrast between the present and an antiquity in which dream and action might be one, in which life did not need to be lived behind a veil of frustrated desire.[32] To Flaubert the antique was not the classical peace of Augustus but a kind of surrealist nirvana which went beyond good and evil. One of the frankest of the early letters to Louise Colet, written before his journey to Egypt, puts clearly his reaction from her brand of sentimental nineteenth-century liberalism:

You have never, I won't say responded, but even had the slightest pity for my instinct for luxury. A heap of needs that eat me up like vermin, which I let you see as little as possible, have only excited in you the disdain with which the bourgeois crushes me. Three quarters of my day is habitually spent in admiring Nero, Heliogabalus or one of the secondary figures who converge like stars around those suns of plastic beauty. What enthusiasm did you expect me to have for petty moral devotions, for the domestic or democratic virtues you wanted me to admire? (Corr., Bruneau, I, p. 446.)

Flaubert's frustration with the modern *bourgeois* was essentially a regret at the dominance of Christendom.

Perhaps a way of placing this cult of the antique and the non-Christian is to cast our minds forward to the more messianic kind of primitivism we find in Lawrence. On the surface Lawrence shared a similar nostalgia for the animal in man which civilised life had stunted. But for Lawrence the animal lies behind civilised life in another way; it provides him not just with ironic contrast but with an inherent numinous quality in man which is still recoverable and can redeem the modern sentimental mess. *Women in Love* could be read as an attempt to find a positive solution to the kind of romantic politics we get in Flaubert; when Birkin and Ursula return to England at the end of the novel they are faced with the task of extending their new-found sense of being within a sterile community.[33] This was a task which, from Emma's suicide to Bouvard and Pécuchet's decision to return to copying, Flaubert shirked from imposing on his characters. There are some revealing letters from 1847 in which he gives his reactions to the current scandal of the murder of the Duchesse de Praslin by her husband:

> It pleased me in this sense, that I saw that man wasn't yet dead and that the animal in him, despite all the wrappings he is covered in, despite the cages he is put in and the ideas his head is stuffed with, was just the same, with his old natural instincts of baseness and blood. In vain have people wished, since civilisations have been built, to falsify the human lyre. One can raise or drop a few of its chords but it still stays complete. (*Corr.*, II, p. 43.)

Humanity satisfied Flaubert if it were only bad enough. His love of antiquity and of the orient shared the appetite for wildness that is found in the superb lion-hunts of Delacroix, an artist whose politics he also shared.[34] And like Delacroix, he enjoyed moralising over the spectacle of destructive energies and passions:

> The contemplation of an existence made miserable by a violent passion, of whatever sort, is always something instructive and loftily moral. It belittles with ferocious irony so many banal passions and vulgar obsessions that one is satisfied in thinking that the human instrument can vibrate so far and reach such an acute pitch. (*Corr.*, II, p. 32.)

The moral is a serious one, not just a piece of bluffing romantic pride. It is what redeems Emma's desperation from being merely the helpless nerve of a beast at bay. Like all hatreds of the present, Flaubert's could be an affirmation.

IV

Flaubert's notion of impersonality may sometimes lead him into bad faith but it testifies most clearly to his immersion in the world that made him suffer, not to a pose of indifference to it. He did not simply recoil from the contemplation of the non-self into some transcendence of the self. On the contrary: 'the ideal is only fruitful

when one makes *everything* enter into it. It is a work of love and
not of exclusion.' (*Corr.*, IV, p. 15.) One can apply to him Santayana's
fine remark on the tragic poet: 'His philosophy can build only
on such knowledge of the world as the world can give.'[35] His search
for 'impassibilité' was impelled by his wish to focus and place the
demands of the ego, to shed the thin and artificial skin that disguised his nakedness from a world that exposed it. 'Impassibilité' is
far deeper than the stony imperviousness it is often imagined to be.
Perhaps it was wrong to see the young Flaubert as watching the
agitated sea of history from the shore? I did not mean that he had
found a technique for the evasion of suffering. Watching from the
shore, he discovered the distance that could make suffering clearer
to him because it was no longer his own. In Flaubert, moments of
understanding or spiritual release always occur at a distance from
the ordinary world, from Smarh carried into the skies by the devil
to Emma looking down from the window of her room in Yonville
and St Julien transported heavenwards by the leper.

A need to distance himself from his characters in order to convey
what is more than personal in their situations does give Flaubert a
bad name for hardness towards them. Henry James, at least in
French Poets and Novelists, comes up with a version of the stony,
impervious Flaubert:

> M. Flaubert's theory as a novelist, briefly expressed, is to begin
> on the outside. Human life, we may imagine his saying, is before
> all things a spectacle, an occupation and entertainment for the
> eyes. (P. 201.)

This Flaubert has the emotional leisure to step back from the world
and coolly decide how to describe it. Surely words like 'spectacle',
'occupation' and 'entertainment' evoke a far less harrowing novel
than *Madame Bovary* – something more like the meticulous, self-
possessed realism of George Moore's *Esther Waters*. James's account
squares neither with what we know of Flaubert's 'affres du style'
nor with what it can feel like to read him. The art he evokes could
hardly have made Zola feel as if he were 'gripped by an iron fist
which makes one cry out in agony'.[36] James's words suggest a cynic,
not a version of the Commendatore in *Don Giovanni*. This is what
gives his case away: he makes it seem too easy to size Flaubert up.
That inviting 'we may imagine' smoothes over too much. The
slightly pompous and airy generalisation attributed to Flaubert is
difficult to imagine in Flaubert's own mouth. It only suggests the
Flaubert whom Joyce is said to have been thinking of in *A Portrait
of the Artist as a Young Man*, when Stephen Dedalus thinks of the
artist as surveying all creation and paring his fingernails.

Jame's implied antithesis between two ways of rendering experience – from the 'outside' or from a more inward psychological perspective – neatly explains his opposition to Flaubert within the restricted terms of a debate about literary methods. This is characteristic of his tendency to disguise human and philosophical issues beneath discussions of technique.[37] James obscures the real issue by his emphasis on method: that he believed that life was most fully rendered as it was seen from the individual consciousness, whereas Flaubert did not. The distance of the narrator in *Madame Bovary* argues not Flaubert's coldness but his refusal to take the individual as the measure for all things. It was this refusal, and not simply an inadequate technique, which James, the apostle of consciousness, needed to contest. To see Flaubert as primarily a psychologist is to underrate him. He aspires to be more than that when he wants to become a 'cœur général', and his true human charity is, in fact, precisely what James tried to dissuade Grace Norton from.

When Flaubert shows us life through Emma's consciousness he never forgets his satiric intention of sabotaging her romantic subjectivity through a view of the world which her own version of it fails to fit. The emphasis on her illusions is more akin to the spirit of Johnson's *The Vanity of Human Wishes* than to the study of the creativeness of illusion which James makes in *The Ambassadors*. She deceives herself as to the real nature of a world which is forever the same, the sport of the same laws of time and change and death. Reality does not, as it can in later James, change with each different interpretation of it: it is as though it still expressed some universal significance despite its extreme materiality, as if that very materiality had become immanent and metaphysical. Imagination in Flaubert is a cross to be borne, the source of that human blindness which is responsible both for the comedy and for the tragedy of life. There are, it is true, rare moments in *Madame Bovary* when we are encouraged to regard Emma's idealism and her imaginativeness as marks of her spiritual superiority but, in general, Flaubert presents them as a symptom of her inability to face the real. The irony of the prose is both the palpable form taken by her relentless fate, an unfriendly medium in which she wriggles unavailingly to escape, and Flaubert's way of constantly prodding her (and us) to attend to the true nature of the reality she is always embroidering.

In James, the real does not dispel the imagined in this way. His heroes and heroines are more pragmatic and conceive of the two together: where there is tension between them it prompts further flights of imagination.[38] Strether's comic naïveté is at the same time the index of his spiritual distinction. Life is most nobly imagined when seeing it as it is does not preclude the seer from seeing it as it might be. This kind of 'spiritual lightness and vigour' is part of

James's Americanness, derived in part from Hawthorne. His mono-graph on Hawthorne is often read as if the James who wanted to be an American Balzac were simply criticising Hawthorne's lack of Balzacian realism, but the book is much more revealing for its account of James's growing understanding of the essential part which 'romance' had to play in his own equipment as a realist:

> His fancy, which was always alive, played a little with the some-what meagre and angular facts of the colonial period and forth-with converted a great many of them into impressive legends and pictures. There is a little infusion of colour, a little vagueness about certain details, but it is very gracefully and discreetly done, and realities are kept in view sufficiently to make us feel that if we are reading romance, it is romance that rather supplements than contradicts history. . . .
> Hawthorne, to say it again, was not in the least a realist – he was not to my mind enough of one; but there is no genuine lover of the good city of Boston but will feel grateful to him for his courage in attempting to recount the 'traditions' of Washington Street, the main thoroughfare of the Puritan capital.[39]

It is a crucial paradox for James. If Hawthorne embroiders reality this does not mean that he distorts or conceals it but, strangely, that he brings it to life. It is precisely this 'romance' freedom with which James was to invest so many of his American centres of con-sciousness in his own novels.

To explain the criticism of Flaubert quoted a few pages ago it may help to turn to the preface to *The American*, the key statement of James's Hawthornian notion of 'romance'. It begins by noticing that in *The American* he had 'been plotting arch-romance without knowing it'[40] giving free scope to his disposition to play im-aginatively with reality. He sees this faculty of recreational invention as typical of youth but he himself perhaps possessed it even more abundantly in maturity, as the serious playing with fancies that we find in late work like *The Beast in the Jungle* goes to show. The most sympathetic side of the late Jamesian concern with 'form' is that it is really a way of liberating this instinct to play with reality. Without this instinct Christopher Newman, the hero of *The American*, would never have fallen in love with Madame de Cintré and James could not have transformed her into a subtly distant and evanescent figure of 'romance'. It is because he does have it that James just gets away with his own indifference to all those things in the heroine which Newman fails to see. For he is prepared to let his central consciousness delimit for him the reality he describes, as a way of achieving a romantic distance from it. He

considers this kind of distance – it is nearer Emma's than Flaubert's
– when he discusses his rendering of Paris: 'The image has had
for the most part to be dim if the reflection was to be, as is proper
for a reflection, both sharp and quiet: one has a horror, I think,
artistically, of agitated reflections.' (P. 27.) Quiet 'reflections' take
off from the outer world of the 'real' to the inner realm of the
'romantic':

> The real represents to my perception the things we cannot
> possibly *not* know, sooner or later, in one way or another; it
> being but one of the accidents of our hampered state, and one of
> the incidents of their quantity and number, that particular
> instances have not yet come our way. The romantic stands, on
> the other hand, for all the things that, with all the facilities
> in the world, all the wealth and all the courage and all the wit
> and all the adventure, we never *can* directly know; the things
> that can reach us only through the beautiful circuit and subter-
> fuge of our thought and our desire. (Pp. 31–2.)

This might almost stand as a description of the 'romantic' Emma's
relation to the 'real' Yonville l'Abbaye, were it not that James is
speaking of a spiritual value rather than of escapism: 'subterfuge'
is qualified by an unironical 'beautiful'. *Madame Bovary* in fact
occurs to James at this point, as an antithesis to his own kind of
'romance': 'It would be impossible to have a more romantic
temper than Flaubert's Madame Bovary, and yet nothing less
resembles a romance than the record of her adventures.' (P. 33.)
Where Flaubert's analysis of Emma's deams brings her up short
against reality, so that we see Rodolphe change from romantic
hero to paltry egotist, James lets Newman's imagination take him
in the opposite direction: Madame de Cintré becomes more, rather
than less, 'romantic'. She is a forever retreating, forever glimpsed
possibility, a tribute to Newman's imagination whereas Rodolphe
underlines the inadequacy of Emma's. Just as this vision of Newman's is what reconciles him to losing her, so the 'romance' of
The American reconciles James to the failure in realism which he
later found in the book:

> The balloon of experience is in fact of course tied to the earth,
> and under that necessity we swing, thanks to a rope of remarkable
> length, in the more or less commodious car of the imagination;
> but it is by the rope we know where we are, and from the moment
> that cable is cut we are at large and unrelated: we only swing
> apart from the globe – though remaining as exhilarated, naturally,
> as we like, especially when all goes well. The art of the romancer

is, 'for the fun of it', insidiously to cut the cable, to cut it without our detecting him. What I have recognised then, in 'The
American', much to my surprise and after long years, is that the
experience here represented is the disconnected and uncontrolled
experience – uncontrolled by our general sense of 'the way things
happen' – which romance alone more or less successfully palms
off on us. (Pp. 33–4.)

In Flaubert, by contrast, the instinct to play with reality – art itself,
perhaps – is tragic. In his most personal book, Saint Antoine is at
the mercy of his dreams and played with by them. They distort the
real world and disqualify him from living in it. He ends, not with
a world elsewhere, but desiring to be absorbed into the materiality
of this world.

Confusing talk describing the self's relation to the world through
references to either outside or inside views of reality occurs in many
other nineteenth-century accounts of Flaubert besides James's.
James's own remarks, besides revealing his admiration of George
Eliot, echo Faguet's notorious division of Flaubert into a romantic
half and a realist half. Zola said of Flaubert that 'it is via the outside
that he makes us know what is inside'[41]; Brunetière thought that
Flaubert could 'not conceive of there being anything within man
which balances the pressure on him, so to speak, of the forces from
outside'.[42] It is a dualism which has always dogged Flaubert and
obscured the real subtleties of *Madame Bovary*. Jules de Gaultier's
analysis of *bovarysme* is, of course, the *locus classicus* of such interpretations. He defines *bovarysme* as 'man's escapist faculty for
conceiving himself as other than he really is' – '*la faculté départie
à l'homme de se concevoir autrement qu'il n'est.*[43] The tendency of
this is to assume that what a person really is, is determinable without reference to that person's environment. A true conception of
the self is shaped by what is external to it, which Gaultier thinks
of as *reality*. To know one's true self is to learn diligently the nature
of this reality which impresses itself on us through our particular
situation: reality and the world become identical. This would mean
that Emma Bovary could only know herself if she were prepared
to buckle down and accept the humdrum life which her situation
offers her. What status do Charles and Homais have as embodi-
ments of reality? Obviously, no more than Emma has herself. The
self is not subject to definition in this way. It is no more a fixed
thing than the world is and Flaubert does not see self-knowledge
for Emma as the upshot of the kind of snug insertion of herself
into her world which Gaultier has at the back of his mind. Emma
finds out more about the limits of her self by refusing to accept
the world as it is than Charles does by taking it as it comes. To

Flaubert the novelist there can be no *one* point – inside, outside or what you will – from which an examination of Emma and her predicament must begin. Only Emma herself, seeing everything from her own pressing consciousness, could start from such a point. It is precisely this which James wishes that Flaubert had done because it is what, with reservations, he would have done himself. Flaubert's own wisdom consisted in more than the self-flattering idea that people can fathom the relation in which they stand to the external reality which is the medium in which they live.

The setting-off of the self against the world outside it is one of the hallmarks of romanticism. Naturalism and symbolism are perhaps both directions taken from its initial statements in Goethe or Rousseau or Byron. It was Flaubert's distinction to have avoided a commitment to either direction. This is the great difference between him and the Baudelaire who could say, 'Poetry is what is most real, it is something which is only completely true in *another world*. This world is just a dictionary of hieroglyphics.'[44] Flaubert only went as far as to wish so radical solution were possible. Those material jolts he gives to the dreams which his characters try to impose on reality – the penknife Emma sees Charles take out of his pocket or the dying stag which arrests the blood-crazed Julien – all come from this world, a far less tractable one than the Baudelairean forest of symbols. It is typical of such pieces of actuality that they cannot be separated from the way they are seen by those they surprise, there is no inside and outside to them as images. Taine, who was researching the psychology of creativeness, once asked Flaubert whether the images created by his imagination became confused with the real objects which prompted them: 'For me the image in question is as true as the objective reality of things, and what reality has furnished me with, after a very little time, becomes indistinguishable in my eyes from the embellishments or modifications which I have given it.'[45] 'As true', not more true: to distinguish the two is to simplify. It was on this ground that Flaubert sometimes doubted that things were separate entities, just as he would surely have doubted what Gaultier said about him. He once asked Maupassant, 'Have you ever believed in the existence of things? Is not everything an illusion? All that is true is relationships ("rapports"), that is to say the manner in which we perceive objects.' (*Corr.*, VIII, p. 135.) His imagination did not leave objects behind in its quest for another world.

'I know nothing more noble than the ardent contemplation of the things of this world.' (*Corr.*, IV, p. 357.) It is one of the central statements of the *Correspondance*: the nobility lay in the intensity of the 'rapports' with things. This is what makes the picture of Yonville l'Abbaye so much more than clinical realism.

With his habitual lack of tact Flaubert once told Louise Colet that 'sometimes by dint of staring at a pebble, an animal or a picture I have felt myself enter into it. Communications between people are not more intense.' (*Corr.*, III, p. 210.) It is a kind of trance, near to hebetude, in which the intellect is in abeyance. Flaubert contemplates the pebble but he does not project himself into it; if he enters into its pebblyness it is not by trying to possess it but by being possessed by it. His regard is neither coolly scientific nor mystically self-forgetting: it is a communication, both quiet and intense, receptive and spellbound like poetry. Flaubert would have understood what Wordsworth meant by 'wise passiveness'. To let the world be was to let himself be; it broke the closed and self-defeating circuit of the imagination. Not for him the Baudelairean exploit of getting up and walking away with the world.

Such receptiveness was the complement of Flaubert's impersonality. It is what the Jamesian word 'spectacle' forgets, perhaps because James was the great chronicler of the struggle of consciousness to interpret and piece together the world so that it would be explicable to the self. For Flaubert, genius consists not in the ability to grasp the world but in a gift for self-exposure to it.

> Genius, after all, is perhaps only a refinement of suffering; that is to say, a more complete and intense penetration of the objective through our soul . . . . The sadness of Molière no doubt came from all the stupidity of Humanity which he felt to be comprised in himself. (*Corr.*, III, p. 358.)

Satire and self-examination boil down to the same thing, as in *Bouvard et Pécuchet*. This 'raffinement de la douleur' is a breaking down of the ego. It is in striking contrast to James's letter to Grace Norton. If I am right to call this Flaubertian receptiveness *poetic*, it becomes a moot point whether it does subvert selfhood at its deepest levels. It is precisely what lies beyond the self which makes possible the extension of the self beyond the cage of the ego. Seen in this light, there is nothing paradoxical in the suggestion that Flaubert's impersonality, his ambition to be a '*cœur général*', is more truly understood as self-fulfilment than as self-abnegation.

V

'To postulate a "tragic experience" or "tragic effect" and then seek to define it is to lay oneself open to the suspicion of proposing a solemn and time-honoured academic game.'[46] Leavis's warning must preface my use of the word 'tragic' to describe Flaubert's art. It is

perhaps easier to apply the word to a novelist than a dramatist.
One feels less hampered by the way it has been used in the past,
less tempted to make one's experience of a writer conform to experiences given by other writers. Every tragedy is a new tragedy which
can never be quite defined by older tragedies. I once saw a bad
performance of *Le Cid* in which Don Rodrigue roared his alexand-
rines so heartily that is was impossible to believe that he was suffering at all. With the buskin-thumping kind of tragedy Flaubert
had nothing to do, save in certain early works written under the
spell of Byron and perhaps in a few operatic scenes in *Salammbô*.
In his twenties he had ploughed through reams of lofty tragedies
by Voltaire and Marmontel and their solemnity prompted him to
join with Du Camp and Bouilhet in composing a mock-classical
tragedy, called *Jenner ou la Découverte de la Vaccine*: 'a tragedy
according to the rules, with the three unities, in which things would
never be called by their names'.[47] The conventional august pathos
diverted him because the tragic idea that man is ennobled by suffering had become the pretext for mere self-glorification. 'Misfortune
is good for nothing, although hypocrites pretend the contrary', he
once told George Sand. (*Corr.*, Supp. III, p. 214.) It is no surprise
that he should have preferred Aristophanes to Racine. His niece
reports that on countless occasions she heard him say that 'he would
have liked more than anything to be a great comic poet'.[48] The
word 'tragic' only applies to his work in the sense in which it can
include the idea of comedy. He once wrote that 'the grotesque and
the tragic . . . are only the same mask which covers the same
nothingness'. (*Corr.*, III, pp. 407–8.)

Flaubert's feelings about modern classical tragedy were not uncommon. Manzoni complained that the formal concentration of
tragedy denatured the passions:

> For a character to come to a final decision within twenty-four
> hours, an altogether different degree of passion is required than
> in the case of one with which he has been battling for a month.
> . . . The tragic poets were in a way reduced to painting only this
> small number of clearcut, dominant passions . . . the theatre
> became filled with fictitious characters who figured as abstract
> types of certain passions rather than as passionate beings. . . .
> Hence the exaggeration, the conventional tone, the uniformity
> of the tragic character. . . .[49]

The extension of human feelings over a protracted time is Flaubert's
great subject but his own interest in it was subtly different. Manzoni
is attacking the impulse to generalise about human nature and its
conditions. The author of *La Tentation de Saint Antoine* and

Salammbô seems, by comparison, intent on writing himself out of the modern world and recapturing, from the excesses of romanticism, art's ability to create universal pictures of the human condition. Whereas Manzoni attends to the rhythm of time in order to achieve a greater psychological particularity, Flaubert's interest in tracing his characters' lives is a means to the end of describing the nature of time itself. He would not have been content simply with Manzoni's humanist emphasis on the realistic description of human emotions as an index of fidelity to the human condition. The character Manzoni imagines is battling with himself; in Flaubert he would also do battle with the conditions of his existence. Time would be not simply his medium but his adversary.

Manzoni's argument looks forward to the new kind of sympathy which George Eliot brought to the humble, undramatic fates of ordinary people like the 'promessi sposi' or Emma and Charles Bovary:

> I find a source of delicious sympathy in those faithful pictures of a monotonous, homely existence, which has been the fate among so many more of my fellow mortals than a life of pomp or of absolute indulgence, of tragic suffering or of world-stirring actions.[30]

Tragedy of the old kind is linked to possibilities of action which are foreign to the unheroic inhabitants of the more circumscribed world she herself portrays. What remains of it, she says in *Middlemarch*, is that 'element of tragedy which lies in the very fact of frequency' but which is not yet 'wrought' into 'the coarse emotion of mankind'. (Chapter 20.) This evokes Flaubert – most of all *L'Education Sentimentale* – and then reminds us of ways in which his novels are different. He did not share George Eliot's deep need to particularise each individual lot, nor did he turn to the small and humdrum for a 'delicious source of sympathy'; Sainte Beuve rebuked him, as she might have done, for saying that the small and humdrum were small and humdrum. He surveyed his 'fellow mortals' in a less cosily consoling manner, reminding us rather of Lear's phrase (it is not necessarily less compassionate) about 'this great stage of fools'. A keener, more piercing wind blows through the 'sympathy' he feels for his people. Even with Félicité, in *Un Cœur Simple*, he is concerned to go beyond 'sympathy', from the pathos of her particular life to the way it reflects something larger for which 'sympathy' would be an inappropriate and shallow response: a sense of life as it always is, whether for heroes or for servants. To do this it was irrelevant, beyond a certain point, to share in the specialness of her own orbit of feeling.

Lukács has spoken of tragedy as a 'game of which God is the
spectator. He is only a spectator though and his words and his
actions never enter into the words and gestures of the actors.'[51].
The distance of an all-seeing and unaiding onlooker creates the
tragic feeling that men's actions are being performed without hope
of response from outside themseves. It is a truism that the great
nineteenth-century novelists, as omniscient narrators, had been
forced into filling a place which God appeared to have vacated.
(One might see their often exaggerated quest for verisimilitude as
a symptom of this.) What distinguishes them is the different ways in
which they discharged this function. Where Flaubert is a God who
is a bystander George Eliot is one who is constantly on a mission
down to earth. In Lukács phrase, she does 'enter' into the lives
of her characters, so that she often becomes a sort of answering
universe to them, a bosom in which their joys and sorrows find
that echo which tragedy so cruelly withholds.

It might be said that although George Eliot was content to be
omniscient the thought of omnipotence made her unhappy, whereas
for Flaubert it was a temptation. She once said that, 'When one
has to work out the dramatic action for one's self under the inspiration of an idea, instead of having a grand myth or an Italian
novel ready to one's hand, one feels anything but omnipotent.'[52]
The reader might ask whether any novelist felt less omnipotent than
Flaubert did, constantly struggling to remember his lines as he
understudied for God. My point, though, is to refer to the element
of false impersonality in his work, that hankering after Godhead
which is so clearly the result of an all too human fantasy. It is
not my point to argue that *this* is tragic, though it may be in-
extricable from the true impersonality in Flaubert which does
justify the word tragic. In the early *Souvenirs, Notes et Pensées
Intimes* there is a passage, in which he imagines the world as it
appears to God, that achieves only a spurious, highly personal
impersonality.

Climb a tower which is high enough for all sounds to be lost
and men to look minute. If, looking down, you see one man
kill another you will hardly feel moved, less moved for certain
than if the blood was spurting over you. Imagine a higher tower
and a greater indifference – a giant watching myrmidons, or a
grain of sand at the base of a pyramid, and imagine that the
myrmidons are cutting each others' throats and the grain of dust
is swept up by the wind. What does all that matter to the giant
or the pyramid? Now you can finally compare nature, God, the
infinite intelligence, in a word, to that man a hundred feet tall,
to that pyramid a hundred thousand foot high – let that be your

model for thinking of the misery of our crimes and virtues, our grandeur and our baseness.[53]

Flaubert seeks a certain exhilarated consolation from this thought of the finiteness of human suffering but he tries to have his tragic feeling on easy terms, like a Macbeth seeing that life is 'but a poor player' without realising that he is strutting and fretting on its 'stage' himself. Yet this passage is premonitory as well as immature; it points toward that satiric element which distinguishes Flaubert's published works from his juvenilia. Every great comic writer has seen the view from the top of the pyramid, and it is dangerous to exaggerate the aloofness of that view for Flaubert also knew the view from the base of the pyramid too. Besides, a phrase like George Eliot's 'monotonous homely existence' perhaps has more real aloofness in it than all Flaubert's self-torturing pride. His comedy, at its best, serves to illuminate suffering, not to deny it, and its ferocity only purges our sentimentality to extend our compassion. Only a careless or a complacent reading can look down on a Bouvard and Pécuchet as from a pyramid.

For all his Voltairean rationalism Flaubert's imagination was sufficiently religious to hark back to a conception of man as subject to the unchanging aegis of fate or the gods. He plunges his characters into a world in which they can never tell whether they are the pawns of some mysterious tragic fate or simply the sport of the arbitrary comic demon of bad luck. This undermines the Romantic desire to set the self off against the world. The essence of Flaubert's tragedy and of his comedy is a stripping-down of the protective coverings of the ego in his characters. The same thing might be said of *Othello* or *King Lear*. Yeats says that 'in mainly tragic art one distinguishes devices to exclude or lessen character, to diminish the power of that daily mood, to cheat or blind its too clear perception.'[54] The Flaubert whom we saw contemplating a pebble would have agreed.

2 James's Reading of *Madame Bovary*

I

Flaubert's novel has perplexed and rankled the Anglo-Saxon sensibility too much for one to pretend that there is any real consensus in this country as to its greatness. No other French novel has given us so apt a cue for defining the very different virtues of our own tradition; none has evoked in us such deeply-felt resistance. Our praise of Flaubert has been invariably double-edged, our criticisms of him have often been conducted as declarations of faith. It seems at times as if he had been more debated here than read. This holds for his friends as well as his enemies. When Pound and Eliot used him as a whip with which to chastise the artistic immaturity of the English they were, in a way, as guilty of making Flaubert subserve their own critical battles as is Dr Leavis in those stern asides which offer him up on the altar of the 'great tradition'. What is there to choose between making Flaubert a war-cry or a *bête noire*? Yet when the English critic of Flaubert comes up against this kind of road-block it hardly helps him if he tries to by-pass it. To by-pass Pound, Eliot, Leavis – perhaps Arnold, James and Lawrence too – is to by-pass part of one's own thought about literature. What seems like a detour is really the most direct route into the subject.

It would be crude to pretend that Flaubert has done no more in England than provide a case over which to fight a running battle between Anglo-Saxon insularity and continental modernism. That is just a colourful fantasy of George Moore's.[1] Since the admonitions of Matthew Arnold, much of our best Flaubert criticism has come from writers who felt his art to be incompatible with the art they themselves sought to create. This is especially true of James and Lawrence. Neither Eliot nor Pound ever felt compelled to discuss the novels in comparable depth: they assumed what the novels meant because what they represented was Art. Both James and Lawrence, on the other hand, brought to them the kind of creative adverse criticism which revives curiosity for what has become classic. Such criticism has been too uncommon in France between Sainte-Beuve and Sartre for it to be ignored. Yet the fruit it has borne, even in this country, has been of a dubious kind. Where James and Lawrence focused on the novels as novels those later critics who have taken up their thought have tended to see the novels as they are refracted through the *Correspondance*. The saint of art has got in the way of his own creations as readers have learnt more about his efforts to keep himself out of them. One sees this beginning to happen in Pater's essay on 'Style' in *Appreciations* – Pater has a lot to say about Flaubert but very little about the novels – and it was a confirmed tendency by the time Murry published his perceptive essay in *Countries of the Mind*, in 1921. Eliot usually speaks of Flaubert more as the initiator of a theory of impersonality than as an artistic experience. With Leavis, who at first seems to tread in the footsteps of James and Lawrence, Flaubert becomes a 'case' who can bring out the qualities of other writers. *Madame Bovary* ceases to be seen as a great book about life and death and gets considered only as a monument to its author's 'perverse heroism' in the pursuit of 'form'.[2] The thought of James and Lawrence leads their disciple to no more than a repetition of Pater and Moore from a more hostile position. In Martin Turnell's disappointing essay in *Scrutiny*, Flaubert's greatness is defined as being that of a 'great literary engineer', a mere quarry of techniques for later novelists to use.[3] Even now, it is still possible for the person who reads *Madame Bovary* in translation and only English criticism of it to be left baffled by the novel's status in France. For us, it is too easily seen as just another classic of the classroom, a good essay subject. For freshness of response to it one still goes back to James and Lawrence.

In *Partial Portraits* James gives a description of Flaubert's friendship with Turgenev in which he attributes Flaubert's concern with form to some emotional inadequacy:

> . . . there was something ungenerous in his genius. He was cold, and he would have given everything he had to be able to glow. There is nothing in his novels like the passion of Elena for Inssaroff, like the purity of Lisa, like the anguish of the parents of Bazaroff, like the hidden wound of Tatiana; and yet Flaubert yearned, with all the accumulations of his vocabulary, to touch the chord of pathos. There were some parts of his mind that did not 'give', that did not render a sound. He had too much of some sorts of experience and not enough of others. And yet this failure of an organ, as I may call it, inspired those who knew him with a kindness. If Flaubert was powerful and limited, there is something human, after all, and even rather august, in a strong man who has not been able completely to express himself.[4]

James's compassion is tinged with complacency because he sees Flaubert as trying unsuccessfully to be the kind of novelist he himself was – in, say, Chapter 42 of *The Portrait of a Lady*. After their meeting in 1876 James had felt that he could 'easily – more than easily – see all round him intellectually'. He wrote to his brother William:

> In poor old Flaubert there is something almost tragic; his big intellectual temperament, machinery, etc., and vainly colossal attempts to press out the least little drop of *passion*. So much talent, and so much naïveté and honesty, and yet so much dryness and coldness.[5]

Did Flaubert yearn to 'touch the chord of pathos', to 'press out the least little drop of *passion*' from the tale of Emma's sufferings? To accept James's word 'coldness' might logically lead one to the odd conclusion of finding *Novembre* more satisfying than *Madame Bovary*.

There is no need, in answering James's case, to deny the presence of a certain coldness in the way *Madame Bovary* is narrated. What has to be explored is whether this coldness is the consequence of the author's inherent poverty of feeling. To follow through this question at all adequately an important distinction has to be kept in mind: in speaking of 'feeling' it will be necessary to separate the humanitarian pity which James seems to have in mind from true tragic pity. It is a distinction which was first made by Hegel.[6] To define the kind of feeling we do get in *Madame Bovary* is also to distinguish it from pity. That is, one will be defining the way an ostensibly private pity for Emma herself becomes the reflection of a more general suffering. For *Madame Bovary*, despite appearances, is not a Romantic tragedy of the kind Balzac wrote, and, although it seems founded on the impossibility of human community, it does in fact involve its reader in the contemplation of a common human condition and not just the tragedy of an individual. It does this especially through irony – part of what James meant by 'coldness' – and so its sense of community is of a negative kind which does not confirm order and justice in the way *Macbeth* does. This negativeness is perhaps the inevitable limitation on tragic art in its period; it nonetheless directs us to see the novel as more than just a liberal tragedy of the kind which James, a champion of Ibsen, would have preferred it to be. A true description of the 'feeling' in the book is, therefore, essential to a true recognition of what makes it so original, so special an achievement of the nineteenth-century novel.

One of the most moving chapters of *Madame Bovary* comes at the conclusion of the *Première Partie*, in my view the most completely successful part of the novel. The chapter describes Emma's life at Tostes, a slow, time-ridden routine which is broken only by her growing capriciousness and nervous illness. It is the kind of poetic chronicling of the unpoetic which Flaubert does so well.

There are many passages one could quote to show what is original
in the kind of pity Emma's life evokes but the most appropriate
here is the chapter's conclusion, because it offers an example of
the sort of prose which gives some purchase for James's idea of
Flaubert's 'coldness'. The Bovarys have just decided to move to
Yonville l'Abbaye in the spring:

> Un jour qu'en prévision de son départ elle faisait des rangements
> dans un tiroir, elle se piqua les doigts à quelque chose. C'était
> un fil de fer de son bouquet de mariage. Les boutons d'oranger
> étaient jaunes de poussière, et les rubans de satin, à liséré d'argent,
> s'effiloquaient par le bord. Elle le jeta dans le feu. Il s'enflamma
> plus vite qu'une paille sèche. Puis ce fut comme un buisson rouge
> sur les cendres, et qui se rongeait lentement. Elle le regarda
> brûler. Les petites baies de carton éclataient, les fils d'archal se
> tordaient, le galon se fondait; et les corolles de papier, racornies,
> se balançant le long de la plaque comme des papillons noirs,
> enfin s'envolèrent par la cheminée.
>
> Quand on partit de Tostes, au mois de mars, Madame Bovary
> était enceinte.[7]
>
> (One day as she was tiding up a drawer in anticipation of her
> departure, she pricked her fingers on something. It was a wire on
> her marriage bouquet. The orange-blossom was yellow with dust,
> the silver-trimmed satin ribbons were fraying at the edges. She
> flung it in the fire. It flared up quicker than dry straw, then
> became like a red bush on the cinders, slowly burning itself out.
> She watched it burn. The little card-board berries popped open,
> the binding wire twisted up, the braid melted and the shrivelled
> paper petals, wavering along the fire-back like black butterflies,
> finally floated up the chimney.
>
> When they left Tostes in March, Madame Bovary was pregnant.)

The reticent last sentence reveals more than just an author whose
relish for the twists of Emma's fortunes makes him withhold his
sympathy from her. The tone may be laconic but it is not incompatible with a muted and even a gentle feeling. It needs to be read
in context. The pregnancy comes at the end of the chapter because
it introduces another element, besides the removal, which will force
a change in the way Emma is feeling. As well as simple narrative
suspense though, there is an implicit sense of Emma's personal
neuroses being opened towards a common, less private experience.
This is what makes it unnecessary for Flaubert to work for a direct
pity here. The news of her pregnancy is a shock to us because it is
a shock to her. A more conventional sympathy would be inappropriate since it would so obviously fail to chime with her feelings.

Nothing would be gained by treating Emma as if she were the first woman ever to expect a baby. After the description of her illness Flaubert needs to bring us back to the chilling sense of normal experience against which it had been a protest. The curtness in his tone is not a pose of impersonality but simply a reflection of the finality with which what happens to Emma clashes with the more languid rhythms of her own reveries. Her own sense of her pathos, caught so subtly by the lingering, almost sighing cadence in the prose as the remnants of the bouquet float up the chimney, is different, a pathos of the emotional surface. There is a deeper feeling than her romantic self-pity. The distance of the conclusion makes articulate something more than a sense of mere unbearableness and it is this which is given to the reader to share. There is, it is true, a blank which Flaubert leaves us to fill in. How does Emma respond to being pregnant? Partly this is a question to sustain curiosity in the novel, partly it is a blank which we can fill in by reflecting on how much more of Emma's soul now has to be engaged by this new experience, how its dreadful suddenness exposes the degree of sentimental attitude in the Emma who burns the bouquet.

This is not to say that the beauty of the passage is free from more cryptic elements. The detachment of the narrator expresses a strange moral need as much as any purely aesthetic intention. If the last sentence is felt as forced this is not because Flaubert is rigging Emma's pregnancy but because his detachment barely sustains him from giving in to a feeling of horror at what has happened. The dead-pan shortness of tone testifies not to lack of feeling but to feelings too strong to be more than half-throttled by the need for impassiveness. Serenity jostles with tension. In a letter of 1853 to Louise Colet Flaubert wrote, rather wishfully, that 'the only way to live in peace, is to place oneself at one bound above the whole of humanity and to have no more in common with it than a connection through the eyes'. (*Corr.*, III, p. 178.) Neither pride nor coldness provides sufficient explanation of such remarks. To Flaubert, peace of mind requires a desperate mysticism which is simply a rebound from his feeling of being implicated in the suffering he depicts. If this is true, it helps account for the strange sense of emotion in the end of the *Première Partie*: the irony is the measure of the ironist's conquest of hysteria. It is the same tight-lipped quality in the prose as we find in the account of Emma's suicide, which Flaubert composed with a taste of poison in his own mouth.

The Flaubert I am setting against James's Flaubert was, then, not so much struggling to 'completely express himself' as struggling to express a more than personal range of feeling. Hence the bourgeois heroine, at first sight so unlike himself, whose self-pitying

demand for compassion could not be supplied by drawing on his
own self-pity, as he had done in *Novembre*. Emma is Flaubert's
means of confirming his own sufferings as more than private and
unique to himself. His most famous reference to his novel is to this
intimation of *lacrimae rerum*:

> Rest assured that everything one invents is true. Poetry is as
> precise a thing as geometry. Induction is as good as deduction,
> and when one gets to a certain point, one no longer mistakes
> the things of the soul. My poor Bovary is no doubt suffering and
> weeping in twenty different French villages, at this very hour.
> (*Corr.*, III, p. 291.)

The thought of the novelist who could speak like this in the mid-
nineteenth century had to go deeper than any wish to 'touch the
chord of pathos'.

A formidable corroboration of James's point about Flaubert's
'coldness' is found in two of the critics he most admired, Sainte-
Beuve and Matthew Arnold. Both viewed his anger against life with
indignation of a humanitarian colour. Sainte-Beuve asks a rhetorical
question:[*]

> Yet is it art's function not to wish to console us, to refuse to
> admit, under the guise of being more true to life, any element of
> clemency and sweetness? Besides, truth, to look only for that,
> is not utterly and necessarily on the side of evil, folly and human
> perversity.[8]

The Flaubert drawn by Arnold is equally incapable of glowing:

> But *Madame Bovary* . . . is a work of *petrified feeling*; over it
> hangs an atmosphere of bitterness, irony, impotence; not a person-
> age in the book to rejoice or console us; the springs of freshness
> and feeling are not there to create such personages. Emma Bovary
> follows a course in some respects like that of Anna [Karenina],
> but where, in Emma Bovary, is Anna's charm? The treasures of
> compassion, tenderness, insight, which alone, amid such guilt and
> misery, can enable charm to subsist and to emerge, are wanting
> to Flaubert. He is cruel, with the cruelty of petrified feeling, to
> his poor heroine; he pursues her without pity or pause, as with
> malignity; he is harder upon her himself than any reader even,
> I think, will be inclined to be.[9]

It is very much James's view spiced with Victorian sternness instead

of Jamesian urbanity. James would have read both Arnold and
Sainte-Beuve by the time he wrote *Partial Portraits* and *Notes on
Novelists*.

Faced with an agreement from three such critics it would be
foolish to simply try to prove them wrong. Their response to the
novel has to stand as a possible one even if it seems to bar our
enjoyment of it. But one can ask whether any novel which did
possess the virtues they find absent from *Madame Bovary* would
really be a greater novel than Flaubert's is. They so patently want
something other than a tragic view of life. The ending they would,
for example, want for the conclusion of the *Première Partie* would
surely entail the inclusion in it of precisely the kind of emotion
which it was Flaubert's distinction not to draw on. Their *Madame
Bovary*, one suspects, would dissipate the sense of Emma's tragedy
with its own sympathetic warmth, replacing our reluctant recognition of *her* humanity by a consoling sense of the author's. What
troubles me in these three critics is that, given the indelible actuality with which Emma's story fills the mind, they should all have
been so confident of the moral rightness of their own feelings, so
eager to import into the novel their alternative ideas of reality.
Their demand for the consolation of pity is purely self-protective.
Arnold reveals most clearly the difference between this pity and the
fellow-feeling for which Emma calls. Though he complains of
Flaubert's 'malignity' he is anxious to dissociate himself from her
'guilt and misery'. Flaubert is 'harder upon her himself than *any
reader even*, I think, will be inclined to be'. (My italics.) In the
light of that 'even' we may ask why Arnold uses the word 'guilt'
and why it should intrude on our compassion for Emma. Why
should we only feel a full commiseration for the innocent? What
Arnold wants is to feel for Emma *as an individual* and so her lack
of that 'charm' (he ignores her sensuousness) which is the solvent
of Anna's 'guilt', is a real barrier to him. Yet it is Flaubert's distinction to have appealed to our fellow-feeling for Emma without
needing to have us charmed by her.[10] This makes Arnold's invoca-
tion of 'the treasures of compassion, tenderness, insight' smack
of a charity which begins at home. His fellow-feeling wants to be
free to choose its own objects. Nevertheless, despite his *ex cathedra*
tone, he does offer the admirer of the novel a challenge which
cannot be simply put to one side as a plea for a morally cosier
book. The debility he sees in Flaubert makes him feel that it is not
life but the author harrying Emma: she appears as the victim of the
irony of Flaubert and not the irony of fate. This criticism is a
damaging one and I will take it up later. It rests, however, on a
speculation about Flaubert's relation to his own novel and it is first
of all necessary to ask what he saw himself as doing in it. Did he,

for example, see any alternative to either 'coldness' or being able
to 'glow'?

II

Flaubert saw the greatest reaches of art in the writings of Cervantes,
Molière, Homer and, above all, Shakespeare. He was re-reading
King Lear in 1854 when he was working towards the end of *Madame
Bovary*:

> This week I re-read the first act of *King Lear*. The more I think
> of him the more frightened I am of that fellow. . . . Taken all
> together his works strike me with the stupefaction and exaltation
> I get from the idea of the stellar system. I see there only an
> immensity in which my gaze loses itself by being dazzled. (*Corr.,*
> IV, p. 46.)

This 'exaltation' is unlike his youthful fantasy of transcendence in
Smarh: Flaubert invokes the stars when he is describing experiences
of a religious nature. His tone is one of wonder and humility. The
letter illuminates a part of his sensibility which the novels sometimes obscure, his readiness to be swept away by great art into a
naïvely self-forgetting exhilaration. Here is what he says about the
storm scene, that *locus classicus* for the liberal view of tragedy as the
individual's battle with his world:

> . . . for two days I have been crushed by a scene from Shakespeare
> (the first [*sic*] in Act III of *King Lear*). The man will drive me
> mad. More than ever all the others seem like children beside
> him. In this scene, everyone, at the end of his tether and in a
> complete paroxysm of being, goes off his head and becomes
> irrational. There are three different madnesses howling at the
> same time, while the fool jokes, the rain falls and the thunder
> claps. . . . Yes, it overwhelmed me. All I did was to think of that
> scene in the forest, where the howling of wolves is heard, and of
> old Lear weeping in the rain and tearing out his beard in the
> wind. (*Corr.,* IV., pp. 18–19.)

The romantic rhetoric which is part of the response should not be
allowed to obscure the fact that Flaubert's pity for Lear expresses
a religious sense of man's place in nature which is essentially
different in kind from the romantic pity his critics charged him
with lacking. His sense of this tragic 'paroxysm of being' goes beyond
any romantic self-projection into Lear to a picture of the wild
immensity of wind and rain in which he suffers. The pity is stiffened

with awe. We can see what makes the scene exhilarating as well as intolerable. Shakespeare, for Flaubert, had to do more than 'glow' to show Lear on his 'wheel of fire'. Underneath the romantic bluster of the prose is an awareness of the distance Shakespeare had to keep Lear at to make him tragic.[11]

In one letter Flaubert's humility before the plays takes the curious form of calling Shakespeare a 'dreadful colossus': 'one can hardly believe that he has been a man'. (*Corr.*, I, p. 386.) He does not subscribe to the familiar sentimentality of seeing Shakespeare as ourselves writ large. Instead, this letter, of 1846, is concerned to define the monstrous impersonality of the great artist which makes him a 'colossus':

> For there are two classes of poets. The greatest and rarest, the true masters, sum up humanity without being pre-occupied either with themselves or their own passions. Putting aside personality to absorb themselves in the passions of others, they reproduce the Universe. It is reflected in their works, glittering, various, multiform, like an entire sky mirrored in the sea with all its stars and all its blueness. There are other men who need only to cry to be harmonious, to weep in order to move us, to go on about themselves in order to remain eternal. (*Corr.*, I, pp. 385–6.)

Shakespeare is the type of the first kind of poet. Byron and Musset of the second. He can separate his own condition from the condition of life. To see life from the perspective he affords is neither to become cold, nor to 'glow' like Musset, but to partake of a peace essential to great art:

> When I read Shakespeare I become greater, more intelligent and more pure. When I reach the summit of one of his plays, I seem to be on a high mountain: everything disappears and yet becomes apparent. One is no longer a man, one is an *eye*; new horizons arise, the perspectives stretch out to infinity; one no longer thinks that one has also lived in one of those huts which can hardly be made out, that one has drunk from all those rivers which seem smaller than streams, that, in short, one has scurried around inside that anthill and is in fact still part of it. (*Corr.*, I, p. 339.)

This is not the same feeling as Flaubert had when he described, in *Souvenirs, Notes et Pensées Intimes*, how the world would look from the top of a pyramid. Shakespeare's art offers a transcendence unalloyed by pride which involves an awareness of and not an escape from the sense of human frailty. It offers, in fact, what love always withholds from Emma Bovary.

This Shakespearian ideal, combining an immersion in life with a transcendence of it, is often elusive for Flaubert. He is apt to mistake the 'high mountain' of Shakespeare for his own pyramid, sometimes in the same work. He can see that Shakespeare gives a general reflection on life which relates back to life:

> What distinguishes great geniuses is generalisation and creation. They bring together a host of scattered personalities in one type and make humanity aware of new characters. Doesn't one believe in the existence of Don Quixote just as one does in Caesar's (*Corr.*, III, p. 31.)

On the other hand, Flaubert can conceive of impersonality as the kind of escape from self which he diagnoses in Frédéric Moreau's wish to write history: 'By plunging into the personalities of others, he forgot his own, which is perhaps the only way not to suffer from it.'[12] We get a less human religiousness, that of the ivory tower:

> Take life from higher up, climb a tower (believing it solid, even if its base begins to give); then you will no longer see anything but the blue ether all round you. When it isn't blue there will be fog; what does it matter, if everything disappears, drowned in a calm vapour. (*Corr.*, II, p. 326.)

The job of the Flaubert critic is therefore to distinguish between these two exaltations, that of 'la généralisation et la création' and that of the Flaubert who wanted to write a book about nothing, a Flaubert much admired by critics like Barthes and Genette. The Flaubert of Arnold and Sainte-Beuve certainly existed – he still appeals to some readers – but this only makes it more important to distinguish the artist who narrates the death of Emma from the one who narrates the death of Mâtho in Salammbô. It is the former of whom Pound, also alerted by James's criticism, said:

> He [James] never manages the classic, I mean as Flaubert gives us in each main character: *Everyman*. One may conceivably be bored by certain pages in Flaubert, but one takes from him a solid and concrete memory, a property. Emma Bovary and Frédéric and M. Arnoux are respectively every woman and every man of their period. Maupassant's *Bel Ami* is not. Neither are Henry James's people. They are always, or nearly always, the bibelots.[13]

Pound's thought would help us more if it explained how Flaubert managed to reconcile his two kinds of exaltation in creating his 'Everyman'. What did he mean by the paradox of seeing Shakespeare as so universal that he could hardly believe him to have been a man?

Flaubert's use of the word 'humanité' is clarified by a famous letter written to Louise Colet in 1852. He has just read *Uncle Tom's Cabin*, which he calls a 'narrow book': 'It is done from a moral and religious point of view when it ought to have been done from a *human* one.' (*Corr.*, III, p. 60.) Flaubert's 'human' is not the same as Harriet Beecher Stowe's humanitarian zeal. This does not mean that he thinks the story should be told without compassion, but that true compassion is made possible by a refusal to be swayed by the kind of pity which Mrs Stowe's morality, with its cult of the noble soul, asks the reader for:

> I don't require, in order to be moved by a tortured slave, that he be a fine fellow, a good father and husband, who sings hymns, reads scripture and pardons his torturers: that becomes the sublime, an exception, and thus something special and false. The qualities of feeling in the book, and they are great, would have been better employed if the intention had been more restrained. When there are no more slaves in America, this novel will be no more true than all those old stories in which mahometans are invariably represented as monsters. No more hatred! no more! Besides, that's what makes the book a success, it is *actual*. Truth alone, the eternal, pure Beauty does not excite the masses to that extent. The bias of giving the moral superiority to the blacks becomes absurd, for example, in the character of George, who dresses his murderer's wounds when he should be treading him underfoot, etc., who dreams of a negro civilisation and of African empire, etc. The death of the young St Clare nun is that of a saint. Why? I would weep more if she were an ordinary child. . . . The reflections of the author irritated me the whole time. Is there any need to make reflections on slavery? Show it, that's all. (*Corr.*, III, pp. 60–1.)

He objects to Mrs Stowe because for her life is so much raw experience to be interpreted (and thus distorted) with the help of her moral categories. Books should not be flame-throwers. For her, a human understanding of the world is the disclosure of ways in which man can change his lot; for Flaubert, only man changes, not his conditon, and a truly human understanding of the world is consummated in a resigned, receptive meditativeness rather than in politics. It is not that he dissents from her views *as* views, he doesn't, but only that he thinks life is better understood through art than propaganda, even when the life to be rendered is political. Art transcends those responses to the world which originate in the self's enmeshment in its limited actuality. This is the same distinction which he made between Shakespeare and Musset.[14]

Flaubert's criticism of *Uncle Tom's Cabin* assumes a solidarity of human feeling: slavery only has to be shown as it is for this feeling to be tapped. The paradox of this position is that a humanness so grounded in a belief in an unchanging and unchangeable world denies all sense to human effort. From the summit of art human nature is not a responsibility but a cross to be borne. It is precisely this notion (which owes more to hysteria than cruelty) that lays Flaubert open to the charge of inhumanity from readers who cannot accept his view of history. Compassion which rests on a negation of all belief in human progress is construed as mere bitterness. For Lukàcs, 'the extraordinarily sensitive and highly moral Flaubert has against his will become the initiator of the inhuman in modern literature.'[15]

The way Flaubert expected *Madame Bovary* to be received follows from his reaction to *Uncle Tom's Cabin*:

It will, I think, be the first time a book will be seen to make fun of its heroine and hero. Irony does not diminish pathos; on the contrary, it intensifies it. In my third part, which will be full of farcical things, I want the reader to weep. (*Corr.*, III, p. 43.)

The tragedy had to be articulated, even manipulated, through the comic. Otherwise, it might have lapsed into the kind of cosmic pessimism which spoils *Smarh*, becoming tragedy of the sort one associates with *The Return of the Native*. Comedy, like the Fool in *King Lear*, would both sharpen its edge and prevent the reader's being engulfed by it. It involved more than sadistically pressing his own 'petrified feeling' onto Emma:

When one is inclined to see the grotesque everywhere one sees it nowhere. Nothing is so sad as the faces of cathedral gargoyles. Yet they are always laughing. There are people whose soul is just the same. (*Corr.*, I, p. 431.)

Without including the laughter of the gargoyle in his response to Emma, Flaubert's poetic generality would have evaporated into the thin air of mysticism in which neither compassion nor irony could have lived. This comedy has not always been given its rightful place in the novel by criticism in English and neither James nor Lawrence really account for it. Yet it was, to Flaubert, a sign of the greatest art and something he always tried for:

. . . no one has breathed in other people more than I have. I have gone off and inhaled unknown dunghills and had compassion for many things which left sensitive people unmoved. If

Bovary is worth something, the book will not lack heart. Yet to me irony seems to dominate life. . . . The comic pushed to an extreme, comedy which doesn't make you laugh and lyricism in jest, these for me are everything I most covet as a writer. The two human elements are there. *Le Malade Imaginaire* goes more deeply into the inner world than all the Agamemnons. The 'N'y aurait-il pas du danger à parler de toutes ces maladies?' is well worth the 'Qu'il mourût!' (*Corr.*, II, p. 407.)

There is good reason to use the words comedy and tragedy almost interchangeably in speaking of Flaubert.

The discussion of Mrs Stowe ends with a conception of the artist as a sort of understudy for God,

> everywhere present and nowhere visible. Art being a second nature, its creator must work by similar means. The reader must feel in each atom, in every aspect of it, a hidden and infinite impassibility. To the spectator the effect must be a kind of astonishment. (*Corr.*, III, pp. 61–2.)

The gargoyle's rôle is to prevent this 'astonishment' from being merely oppressive to us. Such a dream of transcendence would in fact have been undreamable had Flaubert not been immersed in the life his dream sought to transcend:

> I am less of a dreamer than people think, I know how to see and I see as the short-sighted do, right into the pores of things, because they thrust their noses in them. From the literary viewpoint there are two distinct characters in me: one is in love with *rhetoric* [*gueulades*], lyricism, great eagle-flights, all the sonorities of language and the summits of thought; the other burrows and digs into the real as much as he can, enjoys seizing on small facts as powerfully as on great ones, and wants to make you feel almost *materially* the things which he renders. The latter character likes to laugh and relishes man's animalities. (*Corr.*, II, pp. 343–4.)

This is schematic in that, in the art it points to, the two characters are inseparable. The reason for quoting this letter is that critics of *Madame Bovary* often try to separate them. Thus James, under the influence of Faguet, starts his 1902 essay from the assumption that Flaubert 'was formed intellectually of two quite distinct compartments, a sense of the real and a sense of the romantic'.[16]

III

In her memoir of D. H. Lawrence, Jessie Chambers recalls a remark of his which takes us back to the young James's view of Flaubert as an artist who began 'on the outside':

'You see, it was really George Eliot who started it all', Lawrence was saying in the deliberate way he had of speaking when he was trying to work something out in his own mind. 'And how wild they all were with her for doing it. It was she who started putting all the action inside. Before, you know, with Fielding and the others, it had been outside. Now I wonder which is right?'
. . . I ventured the opinion that George Eliot had been right.
'I wonder if she was', Lawrence replied thoughtfully. 'You know I can't help thinking there ought to be a bit of both.'[17]

The question is put in a spirit of open-minded puzzlement: why should a novelist have to choose between these two ways? When James discusses Flaubert he is a true disciple of George Eliot and he argues for 'putting all the action on the inside'. For him, the life rendered by a novel is in a direct ratio to the richness or poverty of consciousness of the character through whom the events of that novel are seen. This life thus becomes less any prevailing common lot than one mind's way of conceiving of its own existence. In the helpful distinction worked out by René Girard, he chooses the 'mensonge romantique' rather than the 'vérité romanesque'.[18] The word 'life' becomes a value rather than being simply descriptive. Even if the value of this 'life' is judged by the individual's receptiveness to the 'outside' world, his mind is its prior source. A novel like *The Sacred Fount* is ample proof that James was no mere idealist, of course, but the tendency of his faith in consciousness is to make life significant only as the romantic faculty of the self comes in to transmute the real. 'Life' and the human condition are made into subtly different things.

The typical problem of a James character is that the 'outside' world tends to overturn the brightest imaginings of the self. Superficially, this seems to be the same problem as Emma Bovary's. But its effect on its victim is very different. In *The Ambassadors*, Strether's ideal Paris may be undercut by an actual Paris on which it pretends to base itself but his awakening is no mere come-down: something is salvaged, because the actual Paris has, nonetheless, vouchsafed him a vision which, true or false, has enlarged his sense of what it is to be alive. To the pragmatic James there is no immanent reality in the world outside the mind to which the mind must adapt if it is to see life truly. Strether is not bound by the real

relations of Chad and Madame de Vionnet in the way that Emma
is bound by the real nature of Charles, Léon and Rodolphe. Neither
is he chastened by what he learns as Jane Austen's Emma is, when
she finally discovers where Jane Fairfax's piano came from. Despite
the irony of his situation, he is still free to make a glad renunciation
of his claims in the 'outside' world, on Mrs Newsome, Marie de
Vionnet and Maria Gostrey: there is no essential truth about life
to which he must capitulate. Strether's sensitive nature provides
James with a case in which a certain measure of idealism can be
vindicated. There is another version of this in the conclusion
to *The Spoils of Poynton*. Fleda's moral triumph would not be
possible without her deliberately allowing Mona Brigstock to win
Owen back from her. Again, renunciation is not resignation. In
Flaubert, the fate of the imaginative person is the reverse of this:
the world fastens its fetters tighter and tighter round the struggling
self until all dreams are dispersed by its almost material insistence
on the transience of life. Milly Theale may have her triumph in
death, in Emma Bovary's death it is the world which triumphs.

This thumbnail sketch of the differences between James and
Flaubert may suggest the way in which a novelist like James was
liable to misunderstand *Madame Bovary*. His description of Emma's
tragedy, though it at first seems to evoke his own novels, in fact
implies their differences from Flaubert's:

M. Faguet has of course excellently noticed this – that the fortune
and felicity of the book were assured by the stroke that made the
central figure an embodiment of helpless romanticism. Flaubert
himself but narrowly escaped being such an embodiment after
all, and he is thus able to express the romantic mind with extraordinary truth. As to the rest of the matter he had the luck of
having been in possession from the first, having begun so early
to nurse and work up his plan that, familiarity and the native
air, the native soil, aiding, he had finally made out to the last
lurking shade the small sordid sunny dusty village picture, its
emptiness constituted and peopled. It is in the background and
the accessories that the real, the real of his theme, abides; and
the romantic, the romantic of his theme, occupies the front.
Emma Bovary's poor adventures are a tragedy for the very reason
that in a world unsuspecting, unassisting, unconsoling, she has
herself to distil the rich and the rare. Ignorant, unguided, un-
diverted, ridden by the very nature and mixture of her consciousness, she makes of the business an inordinate failure, a failure
which in its turn makes for Flaubert the most pointed, the most
told of anecdotes. (P. 60.)

James's perception of Flaubert's inwardness with 'the romantic mind' makes this far subtler than his earlier criticism of him, yet he still gives an obliquely Jamesian version of the novel. The first word to show this is 'emptiness'. In Flaubert, the village is not an 'emptiness': it is already 'constituted and peopled' by nature. One cannot think of Les Bertaux, the silent village, the bleak Norman plain, or the forest where Emma goes riding with Rodolphe as a 'background'. The landscapes and the weather are no more 'accessories' than are the wind and rain in *King Lear*. Emma herself has the same physical reality so it is misleading to make James's distinction between the 'real' in the 'background' and the 'romantic' in the 'front': nature can seem romantic just as Emma is often sharply real, as when Charles sees her finishing her liqueur on his first visit to Les Bertaux. James has a fine sense of the pathos of her dreams, though; it comes out in the beautiful image of Emma distilling 'the rich and the rare' from a 'world unsuspecting, un-assisting, unconsoling'. Yet that phrase does suggest that his pity for her is rather unironical and personal, so that her rêveries seem too wistful and lacking in urgency, too like Hyacinth Robinson's, for Emma. In fact, they cannot be simply set against her 'poor adventures' like this without diluting their sexual intensity. This too helps her individual experience to evoke our own. To miss it is to want, like Arnold, to turn from her 'guilt and misery' and ask for some finer 'charm'. This is what James's word 'romantic' seeks to supply. It is in this way that his word 'tragedy' suggests something more sentimental than Flaubert was after. The result, as James starts to re-think the novel against its own grain, is that his pity becomes nearly contemptuous towards the 'inordinate failure' of her 'poor adventures'. He is reluctant to see that her 'business' with her lovers was as much a search for sexual as for spiritual fulfilment. Thus, out of his own more etiolated sentiment, he concludes that the novel's final effect is a cold one: it is 'the most *told* of anecdotes'. I would argue that, by trying to see Emma too much as she wishes to see herself, too romantically, James imports into the book a coldness which is really his own. In short, Flaubert's sense of tragedy would not let him turn Yonville into a 'background' for Emma's sufferings in the way that in a novel like *The Portrait of a Lady* James makes the far richer world of Rome a sublime backdrop to the sorrows of Isabel Archer.

One of James's own best critics, R. P. Blackmur, has a similar Jamesian reading of *Madame Bovary*:

Bovarysme is an habitual, an infatuated practice of regarding, not the self, but the world as other than it is; it is an attempt to find in the world what is not there. This is not an unworthy effort as is plain if we look not only at Emma but also at Charles.[19]

This is worth balancing against Gaultier but, like James, Blackmur forgets the weight of flesh by which Emma is incorporated into her world despite her dreams. That world is not inimical to her just because of what is absent from it but because what is present in it is present in her too, premonitions of death, the haunting rhythm of passing time. The final irony is that suicide, her last escape from the world, only plunges her deeper into its appalling materiality:

> Le drap se creusait depuis ses seins jusqu'à ses genou, se relevant ensuite à la pointe des orteils; et il semblait à Charles que des masses infinies, qu'un poids énorme pesait sur elle. (P. 454.)
> (The sheet dipped down from her breasts to her knees, lifting again at the tips of her toes; it seemed to Charles that an infinite mass, an enormous weight, was pressing down on her.)

Like her, the reader is forced to attend not just to her 'inordinate failure' but to what is revealed in the quick of her life: her mortality. Hence her despairing question as she discovers that her dreams too are perishable:

> D'où venait donc cette insuffisance de la vie, cette pourriture instantanée des choses où elles s'appuyait? (P. 392.)
> (Then whence came that insufficiency in life, that instantaneous corruption of the things on which she lent for support?)

Does decay begin with the things of the world touching her or with her own touch on them? It was by not attending to the poetry that flows from Emma's question that James was led to stress the form of the novel as its central greatness: 'the most *told* of anecdotes'. Yet an anecdote is confined in its own particularity and, if *Madame Bovary* is 'pointed', as James says it is, its point is more that of a *memento mori* than of a *fait divers* turned into a cautionary tale.

James's discussion of the novel's form is a classic example of the way his criticism gives a free hand to his different responses to a book to work themselves out together. Like many Anglo-Saxon readers he was disturbed by the definiteness of outline of *Madame Bovary*. He suspected Flaubert of demarcating its meaning more clearly than the life in it permitted. Yet this clarity was also his greatest admiration. The following passage therefore has a peculiarly fertile kind of ambiguousness:

'Madame Bovary' has a perfection that not only stamps it but that makes it stand almost alone; it holds itself with such a sup-

reme unapproachable assurance as both excites and defies judgement. For it deals not in the least, as to unapproachability, with
things exalted or refined; it only confers on its sufficiently vulgar
elements of exhibition a final unsurpàssable form. The form is in
itself as interesting, as active, as much of the essence of the subject
as the idea, and yet so close is its fit and so inseparable its life
that we catch it at no moment on any errand of its own. That
verily is to *be* interesting – all round; that is to be genuine and
whole. The work is a classic because the thing, such as it is, is
ideally *done,* and because it shows that in such doing eternal
beauty may dwell. (Pp. 62–3.)

This is fine and subtle praise but it really does nothing to take us
beyond the strictures of Arnold. Throughout the passage phrases
like 'exalted and refined' and 'sufficiently vulgar elements' drop hints
which allow James to take away with his left hand what his right
has just given. *Madame Bovary,* 'such as it is', is 'ideally *done*', but
the insistence on the word '*done*' deliberately withholds any recognition of the profoundly human thought in the novel. The accolade
of 'final unsurpassable form' has an ambiguous ring, not just because James is expressing a reserved admiration, but because he is
rather embarrassed by the words he uses to praise a novel he thinks
so 'classic'.

James does not regard *Madame Bovary,* as an older Flaubert was
to do, as just a great *tour de force.* He feels a real difficulty in
making up his mind about it and his shifting tone shows him
thinking out his own thoughts about the 'art of fiction' to define
Flaubert's:

And yet it is not after all that the place the book has taken is so
overwhelmingly explained by its inherent dignity; for here comes
in the curiosity of the matter. Here comes in especially its fund
of admonition for alien readers. The dignity of its substance is
the dignity of Mme Bovary herself as a vessel of experience – a
question as to which, unmistakeably, I judge, we can only depart
from the consensus of French critical opinion. (P. 62.)

Finding no 'dignity' in the vulgar tragedy of the wife of a country
doctor, he is puzzled by the book's 'inherent dignity'. It must inhere
in its 'form' rather than its 'substance'. He does not ask whether
the narrowness of Emma's soul was necessary to the disciplining of
her story into its 'unsurpassable form'. 'The form is in *itself* as
interesting . . . as the idea, and yet so close is its fit and so inseparable its life that we catch it at no moment on any errand of its
own.' This is elusive because James is not sure whether 'form' can

be a thing 'in *itself*', except in a flight of fancy like this. He speaks
as if, way back, 'form' and 'substance' had been separate, before
Flaubert made of them a 'close fit'. Yet he is really arguing that the
'form' transcends its 'substance' and their 'fit' is just what he is not
interested in. One is left remembering the 'architecture' of *The
Portrait of a Lady* and *The Ambassadors* more than the tragic
action of *Madame Bovary*.

James's notion of the way the novel is *'done'* gives a fresh direction to the slippery evocativeness of his view of Emma herself:

> A pretty young woman who lives, socially and morally speaking,
> in a hole, and who is ignorant, foolish, flimsy, unhappy, takes a
> pair of lovers by whom she is successively deserted; in the midst
> of the bewilderment of which, giving up her husband and her
> child, letting everything go, she sinks deeper into duplicity, debt,
> despair, and arrives on the spot, on the small scene itself of her
> poor depravities, at a pitiful tragic end. In especial she does these
> things while remaining absorbed in romantic intention and vision,
> and she remains absorbed in romantic intention and vision while
> fairly rolling in the dust. That is the triumph of the book as the
> triumph stands, that Emma interests us by the nature of her
> consciousness and the play of her mind, thanks to the reality and
> beauty with which those sources are invested. It is not only that
> they represent *her* state; they are so true, so observed and felt,
> and especially so shown, that they represent the state, actual or
> potential, of all persons like her, persons romantically determined.
> Then her setting, the medium in which she struggles, becomes
> in its way as important, becomes eminent with the eminence
> of art; the tiny world in which she revolves, the contracted cage
> in which she flutters, is hung out in space for her, and her com-
> panions in captivity there are as true as herself. (P. 63.)

This is so sensitive that it is easy not to see that it is slanted and
makes from the novel a picture of its own, as much as describing
Flaubert's picture. To many English readers it will have become
a part of their reading of the novel itself. Yet it Jamesifies the novel
to apply only adjectives like 'pretty' and 'ignorant, foolish, flimsy,
unhappy' to Emma, for there is more to her than they tell. There is
more than 'romantic intention and vision' too: there is innocence,
self-will, *ennui*, anger, voluptuousness and, above all, an intensity
of desire which is both sexual and more than sexual. At the centre
of the novel is a passionateness which James's eloquence no more
suggests than it does those moments when her emotion touches the
mystical. One sign of his missing this quality, a sign related to his
emphasis on 'form', is that he sees Emma's situation more from
above than, as Flaubert came to, from within. He has too much pity

to share much in the irony but is not involved enough by Emma's
fate to avoid a tone of condescension to her. His social feeling about
her class is too evident. One imagines him peering after her with
aloof sympathy as she 'sinks' into 'the small scene . . . of her poor
depravities'; as she 'sinks', he admires her truth to life. And so he
does not seem to feel, as Flaubert surely wanted his reader to feel,
that he might be 'fairly rolling in the dust' himself. He comes out
of the book too clean. That is where the notion of 'form' takes him.

James both wanted to sympathise with Emma too much and
could not sympathise with her enough. It is this uncertainty that
prompts his central criticism of *Madame Bovary*: 'Our complaint
is that Emma Bovary, in spite of the nature of her consciousness
and in spite of her reflecting so much that of her creator, is really
too small an affair.' (P. 64.) 'Small', that is, in relation to the
intended representativeness. This severely reduces the force of the
previous statement that 'Emma interests us by the nature of her
consciousness and the play of her mind, thanks to the reality and
beauty with which those sources are invested'. That phrase was
anyway left purposely vague so that it would seem debatable
whether Emma's 'beauty' is intrinsic or whether it exists mainly in
the evocative 'beauty' with which Flaubert *invests* her. Her smallness seems, in fact, to be repeated by James's sense of the smallness
of her world when he does suggest something of the novel's true
depth: 'the tiny world in which she revolves, the contracted cage
in which she flutters, is hung out in space for her . . .'. Again,
there is a deliberate vagueness in the beautiful phrasing of the
criticism: does the 'tiny world' take on representative largeness of
meaning or is it simply that Emma at last sees it whole? Is it really
Flaubert whose hanging James admires? *Madame Bovary* may still
slip away here, leaving us clutching either at a perfect 'livre sur
rien,' or an art oddly reminiscent of a Jamesian *nouvelle* like *In The
Cage*. It is impossible to be sure whether or not James thinks Emma
can finally go beyond her own smallness.

The crucial argument against James's view of Emma's smallness
is that in one way she is meant to be small. Her view of the life
she lives can never fully describe that life as the novel enables us
to see it. This is quite consonant with her seeming superior to the
other inmates of her world: we are all, more or less, small affairs
in a much vaster life than just our own. It was to escape this thought
that James attributed Emma's smallness to her social position and
limited sensibility. Yet a heroine of greater beauty, seen in Flaubert's
terms, would have been small in the same way. This is why Flaubert
was such a puzzling great novelist to James:

Why did Flaubert choose, as special conduits of the life he pro-

posed to depict, such inferior and in the case of Frédéric such
abject human specimens. I insist only in respect to the latter, the
perfection of 'Madame Bovary' scarce leaving one much warrant
for wishing anything other. . . . He wished in each case to make
a picture of experience – middling experience, it is true – and
of the world close to him; but if he imagined nothing better for
his purpose than such a heroine and such a hero, both such
limited reflectors and registers, we are forced to believe it to have
been by a defect of his mind. (P. 64.)[20]

Flaubert's poetry is not created through Jamesian 'reflectors and
registers', which suggest an art nearer to Musset's emotional effect
than Shakespearean 'généralisation'. His sense of the danger of being
personal made it essential that his 'special conduits' should be
flawed. His point is precisely in seeing what he can feel in common
with them, not in dismissing them as 'abject specimens'. The compassion called forth through Emma for the tragic contradiction
between our desire and its objects is richer for having so ordinary
a source. In *Uncle Tom's Cabin* he objected to the young nun's
death being that of a saint: 'Why? I would weep more if she were
an ordinary child.' Perhaps it needs less compassion to weep over
a Milly Theale than an Emma Bovary? A feeling of what is common
in the human condition can be deeper and more primary than our
moral evaluations of individuals.

James would not accept this argument because for him the richness of a novelist's 'reflector' is an index of its representativeness:

When I speak of the faith in Emma Bovary as proportionately
wasted I reflect on M. Faguet's judgement that she is from the
point of view of deep interest richly or at least roundedly representative. Representative of what? he makes us ask even while
granting all the grounds of misery and tragedy involved. The
plea for her is the plea made for all the figures that live without
evaporation under the painter's hand – that they are not only
particular persons but types of their kind, and as valid in one
light as in the other. It is Emma's 'kind' that I question for this
responsibility. . . . (P. 65.)

The sharp question is blunted by the loaded word 'type'. Why look
for Emma's 'representative' more in her personality than in the
action? James divides types into a sort of class system in a way that
seems to preclude the sense in which, to be typical, a 'type' must also
represent something we find in ourselves as well as a special character of its own:

The book is a picture of the middling . . . but does Emma attain even to *that*? Hers is a narrow middling even for a little imaginative person whose 'social' significance is small. It is greater on the whole than her capacity of consciousness, taking this all round; and so, in a word, we feel her less illustrational than she might have been not only if the world had offered her more points of contact, but if she had had more of these to give it. (P. 66.)

There is a true perception here which Flaubert, whose letters show how hard he often found it to share Emma's experience, would have been the first to see. We may well wonder if that experience is shareable only at the cost of restricting our own experience. We may even ask whether Flaubert was more ready to share in its negative emotions than in the more positive ones it so nearly broaches. Yet these questions are still only secondary to the main recognition that Emma's experience is not supposed to be easy to share while we are nonetheless made to share it. It required courage, humility and compassion to see that, 'Madame Bovary, c'est moi'. To see these things in the creation of Emma is to begin to ask why James himself invariably sought such congenial vessels as Isabel and Strether for his own sense of life.

Despite his reservations James could still call Flaubert 'the novelist's novelist'. (P. 85.) In doing so he even adopts some of Flaubert's more extreme ideas about 'style' and 'form', ideas behind the novel even if they cannot explain its greatness. Again, they help suggest that there was always something in *Madame Bovary* which James could never quite account for:

> ... the way the thing is done not only triumphs over the question of value but in respect to it fairly misleads and confounds us. Where else shall we find in anything proportionately so small such an air of dignity of size? (P. 72.)

The word 'small' now applies to the book itself as well as to Emma and yet this only makes the book's 'dignity' more of a puzzle. He has to take an aesthetic escape from this puzzle in a way that Flaubert the novelist never did:

> His own sense of all this . . . was that beauty comes with expression, that expression is creation, that it *makes* the reality, and only in the degree in which it is, exquisitely, expression; and that we move in literature through a world of different values and relations, a blest world in which we know nothing except by style, but in which also everything is saved by it, and in which the image is thus always superior to the thing itself. (Pp. 78–9.)[21]

This is nearer Pater than the essay on Baudelaire in *French Poets and Novelists*. James's notion of style gets farther and farther away from his real sense of what the prose of *Madame Bovary* is like as Emma's tragedy is 'observed and felt, and especially so shown':

> Style itself moreover, with all respect to Flaubert, never *totally* beguiles; since even when we are so queerly constituted as to be ninety-nine parts literary we are still a hundredth part something else. This hundredth part may, once we possess the book – or the book possesses us – make us imperfect as readers, and yet without it should we want or get the book at all? (P. 79.)

Flaubert would, of course, have assented to this but James is really bringing in the Flaubert who wrote the letters because he has been unable to explain this 'something else'. His question is rhetorical and does not stop him from ending his essay by again praising the novel's 'crowned classicism' as evasively as when he began it:

> . . . I do not mean that 'Madame Bovary' is a classic because the 'thats', the 'its' and the 'tos' are made to march as Orpheus and his lute made the beasts, but because the element of order and harmony works as a symbol of everything else that is preserved for us by the history of the book. The history of the book remains the lesson and the important, the delightful thing, remains above all the drama that moves slowly to its climax. It is what we come back to for the sake of what it shows us. We see – from the present to the past indeed, never alas from the present to the future – how a classic almost inveterately grows. (P. 84.)

It is not just the importation of biography which makes this picture of what is 'classic' in *Madame Bovary* seem too narrow. Between the wit and the sentiment, the novel's 'drama' and 'what it shows' get lost in a circular argument.

IV

James might have looked at other things in the letters for help with *Madame Bovary* and it is worth quoting some of them to put this account of his essay in context. One of their central themes is the artist's relation to his personal emotions and it is often brought out by an exasperated reaction to the poetry of Musset:

> Musset has never separated poetry from the sensations which it completes. According to him, music was made for serenades,

painting for portraits and poetry for the consolations of the heart. When one wants to put the sun in one's pants like this, one burns one's pants and pisses on the sun. That's what has happened to him. Nerves, magnetism, that's poetry. But no, it has a more serene basis. If it were enough to have sensitive nerves to be a poet, I would be better than Shakespeare and Homer, who strikes me as having been a man with few nerves. This confusion is impious. (*Corr.*, II, pp. 460–1.)

For Flaubert, the Mozarts of the future are not those children who are so affected by music that every note makes them writhe with pain: the more personal the artist is, the more feeble will be his art. This was the fault of the first version of his own *La Tentation de Saint Antoine*:

In place of Saint Anthony, for example, I myself am there; the *Temptation* was for me and not for the reader. *The less one feels a thing, the more qualified one is to express it as it is*, (as it *always* is in itself, in its generality, freed from all its transient contingencies). But it is necessary to have the ability *to make one's self feel it*. This ability is nothing else than genius: to see, to have the model, posing before one's eyes. (*Corr.*, II, pp. 461–2. G.F.'s italics.)

Art should not be just 'the chamber pot of the passions'. (*Corr.*, IV, p. 61.) 'We are only worth something because God breathes in us.' (*Corr.*, IH, p. 103.) James may have agreed to much of this and there is no question of assimilating the personal elements in his art to Musset or Lamartine, with whom the young Flaubert had probably more in common. What is significant is that it is not this part of Flaubert's thought which is referred to in James's criticism: where Flaubert's concern is with the 'model', the object as it really is in itself, James concentrates on his 'style', the way the object is seen, so that 'the image is thus always superior to the thing itself'. One might want to add that where Flaubert's style grew increasingly bare, James's grew more and more mannered and personal.

As his attitude to the first *Tentation* shows, Flaubert only put the personal behind him by dint of exploring it. It would be a mistake to attribute to him the kind of flight from self which Eliot, no doubt partly as a result of reading him, presented as a separation between the 'suffering' and the 'creative' minds. It is Frédéric Moreau who does that. Neither is it easy to imagine Flaubert making as much as James did in *The Tragic Muse*, in the figure of Nick Dormer, of the 'turned back' of the artist: he was not interested by

the figure of the artist in that individual way, as Pellerin in
L'Education shows. The true sense of his rejection of the personal
is towards a broader exposure of the self to life. Writing in 1853
from Trouville, a place redolent of the family memories of his
childhood and the scene of his first meeting with Mme Schlésinger,
he said:

> I have reviewed myself a great deal here and here is the con-
> clusion of these four idle weeks: farewell, that is to say, farewell
> forever to the *personal*, the intimate, the relative. My old project
> of writing my memoirs later on has left me. Nothing about my
> own person tempts me. (*Corr.*, III, p. 320.)

What was to give him pleasure in his art was to find life confirming
it, as when he found the words of the speakers at the Comices
Agricoles in *Madame Bovary* re-appearing later, in the newspaper,
in the speech of a Rouen dignitary. It is important to see that this
was quite compatible with his going on to write *L'Education* and
Un Cœur Simple, both of which had their roots in his memories
of Trouville.

The idea of projecting the self into experiences one has never
known, which goes back at least to Jules in the first *Education*,
is always more an extension of the personal than a simple reaction
to it. Whether we see it as stemming from self-hatred, pride or a
need to compensate for the self's finitude is less important than it
is to see that it is more than mere histrionic impersonation. Behind
it is a deep and ambiguous compassion, a feeling that personal
experience is only seen imaginatively when seen as personal to
someone else. This is why Flaubert's compassion for Emma can
be general and not a disguised self-pity. He only feels for himself
when feeling for someone else. It is in this way that it is not mere
paradox to speak of his humanity in the same breath as of his
'impassibilité'. If we do, we can get more from him than the feeling
of 'a strong man who has not been able to completely express
himself'.[22]

Why did James read *Madame Bovary* as he did? It would be
wrong to try to discount his kind of creative misreading, for it is
common to all criticism and something criticism could hardly do
without. It is also easy to see powerful historical reasons for James's
taking the line he did: it is coloured both by the recent impact
made by the publishing of the *Correspondence* and by the currency
at the time of distorted versions of Flaubert's thought, in critics
like Zola or like Pater. Yet the source of his views lay deeper than
literary fashion. One surmises that the eulogy of *Madame Bovary*'s
'form' helped rationalise a more divided response to Flaubert, a

tugging between attraction and repulsion, into a simpler mixture of aesthetic praise and moral criticism. In ways, James must have been attracted by the moral position he rejects and have half-shared it. In *The Portrait of a Lady*, after all, he is only half-conscious that the 'high places of happiness' to which Isabel aspires are the reverse of 'life' in any Lawrentian acceptation of the word. Flaubert would have made him more aware of that side of himself and he may well have resented him for revealing the affinity. One could also speculate along the lines of Vernon Lee's imaginary portrait of James, in her *nouvelle Lady Tal* (1892). She says in it that 'a tendency to withdraw from all personal concerns . . . was mainly because he conceived that this shrinkingness of nature (which foolish persons call egoism) was the necessary complement to his power of intellectual analysis; and that any departure from the position of dispassioned spectator of the world's follies and miseries would mean also a departure from his real duty as a novelist'.[23] This sketches a similar, if more polite, fear of life to that so often attributed to Flaubert by those who see him as stony and impervious.

If James saw 'all round' Flaubert it was perhaps because he needed to. For Flaubert's voice was a dangerous one to listen to, one that echoed in his own feelings of pessimism too disturbingly for him to resist censuring them in someone else. James must also have been disturbed by the immense energy which simmered inside Flaubert's despair. Such a force of life against life may have seemed stronger than the force of life *for* life which he felt and imagined himself. I do not finally think of James as admiring Flaubert from the point of view of a fellow professional, doing obeisance to the 'novelist's novelist'. I think rather of the scene in the cemetery in his late story of *The Beast in the Jungle*, where John Marcher, who has let life pass him by, stares into the grief-ravaged face of another mourner who has given life a firmer hold on him than he has himself. The fellow craftsman is similarly gripped by awe, fear and envy. Flaubert's challenge to his readers is often dodged by explaining' him with hindsight as a 'case', the 'case' of the artist. Whether we define that case, in Lawrence's way, as a fear of life or, in Gourmont's, as an unflinching confronting of the unconfrontable, we too easily slip through the trap-door of mythologising. We forget, because it is easier to forget, that Flaubert's real greatness lay in exposing himself, in spite of his fears, to things in life which brought thoughts of pain and misery. Ironically, the 'case' was the invention of Flaubert's own weakness for pretending that all he exposed to life was a toughness which it would temper like steel. That weakness was only the obverse of a deeper strength, not the whole man.

3   Emma Bovary in her World

James's criticism helps us to see how the irony and compassion of *Madame Bovary* keep each other alive. There may be episodes in which irony outweighs compassion and becomes malice, just as in other episodes Flaubert's feeling for Emma can sap his irony so that he relapses into simple pity; the abiding impression the novel leaves is of irony and compassion indissolubly married – married, that is, in one of those marriages where the strain of cohabitation is only surpassed by the unthinkableness of divorce. A strangely fused tension of opposite emotions is at the source of the book's unique capacity to provoke and move its readers in the same breath. It is, I think, with this tension that criticism must begin.

'Irony does not diminish pathos; on the contrary, it intensifies it. In my third part, which will be full of farcical things, I want the reader to weep.' The tension within the novel is deliberately created; it is not just the consequence of Flaubert's having unintentionally coloured his narrative with his own neuroses. If readers feel as if the author has cast them as a battlefield for the enaction of his own emotional contradictions this is, in part, how it was meant to be felt. Yet it is not obvious how this intermixed laughing and weeping can be gathered up by the reader into a coherent sense of who Emma Bovary is. One reading would say that she is the result of Flaubert's transferring to the reader his own divided and self-punishing feelings about her. This view leads inexorably towards biographical interpretation. James's concern with evaluating the moral life embodied in Emma gives a surer starting point. It has always been felt that, in some sense, Emma is offered as a case or a type. One can agree, as long as we do not bring to the novel any notion that a character of this kind ought, *a priori*, to express some integrated selfhood, some 'finer consciousness'. It is necessary to ask whether Flaubert made Emma as unworthy as James says she is, to forward his critique of the Romantic idea of selfhood.[1]

A good way to begin is by looking at the kind of writing that Flaubert eliminated from the novel's earlier drafts on his way to the final text. One of their most striking features is that they often show him giving in to the temptation to feel sorry for Emma, perhaps in just the way James, Arnold and Sainte-Beuve would have wished. The number of revisions undergone by some of the more pathetic

passages show that he must have felt his pity for Emma rising too
near the surface of his prose. He seems often to guard himself from
facile identification with her when he re-writes. The finished text
usually makes his pity more reticent or terse. For example, at the
end of the draft of the first part comes this sentence:

> Pauvre diamant ignoré qui roulait dans les fanges du ravin sous
> les pieds des pâtres, parmi les cailloux et le sable innombrable,
> aucun bras de pêcheur n'amènerait donc jamais au soleil ses
> facettes multiples et sa pureté splendide! *Et elle exécrait
> l'injustice de Dieu. . . .*[2]
>
> (A poor unconsidered diamond rolling in the mire of the ravine
> beneath the herdsmen's feet, among the pebbles and the number-
> less sands: no fisherman's arm would ever bring into the sunlight
> its multiple facets and splendid purity. *She abhorred the injustice
> of God. . . .*)

The characteristic astringency is missing; the cadences supply a half
approving echo to Emma's self-pity; prose so given to posing is ill-
suited to satirise a heroine who is always posing herself. The final
text is blunt and separate:

> Elle avait vu des duchesses à la Vaubyessard qui avaient la taille
> plus lourde et les façons plus communes, et elle exécrait l'injustice
> de Dieu; elle s'appuyait la tête aux murs pour pleurer. . . .(P. 93.)
>
> (At la Vaubyessard, she had seen duchesses whose waists were
> heavier and whose manner was more common, and, resting her
> head against the wall to weep, she abhorred the injustice of
> God. . . .)

Emma's distress is too bitter to leave her time for wistful sentiments,
so the reader is not enticed into sympathetic complicity with her.
This makes her tears more real: there is now no implicit audience
for them. In pruning, her feelings are not belittled but given
intensity. This is more significant than the fact that her jealousy,
anger and hysteria come over more clearly so that she seems less of
a noble soul, a 'pauvre diamant ignoré'. What such changes do is
to enable Flaubert to include in Emma's story more of the things,
animate and inanimate, which lie beyond herself. Her world
becomes more solidly shaped with each such omission. Flaubert
imagines her most clearly when he imagines her world most clearly.

This continuity of self and world is vividly caught in the description of Emma's petty domestic rounds in chapter seven of the
Première Partie. The *Nouvelle Version* has a long passage, cut
only at the stage of page-proofs, in which Emma retires to her

garden for fresh air after a summer storm. She gives in to her growing unhappiness:

> Elle se renversa la tête contre le dossier du banc, et humait l'air dans une aspiration à faire craquer son corsage; un sanglot alors la prit. Une tristesse liquide lui monta du cœur aux lèvres sans pouvoir couler, puis redescendit en elle et se figea dans tous ses membres en accablement. Elle entendit dans sa tête des roulements qui passaient ou comme les bruits d'un grand vent qui siffle la nuit dans une galerie. Les mains humides, les genoux déliés, le cœur battant, elle ne pensait plus, voyait à peine et, dans des immensités intérieures, sentait seulement défaillir son âme, comme un nageur épuisé qui agonise sur la mer. Quelque chose remua parmi les feuilles. Elle se leva d'un bond en rougissant. C'était une vache dans le clos voisin, qui, la tête passée par-dessus le haie, regardait là, tranquillement, de ses gros yeux ronds.
>
> Charles ne rentra le soir qu'à onze *heures*, n'ayant pas mangé depuis le matin. (P. 197.)
>
> (She threw back her head against the bench-rest, inhaling the air in a breath deep enough to burst her bodice open. Then a sob gripped her. A liquid sorrow rose up from her heart to her lips, unable to flow, then sunk back inside her to set hard through all her limbs as deep dejectedness. Inside her head she heard rumbling wheels going by or sounds like the noise of a great wind whistling at night-time in a gallery. With moist hands, limp knees and a throbbing heart, she could think no longer, could hardly see and felt only her soul swooning in an inner immensity, like an exhausted swimmer in his death throes in the sea. Something among the leaves stirred. She got up suddenly, blushing. It was a cow in the next field, its head lent over the hedge, who was calmly watching her out of its big round eyes.
>
> Charles did not get in until eleven o'clock in the evening, having eaten nothing since the morning.)

There is too much fine writing; the pity for Emma's 'accablement' is, in the same way, like a tap left running. The thing one is sorriest to lose in the final version is the moment when she is aroused from her rêveries by the cow, staring at her with quiet indifference.

In the novel itself the passage where this early version was to have come in is restricted to a narrative of Emma's housekeeping and the credit it reflects on the innocently complacent Charles:

> Quand ils avaient, le dimanche, quelque voisin à dîner, elle trouvait moyen d'offrir un plat coquet, s'entendait à poser sur

les feuilles de vigne les pyramides des reines-Claude, servait renversés les pots de confitures dans une assiette, et même elle parlait d'acheter des rince-bouche pour le dessert. Il rejaillissait de tout cela beaucoup de considération sur Bovary.

Charles finissait par s'estimer davantage de ce qu'il possédait une pareille femme. Il montrait avec orgueil, dans la salle, deux petits croquis d'elle à la mine de plomb, qu'il avait fait encadrer de cadres très larges et suspendu contre le papier de la muraille à de longs cordons verts. Au sortir de la messe, on le voyait sur sa porte avec de belles pantoufles en tapisserie.

Il rentrait tard, à dix heures, minuit quelquefois. Alors il demandait à manger, et comme la bonne était couchée, c'était Emma qui le servait. Il retirait sa redingote pour dîner plus à son aise. Il disait les uns après les autres tous les gens qu'il avait rencontrés, les villages où il avait été, les ordonnances qu'il avait écrites, et, satisfait de lui-même, il mangeait le reste du miroton, épluchait son fromage, croquait une pomme, vidait sa carafe, puis s'allait mettre au lit, se couchait sur le dos et ronflait. (P. 59.)

(When they had one of the neighbours to dinner of a Sunday, she would manage to serve an elegant dish: she knew how to set a pyramid of greengages on a base of vine-leaves, poured her preserves onto a plate to serve them and even talked of buying finger-bowls to go with the dessert. All this reflected much credit on Bovary.

The possession of such a wife came to give Charles a higher opinion of himself. In the drawing room, he would proudly show off two little pencil sketches of hers, which he had had mounted in very large frames and suspended by long green cords against the wall-paper. As one came out of mass, he was to be seen at his door wearing a fine pair of carpet slippers. He came home late, at ten, sometimes at midnight. Then he would ask for something to eat and, since the maid had gone to bed, it was Emma who served him. He took off his frock coat to dine more comfortably. One after another, he related all the people he had met, the villages he had been to, the prescriptions he had written, and, feeling pleased with himself, he would eat up what was left of the onion soup, pare his cheese, munch an apple, empty his decanter, and then go up to bed, lie down on his back and begin to snore.)

The fidelity of this to the texture of Emma's life makes the passage of time almost tangible. The blank catalogue of Charles's supper generates a subdued crescendo of misery which needs no spelling-out by poetical words like 'accablement'. The prose serves the reality of its subject, as the undertone of comic affection for Charles shows.

Flaubert has no need to explain what Emma feels by analysing her state of mind: our own humanity fills in the blanks. The feeling is more of compassion than pity, it is both less pleasurable and less exclusively directed to Emma than in the unrevised passage. We see Emma wincing as Charles munches his apple but we still see his own relish for it. Her isolation is glimpsed through the comic picture of Charles proudly sporting his slippers on the doorstep and congratulating himself on his wife: both are equally alone. The irony achieves vigour without becoming hostile to its objects. It makes us feel penetrated by Emma's surroundings: the sketches in their over-large frames, the vine leaves, the prescriptions, what there is for dinner. This is enough.

I think that Flaubert disciplined his prose in this way in order to keep clear that difficult distinction between fate and character which the nineteenth century, so fertile in variations on the idea that 'Character is fate', was anxious to blur. The irony prevents the reader from confusing pity for Emma as a person with the more general, because shared, compassion that her weakness and mortality evoke. It circumvents the greatest danger inherent in rendering life from a particular 'point-of-view': that the reader will use the main character simply as a kind of continuation of his own relation to himself. Flaubert makes no bid for our disguised self-pity. At the same time, he thwarts any temptation his reader may have to use Emma for making abstract generalisations about 'life': he makes clear what it means to be a separate self *and* what each separate self has in common with other selves. This is something very different from what happens in a novel like Balzac's *Le Père Goriot*. The end of that book shows how pity, excited on behalf of a character because of the particular kind of character he is, can become a pleasurable emotion. We pity Goriot because we don't feel much like him ourselves, even if we are parents. His tragedy is palliated for the reader, as it is for his daughters, by the knowledge that in him parental love has taken an obsessive and extreme form. As Leslie Stephen saw, Balzac makes us eager to turn down our thumbs on him so that he can be satisfyingly consigned to the lions.[3] *Madame Bovary* will not let us wriggle off the hook by gratifying this sort of slightly complacent pity which seeks to put us in Goriot's skin without making us share humanity with him. The fact that Flaubert's irony often focuses on Emma's unintelligence and vanity does not dam up this sympathy, though it makes it more demanding and painful. By contrast, our hearts are meant to bleed for the Christ of Paternity with thoughtless exuberance.[4]

Critics who resent the fact that Emma is only Emma often manage to give the impression of having wanted to identify with her and failed. James is clearly aggrieved that Flaubert has made him feel so intensely for somebody with whom he cannot identify without thinking less well of himself or of human nature. This is partly why he argues that Emma is too 'small' to be 'representative'. Flaubert has an appalling gift for exacerbating his reader's tendencies to self-pity only to revoke them, yet, as James's essay shows, to baulk his tragic satire is to side-step his essential compassion for people who suffer. James was not simply being a moral snob though; Flaubert was himself tempted to see Emma *de haut en bas*, and there are many passages when we are treacherously invited to look on her as a Parisian would. But they are surely there to trap us into the momentary illusion that life in Yonville is somehow essentially different from metropolitan life, mere *mœurs de province* and not the human condition. In the book's terms, such a view is simply the reverse folly from Emma's own. If we ask Flaubert for a less bleak view of human nature than his irony gives, we play Emma's own rôle at the opera and thus fall victim to the practical joke sprung on us by the brilliant use of Homais: we end up seeing her through values uncomfortably similar to those upheld by the most suspect apostle of 'progress' in Yonville. Caught in this trap, it is natural for readers to defend themselves by arging that Flaubert's choice of Emma as his heroine, rather than someone better able to comprehend her own tragedy, is a sophistry for enforcing on us his own hatred and fear of life. It is a reassuring view: by saying, as Lawrence did, that Flaubert 'stood away from life as from a leprosy' one makes the book's horror at life into a projection of its author's neuroses, not a feeling it is possible to understand from personal experience.[5] Flaubert becomes more of a 'case' than an artist. This reaction (it is Leavis's and, in a way, Sartre's too) is one that any reader may sometimes need, just as Emma herself needs her redeeming fantasies of la Vaubyessard. Of course, Flaubert *was* a 'case' (so was the Dr Johnson who wrote *Rasselas*) but to stress the fact becomes reductive when it ushers in the equally reductive Arnoldian view that the book is blighted because Flaubert is reductive about his characters. Bourgeoisophobia is never the deepest note in the novels, which are written by Flaubert the artist and not by Flaubert the Garçon or Flaubert the letter-writer. In fact, *Madame Bovary* never satisfies our need for self-relieving indignation as, say, the Dickens of *Bleak House* does; many readers must have winced at finding how difficult it is to feel comfortable in despising Charles. The novel would be far less painful if we could only dislike him a little more! Even Homais is handled with a rough kindness of mockery which makes it impossible to see him as a 'villain'; as Renan saw, Flaubert knows that without his sort people would still be being burnt at the stake.[6] People pretend he is a caricature in order to make out that Flaubert hates his characters: then they need not feel they have anything in common with them. In fact, Homais is a mystery, not a caricature, and Flaubert is quite as delighted as he is appalled by him. What puzzles humanist critics is that you cannot identify with a mystery.

Flaubert came early to the conclusion that the idea of being a judge is an absurdity, yet, in his long campaign against the *bourgeois*, he was always making judgements or, at least, pretending to make them. It is not, therefore, surprising that *Madame Bovary* should tempt us towards a general thought about life and then withhold it from us. The irony lurks in ambush for the generalising reader as much as it does for the book's characters. It is so intrinsic to everything that to ask what its function is and to ask how Emma should be seen becomes a single question. To understand her it is necessary to see how she is meant to be understood, yet the irony is partly there to make it impossible for one to decide just what she is like. We are tempted into moral judgements on her only to have our confidence in those judgements betrayed in deepest consequence. This accounts for much of the fascination her character has always had for readers; it also compounds her loneliness by making her seem elusively distant from the reader as well as from the people she lives amongst. James was, I think, wrong to speak of her as if she were quite easy to know, a shallow 'middling' person: *Bovarysme*, unlike Swift's Pride and La Rochefoucauld's *amour-propre*, is very much a false scent trailed speculatively across the psychologist's path. Emma remains an enigma, just as Homais does.

She is not, however, problematic just because an aloof novelist keeps her so much at arm's length that her emotions seem merely conjectural. It is all very well to ask where Flaubert stands in relation to his heroine, the novel would have been far less interesting had he felt dogmatically on the subject. After all, where does Shakespeare stand in relation to Hamlet? Eliot was, in a sense, quite right in his notorious description of that play; he simply failed to see that is is precisely the fact that final sense cannot be made of all its facts which justifies its expression of the imponderableness of human character. Emma has something of the Prince of Denmark in her: she never tracks down a firm idea of the kind of self she is, despite being absorbed in herself. Her fantasies reveal how conjectural her real emotions are to herself as well as to us. Flaubert was undermining the 'old stable ego' long before Lawrence was; the process of doing so pained him and is meant to pain his readers. In the many references to Emma in his letters there is always the sense, beneath that exasperation which he could turn on in a trice in order to wind down from a day's solitary work, that he is desperately striving to follow what it is that makes another person tick.

It is therefore misleading to take to the novel any idea of unity of being or 'finer consciousness' in order to define our attitude to Emma. Flaubert proposes a more tragic (and less Protestant) question about the self than James does: May not the notion of selfhood be no more than the heroic illusion of Romantic culture, just the sort of illusion which fosters the posing we have in Emma herself? There is no need to open the book with the expectation of finding a Dorothea Brooke or an Ursula Brangwen.

Passages like the one I quoted from the end of the *Première Partie* make it clear that the problematic depiction of Emma's character reflects Flaubert's own uncertainty and is not a mere trick played on the reader. The apparent coldness of the narrative is in part the self-defensive mask for a subterranean tenderness. I insist on the Lawrentian word 'tenderness': in many ways Flaubert possessed more of that quality than Lawrence did. Lawrence would have treated people like Emma's father or Homais' servant, Justin, far more moralistically. The common reader has always known that the deepest thing about *Madame Bovary* is the way it asks us to share in Emma's suffering, to become almost literally possessed by it. She is not simply a fly to her spider-like creator. The book seeks to expose a nerve of agonised sensitiveness in its reader; it is that which gets it a name for coldness; it asks for an empathy which is doubly appalling, because of its intensity and the unheroic nature of its object, and, faced with this demand, we may well exorcise it with the claim that it is Flaubert, not life, which is brutal. Lawrence saw through this view himself, at least to the extent of seeing that the book is slightly over-tragic, flawed by 'seams of pity'.[7] In the *Troisième Partie*, the note of pathos perhaps becomes too pressing, and the general sense of the world's indifference to Emma's sufferings courts a more self-pitying and Hardyesque view of life as persecution.[8] The criticisms the novel does call for may be quite contrary to those made by James and Arnold and Sainte-Beuve.

An interesting confirmation of Flaubert's tenderness is found in the picture of Canivet, the doctor who attends Hippolyte after Charles' unsuccessful operation on his club foot. He is, like Arnold's version of Flaubert himself, dispassionate to the point of callousness, and he is ridiculed in the most scathing way. He checks that his horse is well cared for before he attends to his patient, then he calmly discusses his work with the sycophantic Homais:

> . . . je ne suis point délicat comme vous, et il m'est aussi parfaitement égal de découper un chrétien que la première volaille venue. Après ca, direz-vous, l'habitude! . . . l'habitude! . . .
>
> Alors, sans aucun égard pour Hippolyte, qui suait d'angoisse entre ses draps, ces messieurs engagèrent une conversation où

l'apothicaire compara le sang-froid d'un chirurgien à celui d'un
général; et ce rapprochement fut agréable à Canivet, qui se
répandit en paroles sur les exigences de son art. Il le considérait
comme un sacerdoce, bien que les officiers de santé le déshonor-
assent. (P. 254.)

(. . . I'm not squeamish like you and it's all one to me whether
I carve up a Christian or the first piece of poultry that comes
my way. Ah! you'll say at that, it's habit, merely habit! . . .

Then, without the slightest concern for Hippolyte, who was
sweating with agony between the sheets, these gentlemen em-
barked upon a conversation in which the chemist compared the
phlegm of a surgeon to that of a general, and Canivet, flattered
by this parallel, overflowed with fine words about the demands
of his art. He regarded it as a sacred vocation, even though it
was dishonoured by half-qualified practitioners.)

As in the prize-giving at the Comices Agricoles or Charles' last
meeting with Rodolphe, heartlessness is the butt of Flaubert's most
devastating comedy. One immediately takes Charles' side against
Canivet and his incompetence evokes far more compassion than
contempt. Why, then, should Flaubert have tried, in revising his
novel, to become a narrator ostensibly like Canivet? For Canivet,
with his sang-froid and his sense of vocation may well be a self-
parody, like the tax collector Binet making serviette rings in his
ivory tower.[9] It is curious that the emotional power of *Madame
Bovary* should so often appear to come from its author's stifling of
his own emotionality. He is perhaps only completely natural in his
pathos when it is articulated through comedy, as here, in the way
Hippolyte's agony is implied as if in passing. If he had been unable
to laugh at Emma he might have become intolerably sentimental
about her. It is therefore natural to wonder, as James did, whether
there were not something in Flaubert which was never completely
expressed. That, after all, is Emma's own deepest source of suffering.

II

One mark of a Romantic reading of *Madame Bovary* is to dwell
too much on its heroine and to take her *Bovarysme* as special to
herself, yet Flaubert's study of the dangers of hope and imagination
is continued through many of the other characters. Emma's mother-
in-law dreaming of her son's future thinks in the same way as
Emma dreaming of going to the opera and Charles himself is the
same; yearning for some better life elsewhere, he looks out of his
window in Rouen and imagines what life would be like if he were
not a student:

La rivière, qui fait de ce quartier de Rouen comme une ignoble petite Venise, coulait en bas, sous lui, jaune, violette ou bleue entre ses ponts et ses grilles. . . . En face, au delà des toits, le grand ciel pur s'étendait, avec le soleil rouge se couchant. Qu'il devait faire bon là-bas! (P. 11.)

(The river, which makes this part of Rouen into a wretched little Venice, ran by beneath him, yellow, violet or blue between its bridges and its railings. . . . Opposite, beyond the rooftops. a great pure sky extended, with a red sun setting in it. How fine things must be, over there!)

Such parallels help explain why Flaubert often draws our attention away from Emma at crucial moments in her life, sometimes giving the impression of being cold to her in doing so. Thus, the departure of Emma and Charles for Tostes, after their wedding, is seen through the eyes of Emma's father, not in terms of the talk and feelings of the young couple. We just see their trap receding into the distance:

Puis il se rappela ses noces, son temps d'autrefois, la première grossesse de sa femme; il était bien joyeux, lui aussi, le jour qu'il l'avait emmenée de chez son père dans sa maison, quand il la portait en croupe en trottant sur la neige; car on était aux environs de Noël et la campagne était toute blanche; elle le tenait par un bras, à l'autre était accroché son panier; le vent agitait les longues dentelles de sa coiffure cauchoise, qui lui passaient quelquefois sur la bouche, et, lorsqu'il tournait la tête, il voyait près de lui, sur son épaule, sa petite mine rosée qui souriait silencieusement, sous la plaque d'or de son bonnet. Pour se réchauffer les doigts, elle les lui mettait, de temps en temps, dans la poitrine. Comme c'était vieux tout cela! Leur fils, à présent, aurait trente ans! Alors il regarda derrière lui, il n'aperçut rien sur la route. (Pp. 41–2.)

(Then he recalled his wedding, his own former days, his wife's first pregnancy. He too had been in high spirits on the day he had taken her from her father's to his own house, carrying her side-saddle as they trotted over the snow. For it was around Christmas-tide, and the countryside was all white. She held on to him by one arm, her basket hooked over the other; the wind was ruffling the long lace strands of her cauchois head-dress, sweeping them across his mouth sometimes, and, when he turned his head, he could see near to him, on his shoulder, her little rosy face smiling silently, under the gold crown of her bonnet. From time to time she would put her fingers inside his coat-front, to warm them up. How long ago all that was! Their son would have been thirty by now! Then he looked behind him: he could see nothing on the road.)

The poetry of this picture of Emma and Charles going forward into an experience which père Rouault is looking back on makes the reader think of marriage in the perspective of the passing generations; it is not simply Emma Bovary's marriage which is at issue. There may not be quite that inwardness with the feelings of the main characters that one gets in most novels of the period, but out of this detachment comes a deeper note of tenderness for human experience in general.

This note of generality is deepest when Flaubert is thinking about death. At the end of the novel there is a scene in which Homais and Bournisien get into an argument as they watch over the dead Emma. It is part of the comedy (or tragedy?) of this scene that when the pair of them drop off to sleep, what is in question is not simply Emma's death but their own deaths, and our's too:

Des aboiements continus se traînaient au loin, quelque part.
– Entendez-vous un chien qui hurle dit le pharmacien.
– On prétend qu'ils sentent les morts, répondit l'ecclésiastique. C'est come les abeilles; elles s'envolent de la ruche au décès des personnes.
Homais ne releva pas ces préjugés, car il s'était rendormi.
M. Bournisien, plus robuste, continua quelque temps à remuer tout bas les lèvres, puis, insensiblement, il baissa le menton, lâcha son gros livre noir et se mit à ronfler.
Ils étaient en face l'un de l'autre, le ventre en avant, la figure bouffie, l'air renfrogné, aprés tant de désaccord se recontrant enfin dans la même faiblesse humaine; et ils ne bougeaient pas plus que le cadavre à côté d'eux qui avait l'air de dormir. (P. 458.)
(A continuous barking tailed off somewhere in the distance. 'Can you hear a dog yelping?' said the chemist.
'It is said that they can sense the dead,' replied the churchman. 'It's the same with bees; they fly out of the hive when people die.'
Homais did not take up these prejudices, for he had gone back to sleep.
M. Bournisien, who was more robust, went on quietly moving his lips for a little while, then, insensibly, his chin dropped, he let fall his big black book and began to snore.
They were seated opposite each other, their stomachs thrust out, puffy-faced and as if frowning, meeting at last after so much discord in the same human frailty, moving no more than the corpse beside them which looked as though it were sleeping too.)

This ability to step back from the pathos of Emma's death is the

kind of thing I mean in speaking of Flaubert's true impersonality.
The feeling is tragic because it is not exclusive, because everything
the scene suggests is rendered without evasion and all of the author's
feelings about these characters, his irony and his compassion, come
together in the same poetry. When Flaubert is impersonal in this
way there is no sense of his comedy and his tragedy working at
cross purposes.[10]

In both of the passages just quoted from *Madame Bovary* one
has the sense of a commotion of human activity and talk being
swallowed up into a non-human silence, the silence of the Norman
landscape or the silence of Yonville at night. This movement pervades the novel, right from its opening, when the schoolmaster
quells the hubbub made by his pupils chanting '*Charbovari! Charbovari!*' (p. 4) at the new boy, and the classroom reassumes its
habitual calm. Such silences absorb the human dramas of the novel
into their own indifference. Often, they are broken ony by non-
human sounds, as when Emma bids goodbye to Charles after one
of his visits to Les Bertaux before their marriage:

> Une fois, par un temps de dégel, l'écorce des arbres suintait dans
> la cour, la neige sur la couverture des bâtiments se fondait. Elle
> était sur le seuil; elle alla chercher son ombrelle, elle l'ouvrit.
> L'ombrelle, de soie gorge-de-pigeon, que traversait le soleil,
> éclairait de reflets mobiles la peau blanche de sa figure. Elle
> souriait là-dessous à la chaleur tiède; et on entendait les gouttes
> d'eau, une à une, tomber sur la moire tendue. (Pp. 22–3.)

> (Once, when there was a thaw, and water was dripping down
> the bark of the trees into the farmyard and snow melting on the
> roofs of the outhouses, she was standing on the doorstep. Then
> she went to get her parasol and opened it out. The dove-grey silk
> parasol, shot through with sunlight, lit up the white skin of her
> face with flickering reflections. She was smiling from under it at
> the mild heat, and one could hear water-drops falling, one by
> one, on the taut watered silk.)

Sounds as quiet as these water-drops are only this distinct because
of the silence they punctuate. The same thing may be said of
Emma's feelings, which we grasp through the effect of her immobility and her smile in relation to the landscape of which she forms
a part. The fragility of her feelings and hopes is more poetically
suggested by seeing her like this than through an analysis of them
from within. If we lost this non-human range her world would seem
too humanised to be a fully human one. In no sense is nature a
backdrop for her emotions. She cannot be extricated from the melt-
ing snow and the sun.

When anything happens to ruffle the monotony of Emma's life, Flaubert's sense of her world tends to suggest that it comes from outside herself, from a country silence broken, as here, only by gusts of wind and rustling leaves:

Il arrivait parfois des rafales de vent, brises de la mer qui, roulant d'un bond sur tout le plateau du pays de Caux, apportaient, jusqu'au loin dans les champs, une fraîcheur salée. Les joncs sifflaient à ras de terre, et les feuilles de hêtres bruissaient en un frisson rapide, tandis que les cimes, se balançant toujours, continuaient leur grand murmure. Emma serrait son châle contre ses épaules et se levait.

Dans l'avenue, un jour vert rabattu par le feuillage éclairait la mousse rase qui craquait doucement sous ses pieds. Le soleil se couchait; le ciel était rouge entre les branches, et les troncs pareils des arbres plantés en ligne droite semblaient une colonnade brune se détachant sur un fond d'or; une peur la prenait, elle appelait Djali, s'en retournait vite à Tostes par la grande route, s'affaissait dans un fauteuil, et de toute la soirée ne parlait pas.

Mais, vers la fin de septembre, quelque chose d'extraordinaire tomba dans sa vie; elle fut invitée à la Vaubyessard, chez le marquis d'Andervilliers. (P. 63.)

(Sometimes gusts of wind reached inland, breezes that surged straight over the whole plateau of Caux, bringing a salty freshness far into the fields. The reeds whistled along the ground and the beech leaves were rustling with a swift shivering sound, whilst the swaying tree-tops kept up their great murmuring. Emma drew her shawl round her shoulders and got up.

In the avenue, the greenish daylight that filtered through the foliage lit up the smooth moss which crackled quietly underfoot. It was sunset; between the branches the sky was red and the straight line of tree-trunks, each alike, seemed like a brown colonnade set off against a golden ground. She was seized by fright, called Djali and went quickly back by the high-road to Tostes, where she slumped into an armchair and, throughout the evening, said not a word.

But towards the end of September, something extraordinary befell her: she was invited to la Vaubyessard, the home of the Marquis d'Andervilliers.)

Emma suffers insecurity and fright at the thought of this world outside her, moving with a life unconnected with hers. Even its beauty, so vivid to the reader of that cadenced prose, exerts only a pressure on her nerves. She tries to retreat from the non-human silence of this world deeper into her own silence and isolation.[11] Yet the narrative sequence of this passage makes it seem as if the events which determine her inner life occur with as little reference to herself as do the gusts of wind. The very syntax makes her passive: 'quelque chose . . . *tomba* dans sa vie'. Her feelings seem external to her will: 'une peur la *prenait*'. It turns out that even the invitation to la Vaubyessard stems from the fact that the marquis had met her when he came to ask for a cutting from the cherry tree in her garden. Everything connects back to her surroundings, even her brief escapes from them.

It is only a step from this for Flaubert to present Emma's inner life as if it too were part of the landscape. Thus, when Charles proposes, père Rouault promises to speak to her for him; if she agrees to the marriage, he will push open one of the farm's shutters as a sign of her acceptance:

. . . vous pourrez le voir par derrière en vous penchant sur la haie.

Et il s'éloigna.

Charles attacha son cheval à un arbre. Il courut se mettre dans le sentier; il attendit. Une demi-heure se passa, puis il compta dix-neuf minutes à sa montre. Tout à coup un bruit se fit contre le mur; l'auvent s'était rabattu, la cliquette tremblait encore. Le lendemain, dès neuf heures, il était à la ferme. (Pp. 33–4.)

'. . . you'll be able to see it from the back by leaning over the hedge.'

And off he went.

Charles tethered his horse to a tree. He ran to position himself in the footpath and waited. Half an hour passed, then he counted off nineteen minutes by his watch. All of a sudden something banged against the wall. The shutter had been thrown open and the rattling was just subsiding.

He was at the farm by nine o'clock the next day.)

Emma's decision becomes a small brief movement on the face of the tranquil landscape. Human actions become a slight interruption of the silence, just noticeable enough to mark the passage of time.

Throughout the novel, the frenzied rhythm of Emma's passions seems nullified by this quietly subversive rhythm of time passing. Our first impression of Yonville is of the imperceptible changes it has seen since the events which are about to be recounted:

Depuis les événements que l'on va raconter, rien, en effet, n'a changé à Yonville. Le drapeau tricolore de fer-blanc tourne toujours au haut du clocher de l'église; la boutique du marchand de nouveautés agite encore au vent ses deux banderoles d'indienne; les foetus du pharmacien, comme des paquets d'amadou blanc, se pourrissent de plus en plus dans leur alcool bourbeux, et, au-dessus de la grande porte de l'auberge, le vieux lion d'or, déteint par les pluies, montre toujours aux passants sa frisure de caniche. (P. 100.)

(Nothing, in fact, has changed at Yonville since the events about to be recounted. The tin-plate tricolour still turns on top of the church steeple, the calico streamers of the linen-draper's shop still flutter in the wind, the chemist's foetuses, like packets of white touchwood, go on steadily rotting in their muddy alcohol, and above the big inn-door the old, rain-faded golden lion still displays its poodle's curliness to passers-by.)

Emma's life will be framed by Yonville and Yonville is framed by time: the indifference of both will survive her. As the rather loaded image of the foetus suggests, Flaubert's imagination is so absorbed by the silent process of time, burying human suffering in silence as it passes, that he does not think in terms of Emma resisting time to make her own future. Just as this Flaubertian foetus decays instead of growing, so Emma seems the pawn of forces outside herself. From the elegiac calm of passages like this last, one comes to suspect that Flaubert was strangely consoled by his heroine's lack of freedom.

We also hear time pass when Hippolyte's sudden strident cry, as his leg is amputated, breaks the silence of Yonville and then is re-absorbed back into it:

Au milieu du silence qui emplissait le village, un cri déchirant traversa l'air. Bovary devint pâle à s'évanouir. Elle fronça les sourcils d'un geste nerveux, puis continua. C'était pour lui cependant, pour cet être, pour cet homme qui ne comprenait rien, qui ne sentait rien! car il était là, tout tranquillement, et sans même se douter que le ridicule de son nom allait désormais la salir comme lui. Elle avait fait des efforts pour l'aimer, et elle s'était repentie en pleurant d'avoir cédé à un autre.

– Mais c'était peut-être un valgus? exclama soudain Bovary, qui méditait.

Au choc imprévu de cette phrase, tombant sur sa pensée comme une balle de plomb dans un plat d'argent, Emma tressaillant leva la tête pour deviner ce qu'il voulait dire; et ils se regardèrent silencieusement, presque ébahis de se voir, tant ils étaient par leur conscience éloignés l'un de l'autre. Charles la considérait avec le regard troublé d'un homme ivre, tout en écoutant, immobile, les derniers cris de l'amputé qui se suivaient en modulations traînantes, coupées de saccades aiguës, comme le hurlement lointain de quelque bête qu'on égorge. (P. 256.)

(In the midst of the silence that filled the village a harrowing
cry pierced the air. Bovary went white as if he would faint. She
knit her brows nervously, then went on to herself: but all for
him, for that creature, that man who understood nothing and felt
nothing! There he was, quite calm, not even suspecting that the
ridicule his name aroused would henceforth defile her as it would
him. She had tried hard to love him, had repented with tears in
her eyes for giving herself to another.

'But perhaps it was a valgus?' Bovary suddenly exclaimed, as
he ruminated.

At the unexpected shock of these words, interrupting her
thoughts like a lead bullet falling into a silver platter, Emma
raised her head, shuddering, to guess at what he could mean.
They looked silently at each other, almost dumbfounded by what
they saw, so estranged were they one from another in their
thoughts. Charles was considering her with the troubled look of
a drunkard, as he listened, motionless, to the last screams of the
amputated man succeeding each other in drawn-out modulations,
punctuated by sharp outbursts of pain, like the faraway howling
of some animal being slaughtered.)

It is silence which fills the village, not Hippolyte's cries, and it is
as if this silence extends itself to the silence between Emma and
Charles, to the quietening of the screams and, finally, to the dying
cadence of the paragraph's last sentence. Without it, the emotions
of Emma and Charles would seem more cursorily rendered and the
screaming would not grate on us, nor its meaning on Emma, as
it does. In the same way, the prose seeks to reverberate in silence;
its rhythm dissociates itself from the emotional rhythm of the
characters. The carefully phrased last sentence, imitating just the
sound of Hippolyte's last cries, has a sonorous music which bears
no relation to what Emma and Charles feel as they hear them.
This music is a kind of veil drawn over their distress, just as the
silence draws in again over the village and restores its non-human
serenity: the painfulness of the scene is partly anaesthetised. There
is a self-consciousness in the description of Hippolyte as 'quelque
bête qu'on égorge' which manages to detach us from his agony
while being satisfyingly unflinching: the way it draws attention to
itself *as a phrase* makes the compassion aroused for Hippolyte
more bearable.[12] Flaubert uses his curt eloquence here to divert a
feeling of panic at the thought of meaningless pain into an
irrelevant, but consoling, beauty. The dying fall of the prose absorbs
the screams just as the village silence does. It is as if Flaubert invests
himself with that very indifference in the world which he describes
so movingly. I make this point, not to criticise a fine passage, but

to suggest the risks he ran in expressing his sense of the non-human vastness and silence within which his characters act and speak. To close his ears to his silence would have been to confine himself to a more local psychological drama, but there was a cost in listening to it without being able to see it through any objective religious or philosophical notion, such as 'fate'. He is tempted to identify himself with this nameless source of tragedy to express it. This is understandable and may have been a necessary safeguard against mere incoherent *angst*; nevertheless, it means that his tragic tone is seldom quite safe from interruption by the tone which, mixing the aesthetic with the tough, interrupts it here.

Flaubert's sense of human destiny places him in an intolerable dilemma. He feels that there is something general and unalterable in human life and yet he cannot substantiate that feeling with any conviction that 'the world' has a meaningful structure. His feeling that life is tragic does not square with his acute awareness that whatever shape particular lives take is random and arbitrary. This is why he needs to temper his sense of *lacrimae rerum* with comedy and irony. Emma's failure to understand her world is something of a screen for his own uncertainty: he needs to keep open the option of laughing at the way she takes herself so tragically. At times, when he is most unsure of what the meaning of her experience can be, this laughter becomes malicious, a sort of surrogate fate which thwarts and mocks her hopes. Thus, at the end of the novel, she is subjected to the indignity of the blind beggar's bawdy song because he can think of no other way of telling us she is doomed.

This feeling that Emma is the victim of a blind fate with which Flaubert is in secret communication is conveyed by the scene where she finally yields to Léon. It begins with her praying in Rouen cathedral as she waits for her lover, intending to break with him. She is listening to 'the silence of the church, which only augmented the tumult in her heart'. (P. 332.) This 'tumult' is not clearly related to her being in church but Flaubert avoids considering how far her doubts about what to do are religious by satirising the vulgarity of her feeling for religion. The cathedral's portentous 'silence' is unfathomed and all he can do is to mimic it in the scene which follows, when Emma and Léon make love in a cab and the narrative is equally silent about what they are feeling behind its drawn blinds. By the end of the chapter, Emma is so transformed into a part of her objective world that she is presented as little more than an image:

Puis, vers six heures, la voiture s'arrêta dans une ruelle du quartier Beauvoisine, et une femme en descendit qui marchait le voile baissé, sans détourner la tête. (P. 338.)

(Then, towards six, the vehicle came to a halt in an alley in the Beauvoisine district, and a woman got down from it and walked off with her veil lowered, without looking back.)

Emma is, of course, unaware of how small and futile her passion seems here, as she disappears into the indifferent silence of the provincial city which the unusual activity of her cab has perturbed for an afternoon. Had she been shown as more aware of herself Flaubert would have had to probe further into what that silence meant. In robbing Emma of her own voice he sustains his own sense of tragedy by sardonically denying her any share in it:

Une fois, au milieu du jour, en pleine campagne, au moment où le soleil dardait le plus fort contre les vieilles lanternes argentées, une main nue passa sous les petits rideaux de toile jaune et jeta des déchirures de papier qui se dispersèrent au vent et s'abattirent plus loin, comme des papillons blancs, sur un champ de trèfle rouge tout en fleurs. (P. 338.)

(Once, in the middle of the day, in open country, when the sun was beating down at its most fierce on the old silver-plated carriage lights, a bare hand passed under the little yellow canvas curtains and threw out some torn-up paper which was scattered in the wind and fell to the ground further off, like white butterflies, on a field of red clover all in bloom.)

Emma's letter of farewell to Léon, full as it was of confused and affected sincerity, is torn up to become, for Flaubert, a pathetic image of inappropriate purity: 'des papillons blancs'. Only the slightly otiose lyricism, which converts drama into description, saves this from seeming cruel. The music of the prose just softens the satire enough to preserve our tenderness for Emma, but this is only because Flaubert has been able to translate her active sexuality into an image of her helplessness. The pathos is more oppressive than cathartic; Flaubert will not look into Emma's passions and she will not look beyond them. We have only ironic distance with which to fill in the blanks and here it is not enough. Emma may be the victim of destiny but her destiny seems too indistinguishable from the prose which relates it.[13]

It would be wrong to generalise from this one passage because *Madame Bovary* is a less even novel than it is sometimes thought to be. Its poetry can vary; sometimes it benefits from Flaubert's compassionate reticence about Emma's feelings but, at other times, it depends on a reticence which is willed and evasive. Neither kind of poetry can be explained as the product of what Arnold called 'petrified feeling' but both kinds reveal Flaubert's inability

to conceive of Emma's relation to her world as other than petrifying
to the life in her. Any reader of the novel could point to places
in it where only the command of a marmoreal phrase rescues
Flaubert's art from becoming the expression of an incoherent fear
of the universe. The clarity and firmness of the language is won
from the death and disintegration it describes and serves as Flaubert's only armour against them. Such a purely literary means of
conserving the strength to live and look squarely at life are not
available to the unreflecting Emma. It is for this reason that Flaubert's poetry is better at communicating the presence of death in
her world than the energy of life with which she faces up to death.
Her sensibility contains much of the sensibility of her creator but,
for her to have been seen as making a sustained stand against the
world in which she is trapped, she would have had to share in his
impersonal view of her own sufferings. She is therefore doubly
trapped. Flaubert can only view those sufferings impersonally on
condition that she remains irredeemably personal in her own view
of them. Hence, the strange and disturbing friction that we constantly feel between the author of *Madame Bovary* and its heroine.

III

Although Flaubert can deploy his irony to avoid troubling questions
– just as he so often falls back on *Saeva indignatio* in his letters –
it is not possible to leave the scene of Emma and Léon's cab-ride
with an inquisitorial, Sartrean reading and feel that everything has
been explained. Emma is more than a vehicle for Flaubert's pessimism; she is too creatively felt to seem just a victim of the universe.
In the snapshot of her bare hand as it passes through the curtain
of the cab-window we at once see a hand of flesh and blood, making
a living gesture. Much of our compassion for Emma springs from
her vivid physical presence. That is why it goes deeper than vicarious self-pity: she is always *there* as its object.[14] It is misleading to
speak of Flaubert's failures in psychological penetration without
acknowledging this. A great deal of his psychological art consists
in seeing when psychologising can be dispensed with. More metaphysical psychologists, like Dostoievski or Lawrence, seem sometimes
so exhilarated by the emotions they describe that those emotions
tend to pulsate in a physical vacuum. Yet the apparently clinical
sighting of Emma's bare hand evokes both sensuality and a tenderness for the frailty of sensuality; Lawrence often does much less
with Ursula Brangwen, for all his rhetoric about her mystic darkness
and her golden lambency. Flaubert's extraordinary, almost hal-
lucinatory, gift for rendering Emma's emotions through physical

imagery redeems his novel from melodrama. At the Comices Agricoles there is a beautiful moment when she is reminded by the
scent of Rodolphe's hair of the *vicomte* with whom she danced at
la Vaubyessard. Her memory and her sexuality fuse for a moment
with her world:

> Alors une mollesse la saisit, elle se rappela ce vicomte qui l'avait
> fait valser à la Vaubyessard, et dont la barbe exhalait, comme
> ces cheveux-là, cette odeur de vanille et de citron; et, machinale-
> ment, elle entreferma les paupièrs pour la mieux respirer. Mais,
> dans ce geste qu'elle fit en se cambrant sur sa chaise, elle aperçut
> au loin, tout au fond de l'horizon, la vieille diligence l'*Hirondelle*,
> qui descendait lentement la côte des Leux, en traînant après soi
> un long panache de poussière. C'etait dans cette voiture jaune que
> Léon, si souvent, était revenu vers elle; et par cette route là-bas
> qu'il était parti pour toujours! (Pp. 203–4.)
>
> (Then a languid feeling took hold of her and she recalled the
> Viscount who had waltzed with her at la Vaubyessard: his beard
> had given off that same scent of vanilla and lemon as the hair
> did. Involuntarily, her eye-lids closed together the better to
> breathe it in. But, in the movement of pulling herself up in her
> chair, she caught sight of the ancient stagecoach, the *Hirondelle*,
> far away on the edge of the horizon, going slowly down the hill-
> side at Leux, with a long plume of dust trailing away behind
> it. It was in that same yellow coach that Léon had so often come
> back to her, by that same road that he had left forever!)

A critic cannot describe the effect of this re-appearance of the
familiar, battered *Hirondelle* which has become so much a part of
Emma's innermost thoughts. By the end of the novel it has almost
become one of the characters. Its prosaic poetry, more than a thing
but less than an image, is shared by so much of Yonville and the
country round it, even by the inhabitants, who become parts of the
place. Binet is more monotonously punctual at the Lion d'Or than
the *Hirondelle* and seems like a fixture in its dining-room. In
Tostes, there is the hairdresser who lives opposite Emma:

> Lui aussi, le perruquier, il se lamentait de sa vocation arrêtée, de
> son avenir perdu, et, rêvant quelque boutique dans une grande
> ville, comme à Rouen, par exemple, sur le port, près du théâtre,
> il restait toute la journée à se promener en long, depuis la mairie
> jusqu'à l'église, sombre, et attendant la clientéle. Lorsque Mme
> Bovary levait les yeux, elle le voyait toujours là comme une
> sentinelle en faction, avec son bonnet grec sur l'oreille et sa veste
> de lasting. (Pp. 89–90.)

(The hairdresser too would grieve over his unfulfilled vocation
and his lost future, and dreaming of having a shop in a big town
– in Rouen, for instance, by the harbour or near the theatre – he
would spend the whole day in pacing back and forth from the
townhall to the church, gloomily waiting for customers. When
Mme Bovary raised her eyes she would always see him there, like
a sentry on duty, with his smoking cap over his ear, in his jacket
made of lasting.)

The beauty of such things is that, by embedding people so deeply in
their place, they create a sense of common experience between them,
even though they are each isolated. Emma's feelings here are conveyed by the hairdresser's. It is because of such detached, muted
poetry that we can think of her as having a consciousness.

Emma's feelings would not be the same if her world were different but this does not mean that her world is ever merely their
echo. Its otherness is substantial in a blunt, irrevocable way, un-
respondingly silent, resistant to all her efforts to project herself onto
it. Quite early on in the novel she feels that everything around
her is 'enveloped by a black atmosphere floating confusedly on the
exterior of things'. (P. 171.) The only escape from self this 'exterior'
offers is nothingness. This is made most clear when Charles visits
Emma for the last time, when she is dead, with Homais and
Bournisien peacefully sleeping by her bedside:

Il y avait quelques étoiles, et la nuit était douce.
La cire des cierges tombait par grosses larmes sur les draps du
lit. Charles les regardait brûler, fatiguant ses yeux contre le
rayonnement de leur flamme jaune.
Des moires frissonnaient sur la robe de satin, blanche comme
un clair de lune. Emma disparaissait dessous; et il lui semblait
que, *s'épandant au dehors d'elle-même, elle se perdait confusément
dans l'entourage des choses, dans le silence, dans la nuit, dans le
vent qui passait, dans les senteurs humides qui montaient.* (P. 459,
my italics.)
(A few stars shone and the night was mild.
The wax of the candles dropped in big tears onto the bed-
clothes. Charles watched them as they burnt, tiring his eyes in the
glow of their yellow flames.
The watery shimmering of her satin gown made it white as a
moonbeam. Emma was disappearing beneath, and it seemed to
him as if she were spreading out beyond herself, confusedly
merging into everything around her, the silence, the night, the
wind as it passed, the humid scents rising up to her.)

Flaubert begins and ends with the calm night outside the room in which Emma lies dead. The only tears he describes are the drops of candle wax falling on the sheets. In a sense, the whole novel has been building towards this sense of Emma's dissolution into 'l'entourage des choses'. Yet she is not exactly destroyed by her world, there are no furies in it. She has always had her own silence too and, paradoxically, she has longed for this final nothingness as deeply as she has ever longed for her lovers. She is reconciled to the night and the wind from which she previously withdrew in fear becoming one with matter as Saint Antoine longed to. Or so, at least, it may seem as we look through the eyes of the grieving Charles.

But less harmonious notes are sounded at the end of the novel. Flaubert's unflagging sense of the people and things around her is too acute for this almost Romantic sense of the 'entourage des choses' into which she is absorbed to sound a consoling last chord to her tragedy. At Emma's funeral there is no accord between Charles's feeling of her death and the life beyond the grave-side. The sounds heard across the fields have an effect like silence because they have nothing at all to do with Emma:

Toutes sortes de bruits joyeux emplissaient l'horizon: le claque-ment d'une charrette roulant au loin dans les ornières, le cri d'un coq qui se répétait ou la galopade d'un poulain que l'on voyait s'enfuir sous les pommiers. . . .

Le drap noir, semé de larmes blanches, se levait de temps à autre en découvrant la bière. Les porteurs fatigués se ralentissai-ent, et elle avançait par saccades continues, comme une chaloupe qui tangue à chaque flot.

On arriva.

Les hommes continuèrent jusqu'en bas, à une place dans le gazon où la fosse était creusée.

On se rangea tout autour; et, tandis que le prêtre parlait, la terre rouge, rejetée sur les bords, coulait par les coins, sans bruit, continuellement.

Puis, quand les quatre cordes furent disposées, on poussa la bière dessus. Il la regarda descendre. Elle descendait toujours.

Enfin, on entendit un choc; les cordes en grinçant remontèrent. Alors Bournisien prit la bêche que lui tendait Lestiboudois; de sa main gauche, tout en aspergeant de la droite, il poussa vigoureusement une large pelletée; et le bois du cercueil, heurté par les cailloux, fit ce bruit formidable qui nous semble être le retentissement de l'éternité. (Pp. 466–7.)

(The horizon was filled with all sorts of cheerful sounds: the faraway rattle of a cart jolting along over the ruts, the repetitious

crow of a cock or the galloping of a foal that could be seen running away beneath the apple-trees. . . .

From time to time the black pall, strewn with white tear-like
beads, was lifted up to reveal the bier. The weary bearers were
slowing down and it moved on with unbroken jolting, like a
longboat tossed by every wave.

Then they arrived.

The men went on down to the bottom to a place in the grass
where a grave had been dug.

People gathered round, and, as the priest was speaking, the red
earth thrown up at the sides ran noiselessly back at the corners,
never ceasing.

Then, when the four ropes were laid out, they pushed the
coffin on them. He watched it as it went down and still down.

At last, a bump was heard and the ropes came creaking back
up. Then Bournisien took the spade that Lestiboudois handed
to him, and, as he sprinkled holy-water with his right hand, with
his left he vigorously pushed in a large spadeful, so that the wood
of the coffin, with the pebbles battering on it, gave out that fearful sound which strikes us as the resounding of eternity.)

The farmyard noises in the distance and precise sounds like the
thud of the coffin or the noiseless running away of the earth have
the most tragic effect, because they are most independent of Emma
and of any emotion stirred up on her behalf. They confirm her
death while giving normality to it. The lugubrious final image was
not needed and has little relevance to an Emma lost in an eternity
which does not resound. At his best – and also his least literary –
Flaubert sees Emma in her world without flinching at the distance
between her and that world or trying to bridge it. The point is
worth stressing since tragedy is sometimes seen as a kind of insidious
bridge between the self and the world. Robbe-Grillet calls it:

> an attempt to retrieve the distance that exists between man and
> things in the form of a new value . . . a test in which victory
> consists in being vanquished. Tragedy thus appears as the last
> invention of humanism to prevent anything from escaping it:
> since the accord between man and things has been finally ex-
> posed, the humanist saves his empire by at once establishing a
> new form of solidarity, with divorce itself becoming a highway
> for redemption.[15]

This is true of *Quidquid Volueris* but not of *Madame Bovary*. It is
because Flaubert refrains from any attempt to cement the 'divorce'
to which Robbe-Grillet refers that *Madame Bovary* can achieve
the unevasive clarity of tragic art.

Emma's death, like all deaths, takes the breath away:

Il y a toujours, après la mort de quelqu'un, comme une stupé-
faction qui se dégage, tant il est difficile de comprendre cette
survenue du néant et de se résigner à y croire. Mais quand il
s'aperçut pourtant de son immobilité, Charles se jeta sur elle en
criant:
—Adieu! adieu!
Homais et Canivet l'entraînèrent hors de la chambre.
— Modérez-vous!
— Oui, disait-il en se débattant, je serai raisonnable, je ne ferai
pas de mal. Mais laissez-moi! je veux la voir! c'est ma femme!
Et il pleurait.
— Pleurez, reprit le pharmacien, donnez cours à la nature, cela
vous soulagera! (P. 450.)
(After somebody dies there is always a kind of stupefied feeling
unloosed, so hard is it for us to understand the advent of nothing-
ness and resign ourselves to credit it. Yet when he saw how
motionless she was, Charles threw himself on her, crying out:
'Farewell! farwell!'
Homais and Canivet drew him out of the room.
'Calm yourself down!'
'Yes,' he said, struggling, 'I'll be reasonable, I won't do any
harm. But let me go, I want to see her, she's my wife!'
And he wept.
'Have a good cry,' the chemist went on, 'let Nature have her
way and she will bring you relief.')

It is 'la mort de quelqu'un' – anybody's death – but not in any
pompously general way. The gentle and precise thought about the
'condition humaine', is made accessible by the comedy of Homais'
spendidly trite way of bringing in 'la nature'. Why should Flaubert's
sense of a common humanity be strongest when he is writing about
death, about *le néant* and *l'anéantissement*? Why is it at moments
like this that he can enter most completely into what his characters
are feeling. Pathos is certainly there in the scene of Emma's death
yet Flaubert also seems to want to stupefy his reader, to *inflict* on
him the thought of death, as well as to share it with him. It seems
that, just as Flaubert's compassion is only made possible by his irony,
so his pathos depends on a strange kind of determinism.

Our sense that Emma's true destination is always death is most
insistent at those moments when Flaubert suddenly confronts her
with the unrespondingness of the world around her. It is far blanker
than the half-humanised 'indifference' which Hardy pits against
his Tess. No such moment is more moving than the one in which

Emma looks back at Rodolphe's château after her last humiliating visit to him to ask for money:

> Elle sortit. Les murs tremblaient, le plafond l'écrasait; et elle repassa par la longue allée, en trébuchant contre les tas de feuilles mortes que le vent dispersait. Enfin elle arriva au saut-de-loup devant la grille; elle se cassa les ongles contre la serrure, tant elle se dépêchait pour l'ouvrir. Puis, cent pas plus loin, essoufflée, près de tomber, elle s'arrêta. Et alors, se détournant, elle aperçut encore une fois l'impassible château, avec le parc, les jardins, les trois cours, et toutes les fenêtres de la façade.
>
> Elle resta perdue de stupeur, et n'ayant plus conscience d'elle-même que par le battement de ses artères, qu'elle croyait entendre s'échapper comme une assourdissante musique qui emplissait la campagne. (Pp. 431–2.)
>
> (She went out. The walls were shuddering and the ceiling seemed to be crushing her. She went back down the long drive, stumbling through piles of dead leaves that were being scattered by the wind. At last she reached the ha-ha in front of the gate; she broke her nails on the lock in her haste to open it. Then, a hundred paces further on, breathless and ready to drop, she came to a halt. And as she looked back she saw for one last time the impassive mansion, with its park, its gardens, its three courtyards and all the windows of its façade.
>
> She stood lost in a stupor, no longer aware of herself save through the beating of her arteries, which she seemed to hear breaking out like a deafening music that was filling the country-side.)

Emma's experience, arrested by an alien world, her sense of self narrowing down to the panic-stricken sound of her own heart-beat, might almost epitomise the experience of reading *Madame Bovary* itself. Two crucial Flaubertian words show that this is not simply fanciful. She stands 'perdue de stupeur' at the sight of the 'impassible château'. One need not look far in the *Correspondence* to find Flaubert saying that his own 'impassibilité' is meant to strike his readers with 'stupeur' or 'ébahissement'.[10] *Madame Bovary* does work like that – it is a book one does not willingly begin and a book one can not willingly put down, a book that grips us and leaves us stunned, *envahissant* as Flaubert himself was. It is not that Flaubert is persecuting Emma. The 'impassible château' embodies something alien *in life* which speaks through the prose, not a force which the author seeks to control as an expression of his own will. One may reach out for some notion like 'Fate' to describe the effect but Flaubert is deeply agnostic and, despite the irony of the château's belonging to Rodolphe, there is none of that sign-posting of Nemesis that is found in the George Eliot of *Felix Holt* and *Romola*. Yet this very agnosticism makes for problems. In earlier tragedies man is up against the gods or fate, but Yonville is plainly unvisited by any gods: it is just surrounded by the blank landscape which contains La Huchette. It is, I think, precisely this emptiness which encourages the impassive artist to, as it were, step into the shoes of a non-existent God. It is difficult to play God without seeming to subscribe to a kind of determinism; otherwise, the artist seems to deny even negative coherence to his world.

However well the La Huchette passage may transcend or disguise this dilemma, it inevitably reads as one more expression of something we have long felt in the novel's world, the way it acts so unvaryingly as a block to Emma's achieving any true being, as if some vaguely cosmic malediction unremittingly subverts *all* her dreams. So rich a novel is more than an illustration of its author's own *a priori* pessimism, yet it would be naïve to see Emma as only the victim of her own bad luck. How is it that her tragedy can seem both an inevitable destiny and the result of unique combinations of chance? One answer is provided by the novel's overwhelming sense that life is like this, bounded as Emma's is by death, and that death *is* pre-determined. Chance may conspire at her death but there is no chance in her dying. In a world without gods, death becomes the only absolute. It is this that Emma eventually discovers, but, because Flaubert implants it in our minds long before, her spiritual life seems less an exploration of her world than a desperate, protracted resistance to his pre-established truth.[17] The element of determinism in the book arises from a feeling of doom present already in Flaubert's juvenilia.

The word 'fatalité' does occur in *Madame Bovary* but Flaubert is too sly to use it straight as he did in his *Oeuvres de Jeunesse*. It is introduced to debunk the Romantic idea that people can blame their misfortunes on some supernatural power. Thus, when Rodolphe writes to Emma to give her up:

> 'Est-ce ma faute? O mon Dieu! non, non, n'en accusez que la fatalité!'
> – Voilà un mot qui fait toujours de l'effet, se dit-il. (P. 281.)
> ('Is it my fault? Oh God! no, no, blame only fate for it!'
> 'There's a word that always sounds good,' he said to himself.)

The word returns at the end of the book when Charles meets Rodolphe for the last time:

> – Non, ne vous en veux plus!

Il ajouta même un grand mot, le seul qu'il ait jamais dit:
– C'est la faute de la fatalité!

Rodolphe, qui avait conduit cette fatalité, le trouva bien
débonnaire pour un homme dans sa situation, comique même et
un peu vil. (P. 480.)

('No, I no longer bear you a grudge!'
He even added a fine phrase, the only one he had ever made:
'It is fate that's to blame!'
Rodolphe, who had been the instrument of this fate, thought
it was very meek and mild coming from a man in his situation,
comical even and a little base.)

It is not just the gentleness Flaubert has for Charles here which
makes Rodolphe's view of things questionable. That acid 'qui avait
conduit cette fatalité' does not mean what Rodolphe thinks. He has
only been the agent through which fate has worked but what has
happened has not been simply the effect of human agency. Flaubert
half subscribes to the idea of 'la fatalité' while exploding it. Charles
is in a sense right to feel that the wheel has come full circle. After
all, its latest turn has been to confront him with Rodolphe at this
crucial moment. This chimes with the way in which, although
Flaubert always conceives his world as oblivious to Emma, it constantly seems to predict what will happen to her. For example, when
Charles arrives at Les Bertaux for the first time his horse rears and
draws away in fear, as if sensing an unseen danger; in the description
of Emma's adolescence at the start we see her with her father at an
inn, eating off plates decorated with pictures of the career of Mlle
de La Vallière. The imagery sometimes works rather like the clamp
which Charles puts on Hippolyte's leg.

This undercurrent of premonition is most insistent at the start
of the *Troisième Partie*. We begin with Emma and Léon telling
each other how they have suffered during his absence in Paris. Léon
talks sentimentally of 'the calm of the tomb' (P. 324.) and tells her
how he had made a will. Later, when they meet in Rouen cathedral,
a lugubrious verger conducts them round the funeral monuments,
and, as they try to escape him, draws their attention to the Last
Judgement and the Damned in hellfire represented on the north
portal, by which they leave. The comedy serves a sense of doom.
When Emma returns to Yonville she is greeted with the news of
the death of Charles's father. The news must have arrived when
she and Léon were making love in the *fiacre* (which was described
as 'more enclosed than a tomb'. (P. 338.) The news of the death is
so well managed – Emma hears it from Homais at his most comic –
that it has the surprisingness of chance. At the time, one does not
suspect that Emma will eventually kill herself with the arsenic she

discovers in Homais' shop as a result of going there to have the news broken to her. But looking back at these chance happenings and remarks, it becomes impossible to see them as pure accidents. As Jean-Pierre Richard has said, 'the determinist option is one aspect of the temptation Flaubert sometimes undergoes to reduce the formlessness of life by imposing an arbitrary discipline on it from outside'.[18]

The world of *Madame Bovary* may be ostensibly governed by chance but chance itself is apt to turn into one of Emma's most self-pitying illusions:

> Elle se demandait s'il n'y aurait pas eu moyen, par d'autres com-
> binaisons du hasard, de rencontrer un autre homme; et elle
> cherchait à imaginer quels eussent été ces événements non sur-
> venus, cette vie différente, ce mari qu'elle ne connaissait pas.
> (P. 62.)
> (She wondered if, through other combinations of chance, there
> would not have been a way for her to meet some other man, and
> she strove to imagine those events that might have been but had
> never been, that different life, that husband she would never
> know.)

She regards the bourgeois mediocrity of her surroundings as excep-tional, 'the particular chance in which she found herself trapped'. (P. 82.) Her refreshingly green belief in her own bad luck becomes a refusal to face life as it is. Would life have been any different if chance had placed her in Paris? When the dice always fall like this, in the wrong way, they cease to be symbols of chance and one sus-pects the author of loading them. There is therefore something peculiarly passive in the response *Madame Bovary* comes to evoke in us: the sense of tragedy seems to precede the actual tragedy itself.[19] One may take, as an illustration, the highly un-Balzacian scene when Emma goes to la Vaubyessard. She is trembling with the excitement of actually entering the world of which she dreams; she even sits down to dinner in the presence of the old duc de Laverdière, who is said to have been a lover of Marie-Antoinette's:

> Il avait mené une vie bruyante de débauches, pleine de duels, de
> paris, de femmes enlevées, avait dévoré sa fortune et effrayé toute
> sa famille. Un domestique, derrière sa chaise, lui nommait tout
> haut, dans l'oreille, les plats qu'il désignait du doigt en bégayant;
> et sans cesse les yeux d'Emma revenaient d'eux-mêmes sur ce
> vieil homme à lèvres pendantes, comme sur quelque chose
> d'extraordinaire et d'auguste. Il avait vécu à la Cour et couché
> dans le lit des reines! (P. 68.)
> (He had led a life of tumultuous debauchery, filled with duels,

gambling and abducted women, had eaten up his fortune and terrified all his family. Behind his chair was a servant who named each dish out loud in his ear as he pointed his finger at it, stammering. Involuntarily, Emma's eyes kept coming back to rest on this old man with drooping lips, as if upon something august and extraordinary. He had lived at Court and lain in the bed of queens!)

Life and passion and gaiety figure as a survival from a 'belle époque' gone forever. We are left with a *memento mori*. Hence the sheer finality of the prose.[20]

Madame Bovary is full of small things which make this sense of decay pervasive enough to give its life a pattern. The foetus in Homais' window rots a little more each year, the *Hirondelle* looks more and more dilapidated, even Lestiboudois' potato patch is reduced to make room for the expansion of the graveyard. The novel's half-comic, half-lyrical feeling of quotidian tragedy inevitably tones down in Emma's death such feelings of awe and shock as might be felt at the end of other tragedies. Catharsis, it is true, would be an indulgence at the end of *Madame Bovary* but one still suspects Flaubert of indulgence of another kind. The streak of determinism in the book leaves us crushed but it does not throw us off balance. We may even feel subtly reassured by an element of lugubrious moralising over life and death which takes the place of catharsis. The feeling of foregone conclusion robs Emma's death of some of its mystery.

It may seem strange that this tendency for tragic mystery to be sacrificed to a pre-determined moral should have its source in so mystical an ideal as 'impassibilité'. Doubt is turned into a deliberate belief, which is, perhaps, what 'impassibilité' really is too. My own explanation of this paradox hinges on the therapeutic value Flaubert found in art. He told Le Poittevin, in 1845, that, 'the weariness of existence does not weigh on our shoulders when we are composing'. (*Corr.*, I, p. 191.) The artistic reflection of life will, he hopes, absolve and liberate him from its tragedy. In places like the *fiacre* scene (and it is only of such places that I am thinking now) one doubts whether he himself is sufficiently engaged at the core of the experience of which he writes. He may have immolated himself *to* his art, he is not always prepared to immolate himself *in* it. This doubt perhaps arises from a discrepancy between our own agonised suspense and an almost wilful serenity in the narrative which is very different from the un-pressuring feeling of the best parts of the novel. Flaubert once criticised Michelet because his description of the French Revolution was too much affected by the turbulence of the subject:

It is not clear, it is even less calm, and the character of beauty is calmness, just as serenity is of innocence and virtue. Repose is the attitude of God. (*Corr.*, III, p. 340.)

It is disturbing to think of Flaubert exploring his deep sense of mortality from any such position of God-like repose. Mysteries cease to be mysterious to the eyes of God.

The ideal of 'impassibilité' does not explain Flaubert's finest work and should not encourage the idea that he puts an immeasurable gulf between Emma and himself. In fact, 'impassibilité' could be seen as a successful version of *Bovarysme*, equally wishful, but seeking transcendence in art and not in life. It is possible to think of Emma's experience as an experience Flaubert himself had to live through first in order to be able to conceive *Madame Bovary* at all:

I am turning towards a kind of aesthetic mysticism (if the two words can go together) and I want it to become stronger. When no encouragement comes to us from others, when the outside world disgusts and enfeebles and corrupts and deadens us, people who are *honest* and *delicate* are forced to seek somewhere in themselves for a purer place to live in. If society continues as it is going, we shall, I think, again see mystics such as there have been in all periods of darkness. Unable to overflow, the soul will concentrate itself. (*Corr.*, III, p. 16.)

It is the same route that Emma herself, whether in sex or in religion, tries to take. Two short quotations will clinch the point. In the first, Flaubert is writing to Louise Colet, in 1853:

A fact is distilled into Form and rises upwards, like a pure incense of the Spirit, towards the Eternal, the Immutable, the Absolute, the Ideal.' (*Corr.*, III, p. 407.)

In the second, from the *Nouvelle Version*, Rodophe is initiating an admiring Emma into the higher duties of romantic love:

And so Truth, Passion, eternal Beauty and Love hover on high, above social conventions and the ephemeral interests of society. (P. 357.)

Substitute the word 'Forme' for Rodolphe's 'Passion' and 'Amour' and you get the same idea.

This takes us to the roots of the feeling of 'fatalité' in *Madame Bovary*. Flaubert has lived through Emma's experience *in advance*, in the very process of becoming an artist, and so his recoil from 'the outside world' makes him disbelieve that Emma's desire for transcendence within life is ever possible. He may find his own destiny in the act of writing but, in a way, he finds it at Emma's expense: how can she herself, disqualified by his knowledge, try freely to make her own fate, like one of Stendhal's heroes? Only, it seems, by challenging her creator, by unsettling the view of her which he needs to hold.

4 Through Lawrence to Flaubert

I

Flaubert is seldom truly impersonal when he is trying to be impersonal, nor truly tragic when insisting that life is a tragedy. At such times his aspiration beyond self is perverted into a strategy for by-passing self and he surreptitiously clings to his more superficial personality. In the blind beggar episodes he even seems to be clutching at a pose. Tragic emotion emanates from within the tragic action itself and not, as Flaubert knew when he criticised *Uncle Tom's Cabin*, from the attitudes the artist adopts towards it. Those parts of Flaubert's work in which, in Lawrence's phrase, the artist's thumb is in the pan therefore need to be distinguished from his genuinely impersonal art.

The tendency of Flaubert's irony to convert into an implicit fatalism provides his falsely impersonal self with an insurance against tragic knowledge. In pre-empting Emma's own final response to her sufferings it risks disqualifying her from mediating to us any total exposure to tragic experience. For it sometimes seems that she can win through to no knowledge of life which is not a mere echo of a tune we have already learnt from listening to Flaubert's irony. Sometimes, she does not even seem to learn that much. This is why Lawrence took *Madame Bovary* to be a tragic novel without tragic actors, and it is this reading that I want to explore now. If Emma were completely protected from tragic knowledge by the irony she would be exposed, not to tragedy, but simply to misery, since she would be incapable of seeing clearly what she is exposed to. Is that what the wisdom of the ironic narrator comes down to?

In Shakespeare's tragedies man sometimes sees his condition with a spiritual clarity conferred by defeat. Such insight, rarely manifested in feelings of uplift or consolation, may entail just a more articulate sense of pain, but it is vouchsafed only to characters who are fully alive to their sufferings. In *King Lear*, for example, there is Gloucester's moving comparison of his own mental anguish with his master's:

> The King is mad; how stiff is my vile sense,
> That I stand up, and have ingenious feeling
> Of my huge sorrows! Better I were distract;
> So should my thoughts be sever'd from my griefs,
> And woes by wrong imaginations lose
> The knowledge of themselves.   (Act IV, scene 6.)

His spirit vindicates itself as he is being crushed. If, in Emma Bovary's end, we witness only the final bankruptcy of her spirit, a death suffered, like her life, in blindness and delusion, then, however tragic her world appears to be, she herself cannot be a tragic character.

I think that such a view needs much qualifying. Determinism does not govern *Madame Bovary*, it is rather an inner abscess in the book which, in certain scenes, infects its authentic creativeness. Emma is not crushed as Mâtho is in the more spuriously impersonal *Salammbô*; even though she kills herself she does not quite capitulate. She rather gives herself up to a final radical rebellion against the brutal nature of things as they are. If, as James thought, she is less 'abject' than Frédéric Moreau, this is because she is capable of suicide where he is ony capable of living suicidally. Flaubert may pretend sometimes that she is the victim of fate but, when her fate is not rigged, it is merely impotent until she decides to collaborate with it and give it a form at all. The intense pitch of desire at which she lives makes her seem to mock the fatalistic narrator as much as he mocks her. Perhaps this is why she exasperated Flaubert so much as he wrote, for she obstinately refuses to espouse his own stoicism. The complexity of the *Troisième Partie* is that when Emma is nearest to defying her creator she becomes most like him. Rémy de Gourmont once said that 'all Flaubert's efforts to withdraw from his books have only resulted in his appearing to lurk under cover behind each word, each sentence, each scene'.[1] Nowhere is this more true than in those pregnant moments at the end of the book when Emma seems about to fly in the face of her society out of sheer contempt for it:

> . . . il lui semblait que la Providence s'acharnait à la poursuivre, et, s'en rehaussant d'orgueil, jamais elle n'avait eu tant d'estime pour elle-même ni tant de mépris pour les autres. Quelque chose de belliqueux la transportait. Elle aurait voulu battre les hommes, leur cracher au visage, les broyer tous; elle continuait à marcher rapidement devant elle, pâle, frémissante, enragée, furetant d'un œil en pleurs l'horizon vide, et comme se délectant à la haine qui l'entouffait. (P. 420.)
>
> . . . it seemed to her that Providence was determined to hound her, and, swelling with pride at the thought, she had never held herself in such high esteem nor felt so much contempt for other people. She was consumed by a feeling of belligerence. She would have liked to hit men, spit in their faces, grind them all down; she went on walking rapidly forward, pale, trembling and wild with rage, peering through her tears at the blank horizon, as if she were relishing the hatred that was choking her.)

At this moment (she has just left the contemptible Guillaumin) she seems of the same kin as Medea or Phèdre. More intriguingly, she seems significantly like her creator. According to a common reading, it was in some such mood of helpless rage, looking at a similarly blank horizon, that Flaubert sat down to write *Madame Bovary*. It is in this way that she may be said to undermine his irony.

As we put down *Madame Bovary* a crucial unanswered question persists despite the power of the ending: if Emma had not taken the arsenic from Homais' conveniently unguarded medicine cabinet, would she have been able to face life as the guilty wife of the bankrupt yet forgiving Charles? My own guess is that Flaubert was afraid that she could. It becomes rather difficult, given her final attitude to Yonville, to conceive that she can bear the thought of being defeated by someone like the usurer Lheureux. Flaubert, I believe, found the thought of her death a less painful one than the thought of her continuing to live. He chose death for her to avoid imagining what might have been her struggle to accept self-responsibility in life. The real duplicity of his streak of fatalism is only grasped when we see that he has contrived to pass it off as Emma's own feeling. In this way, the conventionally tragic solution to the novel short-circuits its deepest implications of tragedy. He risks showing us an Emma who will seem only half-changed by an experience she lives through in deep earnest. It is strange, given his reputation for sadism towards her, that she should, as it were, be crucified without the nails being hammered right in. It is not simply that she refuses to admit that the natural reaction to the disheartingness of life is resignation. She is not a Frédéric Moreau (nor, perhaps, an Isabel Archer?) who virtually needs the sensation of giving in. She has already shown, in her affair with Rodolphe, that she is prepared to try to change her life, even if only through a phoney kind of love. It was Rodolphe himself who was too weak to second her bid to renew her life, not her. Moreover, it was precisely because of this strength in her that Flaubert was compelled to take her seriously and see her with compassion as well as satire. Therefore, when she dies, there must remain a lurking doubt as to whether she dies because Flaubert wishes her to die or because she herself in a real suicide.

Such clarity as Emma has consists mostly in seeing through other people – Charles, Rodolphe, Léon, Guillaumin; she is too intent on conjuring up flattering self-images to see herself as those people see her. So she cannot see what she has in common with them, even though, as Flaubert sees, her fantasy works in the same ways as their's does.[2] She cannot, for example, see that she shares the despondency of the hairdresser in Tostes; to her, he is just another aspect of the surrounding mediocrity. This reinforces the sense that the will to live is the purely individual illusion of an Emma or, indeed, of a Homais. If we ordinarily think of tragedy as vindicating that will to live in the face of everything life does to wear it down, then in *Madame Bovary* tragic emotion will seem diminished by a reliance on the softer alternative of nihilism. Is Flaubert's own sense of life only sustained on condition that Emma shall not expose it as a retreat from life by herself battling to live? Emma, of course, can be resilient – much more so, for instance, than Charles can – and so one is only half-convinced when she gives up. She was less prone to fear and shame when she walked through Rouen on Léon's arm, 'her head held high, without fear . . . of compromising herself'. (P. 381.) It was Léon who was afraid of being compromised then. There is therefore good reason to remember Flaubert's own words in one of his letters:

> neither sorrows nor despondency [l'ennui] can make you ill and kill you. One doesn't die from misfortune, one lives on it and it fattens one up. (*Corr.*, I, p. 426.)

To suggest that Flaubert conceals Emma's true resilience is not to repeat the Jamesian argument that she herself is intrinsically too mean a person to figure in tragedy. James, as I shall argue from the example of *The Portrait of a Lady*, felt an untragic need to find a reassuring consolation in the thought of human dignity even in situations like Emma's death, when any human being – noble or ignoble – is at the mercy of something stronger than they are. It is not, however, a necessary part of tragedy that the hero should be reconciled either to the world that makes him suffer or to himself: neither Macbeth nor Lear is so reconciled and, if Othello is, it is only by self-deception. By 'resilience' I mean the courage to face things as they are, which may consist as much in what Gloucester calls his 'vile sense' as in the intelligent awareness that James speaks of. This crucial distinction may be made clearer by a quotation from his dialogue on *Daniel Deronda*, a novel which he thinks shows a character who, in suffering as much as Emma does, becomes more representative than Emma is because she understands better what is happening to her:

> . . . What is it [human life] made of but the discovery by each of us that we are at the best but a rather ridiculous fifth wheel to the coach, after we have sat cracking our whip and believing that we are at least the coachman in person? We think we are the main hoop to the barrel, and we turn out to be but a very incidental splinter in one of the staves. The universe forcing itself with a

slow, inexorable pressure into a narrow, complacent, and yet after all extremely sensitive mind, and making it ache with the pain of the process – that is Gwendolen's story. And it becomes completely characteristic in that her supreme perception of the fact that the world is whirring past her is in the disappointment not of a base but of an exalted passion. The very chance to embrace what the author is so fond of calling a 'larger life' seems refused to her.[3]

This seems to me to tilt slightly, but very significantly, away from tragedy. We may need to feel that Gwendolen was capable of that 'larger life' which she is denied, if its tragic denial is to have its effect. What is suspect in the interpretation is the way the thought of her 'supreme perception' leads James to speak of life as 'whirring past her'. It may be that, as Theodora says, 'it is the tragedy that makes her conscience' but that should not be used to imply that she is somehow detached from it. Life does not whirr past Gloucester, neither do we think of him as having a 'supreme perception', not, that is, if that phrase is intended as a tribute to Gwendolen's *intelligence*. Gloucester is aware of a suffering which rather consumes his intelligence into sheer awe and horror. He learns why sometimes it is necessary to hate life in order to live it. In this, Emma resembles him more even though, unlike Gwendolen, she never clearly sees the full irony of her own frustration.

That Emma comes to share Flaubert's own sense of the mysterious emptiness of life is not, in itself, testimony to her capacity to give herself to life, but only a sign of her readiness to give life up. Tragedy occurs when someone loses something of real value in life, something that may be still desired after it has been lost. It is not just about thwarted desires that were never realisable but about desires which, though we can imagine them being realised or even have seen them realised at an earlier point in the drama, are irrevocably thwarted in one particular case. To feel that such thwarting is a perennial possibility we need to believe that what is thwarted is a real and not an illusory desire. Thus, in *Othello*, we may feel that Othello's love for Desdemona is in many ways a false kind of love but the play does not make us feel that love itself is false; indeed, the falseness of Othello's love has the effect of making Desdemona's genuine love seem even more priceless. This contrasts with the feeling that Emma would have been doomed to failure whoever she had loved or married, because for Flaubert failure is the inevitable rule of life. If nothing that Emma desires is worthy of the energy she expends on desiring it, the novel is bound to seem less tragic: if she has nothing essential to gain from life, then there is nothing vital for her to lose through death. It is,

I think, because of this idea implanted in the book that its life seems sometimes to be a repetitive mechanism in which futile human aspirations are monotonously washed out by the ebb and flow of time, leaving only a stagnant deposit of that dejection so often described in Flaubert's letters. 'My sorrow', he says in one of them, 'is stupid and colourless, a storm with dirty rain but without lightning.' (*Corr.*, I, p. 182.)⁴ There is, however, a crucial reservation to be made against this view of the narrator's mood: it forgets the comedy. For it is perhaps the comedy in the novel which in the long run is the hardest thing to bear with resignation. The novel is not a picture of a world in which success is an impossibility. In its famous last line we learn that Homais has just been awarded 'la croix d'honneur'. (P. 481.) All *his* hopes are crowned. This most bitter moment in the whole book is, however, borne only by Flaubert and the reader; Emma is already dead.

There may be no Bradleian uplift in Gloucester's perception of his 'huge sorrows' – he is trapped in his 'vile sense' and sees them whether he will or no – but his mood is deeper than the anguish of depression. There is a muted note of exhilaration in his lines which comes, not from pride in his own perception, but from an assured knowledge of the truth of what he is seeing. It is a very different feeling from that *ennui* which Flaubert sometimes liked to cultivate in order to numb in himself the open nerve of sensibility which made him feel pain so acutely. Tragedy exhilarates as well as appals us because there is a kind of exhilaration which is inherent in the emotion of awe. Another way of putting my argument about the *Troisième Partie* is to say that Flaubert attempts to pass off Emma's moments of tragic exhilaration as fits of self-suffocating hysteria or languid resignation. But Flaubert cannot suppress everything. Emma is not hysterical when she summons the strength to tell Rodolphe some home-truths about himself after he has coldly spurned her plea for help at the end. At that moment it is as if she finds a true voice for the first, perhaps the only time in the novel. The irony is purged away and she is no longer a pitiable provincial housewife trying to play the Romantic heroine:

— Mais, moi, je t'aurais tout donné, j'aurais tout vendu, j'aurais travaillé de mes mains, j'aurais mendié sur les routes, pour un sourire, pour un regard, pour t'entendre dire: 'Merci!' Et tu restes là tranquillement dans ton fauteuil, comme si déjà tu ne m'avais pas fait assez souffrir! . . . Hein! nos projets de voyage, tu te rappelles? oh! ta lettre, ta lettre! elle m'a déchiré le cœur! . . . Et puis, quand je reviens vers lui, vers lui, qui est riche, heureux, libre! pour implorer un secours que le premier venu rendrait, suppliante et lui rapportant toute ma tendresse, il me repousse, parce que ça lui coûterait trois mille francs! (Pp. 430–1.)

('As for me, I would have given you everything, sold all I had, worked with my bare hands and begged by the road-side, for one smile, one look, just to hear you say "Thank you!" And there you sit at your ease in your armchair, as if you hadn't made me suffer enough already! . . . And what about our plans of travelling, do you remember them? Oh! your letter, your letter! it tore my heart in two! . . . And then, when I come back to him, to find him rich and happy and free, and plead for help that the first-comer would give, entreating him and bringing him back all my tenderness, he casts me off, because it would cost him three thousand francs!')

She is superbly articulate and clear about what he is (one of the joys of the passage is in Flaubert's marvellous ear for the rhythms of anger) and her exalted feeling does not come from self, from mere wounded feelings or posing: there is no art in her tone. It resides in her conscious possession of real human feelings and it forges a natural sense of the human mind in general. An Oedipus gathered up into his own passionate outcry against fate all those lesser protests which stay submerged in the breasts of those he lives amongst: Emma, here, is a nineteenth-century equivalent whom the novel-reader comes to regard as the chorus regards Oedipus. Flaubert, however, does not build on this scene but chooses instead to stress Emma's self-pity and the way she thinks her own feelings finer than those of her neighbours, so that she resents the fact that she is made to suffer so much more than they do. We forget that she has also been more capable of joy because it is part of her malady to be unable to see that suffering creates a bond between her and other people. In this, she is a true descendant of Vigny's Chatterton. Her inability to get beyond her own ego, except in moments like her tirade at Rodolphe, makes it difficult for the reader to feel a positive solidarity with her humanity. Ony partially does defeat reveal in her a strength of mind which, without defeat, she would not have attained. Exhilaration is at least fleetingly there in her, but, is it sufficiently there for her to become more than a typical case of a common malady? It is this question which Lawrence can help us explore. On it depends our final judgement of the novel's success, of whether it realises the potential of its *Première Partie* or whether, for all its greatness, the latter part of the book is in vital ways redundant to its total meaning.

II

Lawrence gives a very valuable account of tragedy in *Madame Bovary* but, to reap the harvest of his insights, it is necessary to see how, as well as quarrelling with Flaubert, he was quarrelling too with tragedy itself. I would agree with Raymond Williams that *Women in Love* is his own most tragic novel (his only successful one, I think) but that view of it has to be qualified by saying that it all the time tries to break away from the tragic and go beyond it, that Lawrence was only willing to have tragedy *on his own terms*. These terms, I believe, were too salvationist and Protestant for him to be a tragic writer for long and he became a prophet and paradisal visionary instead, not unlike Shelley in some respects. It is, nonetheless, precisely his instinct for self-renewal which enables him to say something profound about Flaubert and about tragedy in general.

Lawrence always made a firm distinction between the tragic and the depressing, as in this letter of 1912 :

> I hate England and its hopelessness. I hate Bennett's resignation. Tragedy ought really to be a great kick at misery. But *Anna of the Five Towns* seems like an acceptance – so does all the modern stuff since Flaubert. I hate it. I want to wash again quickly, wash off England, the oldness and grubbiness and despair.[5]

It may be countered that in *Madame Bovary* there is a constant ground-swell of rage at life beneath the bitter comedy. Lawrence, though, is really thinking of the tragic hero, not the tragedian, making a 'great kick at misery'. But the phrase suggests an element of the wiful and Nietzschean in tragic terror and may not be much nearer confronting that terror than weak submission is. Lawrence often tried to wish away the tragic by pretending that it existed only in the souls of the dejected, as we see in Ursula's impatience with her melancholy friend Maggie Schofield, in *The Rainbow*. One nevertheless takes his point that an affirmation of the human is an essential part of the tragic emotion. Only through such affirmation is a true resignation to the non-human possible. For the human is affirmed, as sometimes in Wordsworth, when the self becomes lost in awe at the world. Without this, 'resignation' easily becomes a dramatic posture to disguise a disbelief in man. There must, in short, be something positive to be resigned in the first place. Lawrence prompts the question of whether we can find in Emma a sufficiently strong will to live to be able to see her death as a dispossession of the most tragic kind.

Lawrence does not deny a tragic sense to Flaubert but only to his characters and, because of this discrepancy, he sees the pathos of

Madame Bovary as overdone. He develops this criticism in a brilliant passage in his preface to Verga's *Mastro-don Gesualdo,* in the course of an attack on *I Malavoglia* for 'wallowing in tragedy':

> In most books of the period – even in *Madame Bovary,* to say nothing of Balzac's earlier *Lys dans la Vallée* – one has to take off about twenty per cent of the tragedy. One does it in Dickens, one does it in Hawthorne, one does it all the time, with all the great writers. Then why not with Verga? Just knock off about twenty per cent of the tragedy in *I Malavoglia,* and see what a great book remains. Most books that live, live in spite of the author's laying it on thick. Think of *Wuthering Heights.* It is quite as impossible to an Italian as even *I Malavoglia* is to us. But it is a great book.
>
> The trouble with realism – and Verga was a realist – is that the writer, when he is a truly exceptional man like Flaubert or like Verga, tries to read his own sense of tragedy into people much smaller than himself. I think it is a final criticism against *Madame Bovary* that people such as Emma Bovary and her husband Charles simply are too insignificant to carry the full weight of Gustave Flaubert's sense of tragedy. Emma and Charles Bovary are a couple of little people. Gustave Flaubert is not a little person. But, because he is a realist and does not believe in 'heroes', Flaubert insists on pouring his own deep and bitter tragic consciousness into the little skins of the country doctor and his uneasy wife. The result is a discrepancy. *Madame Bovary* is a great book and a very wonderful picture of life. But we cannot help resenting the fact that the great tragic soul of Gustave Flaubert is, so to speak, given only the rather commonplace bodies of Emma and Charles Bovary. There's a misfit. And to get over the misfit, you have to let in all sorts of seams of pity. Seams of pity, which won't be hidden.
>
> The great tragic soul of Shakespeare borrows the bodies of kings and princes – not out of snobbism, but out of natural affinity. You can't put a great soul into a commonplace person. Commonplace persons have commonplace souls.[6]

This is no less suggestive for being, as far I can see, quite wrong. It is not simply that Lawrence imports into his reading his own religious view of the hero as aristocrat, though he does do that. He is in many ways right in saying that we feel resentment against the determinist in Flaubert. Yet the real 'discrepancy' of which he speaks is rather different: it comes not from Flaubert's trying unsuccessfully to pour his 'tragic consciousness' into Emma but from his withholding from her a full share in it. He seems more at ease depicting the kind of tragedy enacted by 'commonplace persons' only ordinarily aware of their fates. In other words, he prefers to put comic characters into tragic situations. (One thinks of his admiration for Molière.) Lawrence does not give any precise description of Flaubert's 'great tragic soul' (he is mainly concerned with Verga in this essay) but it seems unlikely that he would have seen a sense of the *grotesque triste* as part of it. He never mentions Homais: the novel's comedy seems to have impressed him no more than it did James or Arnold. Had it done so, he would have seen that Flaubert expends far more energy on keeping 'commonplace persons' little than in breathing greatness into them. But the most interesting perception Lawrence has is that the presence of these 'little people' lets 'seams of pity' into the book. If Emma has no creative understanding of her fate to draw on, then we can only relate to her through 'pity'. Lawrence's criticism of the novel therefore has quite a lot in common with my own criticisms of the *Nouvelle Version*. He laments the presence in *Madame Bovary* of just that element which James missed in it.

One cannot defend Flaubert against Lawrence by arguing that it is wishfully un-historical to contrast the anti-heroic Emma and Charles with Shakespeare's kings and princes, even allowing for Lawrence's silènce about his satirical purpose.[7] What concerns Lawrence is a kingly spirit which dwells beyond class at a more essential and impersonal level than pomp and circumstance. In the *Study of Thomas Hardy* he sees this spirit as man's power to wrest from tragedy an inner assurance of his own creativeness. The 'great kick at misery' comes in the very act of recognising the supra-human power of the universe:

> That is the whole point: something is which was not. And I wish it were true of us. I wish we were all like kindled bonfires on the edge of space, marking out the advance-posts. What is the aim of self-preservation, but to carry us right out to the firing line; there, what *is* is in contact with what is not. If many lives be lost by the way, it cannot be helped, nor if much suffering be entailed. I do not go out to war in the intention of avoiding all danger or discomfort: I go to fight for myself. Every step I move forward into being brings a newer, juster proportion into the world, gives me less need of storehouse and barn, allows me to leave all, and to take what I want by the way, sure that it will always be there; allows me in the end to fly the flag of myself, at the extreme tip of life.
> He who would save his life must lose it.[8]

There is, in fact, more than just a 'great kick at misery' here: misery is welcomed as a crucible in which the self can be tested but, in itself, misery is a side-issue. The impulse to dwell on it – as Lawrence thought Flaubert did – is the mark of those who draw back from the 'extreme tip of life' in themselves. Flaubert's determination to keep Emma little was just such a drawing back, as, in this mood, all 'pity' was to Lawrence. It is at this point that the argument dons the garb of salvationism, reminding us as it does so of Lawrence's non-conformist upbringing [9] He begins from the image of man as a budding flower:

> But like a poppy that has come to bud, when he [i.e. 'he who would save his life'] reaches the shore, when he has traversed his known and come to the beach to meet the unknown, he must strip himself naked and plunge in, and pass out: if he dare. And the rest of his life he will be staring at the unknown, cast out upon the waters. But if he dare not plunge in, if he dare not take off his clothes and give himself naked to the flood, then let him prowl in rotten safety, weeping for the pity of those he imagines worse off than himself. He dare not weep aloud for his own cowardice. And weep he must. So he will find him objects of pity.[10]

This is more penetrating as psychological insight than as a view of tragedy. It is true that in the end of some tragedies man may be left 'staring at the unknown' but, in that case, there is usually no more life to be lived. Yet Lawrence is surely right to imply that we are in no position to pity a true tragic character, for such characters exist beyond their audiences, 'at the extreme tip of life', creatively discovering their fates and making of them beacons which shine back on us from beyond their individual 'misery'. Tragic experience is not destruction only but a clarification of being in which the destruction is a stepping-stone to the clarification. A quotation from another of Lawrence's essays will make this clearer:

> In tragedy the man is more than his part. Hamlet is more than Prince of Denmark, Macbeth is more than the murderer of Duncan. The man is caught in the wheels of his part, his fate, he may be torn asunder. He may be killed, but the resistant integral soul in him is not destroyed. He comes through though he dies. He goes through with his fate though death swallows him. And it is in this facing of fate, this going right through with it, that tragedy lies. Tragedy is not disaster. . . . Tragedy is the working out of some immediate passional problem within the soul of man.[11]

For Hamlet and Macbeth, that is, tragedy is a stripping away of self in which they fathom a new, more essential ground of being, a broadening of the limitedly personal towards the generally human. This gives us a valuable notion to take back to the reading of *Madame Bovary* but, to see its value, it is necessary to raise a doubt about whether tragedy really does work as Lawrence says. Surely disaster also is present in tragedy? For the 'resistant integral soul' in Macbeth or Lear *is* destroyed; they do not just experience fate as a vehicle for self-discovery, a quasi-mystical process which they live 'through'. Fate also works 'through' them, penetrates their very existence and finally consumes it. To resolve a 'passional problem within the soul of man' is the province not of tragedy but of religion.

I do not wish to take Lawrence's thought and make strained parallels and distinctions between it and Flaubert's: no original work of art will dove-tail with another artist's theories. But Lawrence does raise questions which this book may hitherto have obscured slightly. In discussing James's criticism of Flaubert it was possible to argue that Flaubert's non-attachment to Emma represented a positive alternative to the ostensibly more human art for which James sought himself. This argument depended on the view that the art he desiderated centred on the superior individual character who could serve as a magnet for drawing from us a kind of pity which is essentially disguised self-pity. It will not hold against Lawrence, since he distrusts the instinct to seek out 'objects of pity' and, in fact, detects its presence in Flaubert. By prompting a distinction between self and being Lawrence can make Flaubert's non-attachment seem too negative. Reticence is not the only way of transcending the personal. Lawrence, unlike James, would have hated Flaubert if he had been ready to 'glow' but he considered the Flaubertian divesting of self as no more than a beginning, which should have ended in more than that aesthetic calm of Sirius of which Flaubert was so fond of dreaming. He would not have seen that calm as an end in itself.

III

Out of exasperation with the *muflisme* of his times, Flaubert lamented that, 'The XVIIIth century denied the soul, and the work of the XIXth will perhaps be to kill man.' (*Corr.*, III, p. 397.) Emma, at the end, might have agreed, just as she might also have felt, when faced with the bailiffs, that, 'in bourgeois subjects *hideousness* must replace the *tragic*, which is incompatible with them'. (*Corr.*, III, p. 388.) Tragic affirmation of the human lay outside the actual; for Emma, in fantasy, for Flaubert, in art:

I want to do two or three long, epic books, novels in a grandiose setting in which the action will inevitably be fruitful and the details rich in themselves, books with great walls and painted from high to low. (*Corr.*, III, p. 337.)

Flaubert knew intimately how Emma felt when she went to the opera. Planning *Salammbô*, he feels the same nostalgia for his own first version of *La Tentation de Saint Antoine* as Emma feels as she tries to resuscitate Romantic passions in herself. *Salammbô* is a dream of a short-cut to tragic exhilaration. Flaubert was more honest about how far the dream was also a flight from tragedy (the modern kind of tragedy he knew at first-hand) when he confessed that:

Few people will guess how sad one had to be to undertake the resuscitation of Carthage; it is a Thebiad which disgust with modern life has pushed me into. (*Corr.*, IV, p. 348.)

Madame Bovary is the greater novel because it studies such feelings in their true context. Yonville tormented Flaubert as much as it did Emma: when it frustrated her dreams it frustrated his too. 'Hideousness' was a salutary discipline because it helped Flaubert transform melancholy into the comic rage of the satirist, a version of Lawrence's 'great kick at misery', and gave him what he always needed more than exotic escape: something to write *against*. By inventing Yonville he was perhaps constricting and punishing himself for the excesses of the first *Tentation*. He scrutinises it out of more than a simple fidelity to the real. It is also the arena of a self-victimising complicity in the nineteenth century's work of killing humanism. Emma made any idea of attempting to transcend the actual seem illusory, relegating imagination (Flaubert's own hated god) to a desire for what could not exist in the present. Where Proust's Marcel can travel freely through his own inner time, she feels her time as an unlit prison.[12] By taking up the modern life of Yonville as a yardstick to measure her dreams by Flaubert resigned his own, and capitulated on Emma's behalf. In Lawrence's language, he represented the 'extreme tip of life' as a sentimental nirvana of cloudless Italian skies, outside life itself. This is why she must 'fly the flag' of herself in the face of her creator if the book is to vindicate spirit at all. I think myself, that in spite of all the irony can do, she succeeds and that *Madame Bovary* emerges an even greater book because of the near-intolerable tension that Flaubert's feelings for his century set up in it.

The essence of the novel's satire is that in writing against Emma's spirit Flaubert could not help writing against his own. In the last chapter I suggest that his faith in Art closely resembles her faith in Passion. A letter he wrote to Louise Colet in 1853 shows how deep his faith was and how far *Madame Bovary* was an exploration of it:

> Isn't the life of an artist, or rather a work of art to be accomplished, like a great mountain to be scaled? A hard voyage which demands an iron will. At first one sees a high summit from below. In the skies, it glitters with purity, frighteningly high, yet solicits you precisely for that reason. You set off. But at each plateau on the way the peak gets bigger, the horizon recedes, one proceeds by precipices, vertigo and discouragements. It is cold and the eternal hurricane of the high regions strips the last tatter of clothing off you as it passes. The earth is lost forever and no doubt the goal will never be reached. It is the time when one adds up one's weariness and looks with horror at *one's chapped skin*. One has nothing but an indomitable desire to climb higher, to finish with things, to die. Yet sometimes a gust of wind in the sky comes to unveil to your wonder perspectives which are numberless, infinite, marvellous. Men appear twenty thousand feet below one, an olympian breeze fills your giant lungs and one feels like a colossus who has the entire world as a pedestal. Then, fog returns and one crawls forward on all fours, scraping one's nails on the rocks and weeping in solitude. No matter. Let us die in the snow, let us perish in the white sorrow of our desire, to the murmurings of the torrents of the Spirit, faces turned to the sun. (*Corr.*, III, pp. 342–3.)

Madame Bovary was written for this wonder and not out of some sublime literary doggedness. The feeling is more profound than rhetoric: a hymn of thanksgiving for being enabled to wring joy and beauty from the contemplation of the insupportable reality of the nineteenth century. The heroism is only Flaubertian hyperbole which testifies to his sense of wonder. The object of this wonder is that desire and imagination can, in spite of everything more real, retrieve an habitual frustration so that the spirit may sometimes, however rarely, sustain conceptions through which the world is transcended. The tragi-comedy of *Bovarysme* is not an inevitable fate. That this transcendence is very near to death and nothingness – 'the white sorrow of our desire' – is part of the Lawrentian paradox in which the tragic hero 'comes through though he dies'. Thomas Mann summed up such devotion to art pithily when he wrote that, 'He whose preoccupation is with excellence longs fervently to find rest in perfection; and is not nothingness a form of perfection?'[13] If, as I think, Emma Bovary ends by yearning for nothingness, it is for a nothingness of this kind. The Flaubert who wrote this letter could not really convince us that she sought only emptiness. Emma may begin the novel at the foot of Flaubert's pedestal, by the end she finds through suffering a small imaginative space of solitude from which to regard Yonville herself. Yet this is difficult to show since Flaubert has made it possible to give two very different interpretations of her death and prevented us from choosing between them.

The critic who arises like a road-block on the course of this argument is, of course, F. R. Leavis. Leavis considers that James is representative of an English tradition in fiction whose distinctive virtues supply an antithesis to the tradition of Flaubert and his successors. He says of the novelists in his 'great tradition' (a tradition avowedly less European) that: 'far from having anything of Flaubert's disgust or disdain or boredom, they are all distinguished by a vital capacity for experience, a kind of reverent openness before life, and a marked moral intensity.'[14] He twists the Lawrentian view of a Flaubert turning away from life as from a leprosy by ignoring the fact that Flaubert did not turn away from leprosy. Lawrence's value-meaning of the word 'life' is near to becoming a general descriptive word too. It is a way of eliminating the tragic which is wholly consonant with the nineteenth century traditions of which Leavis is an heir. Yet a true 'openness before life' includes irreverence too. How else can comedy and satire survive? Art also needs to recognise the response life provokes in Hamlet when he cries:

> O God, God,
> How weary, stale, flat, and unprofitable
> Seem to me all the uses of this world!
> Fie on't, ah, fie, 'tis an unweeded garden
> That grows to seed. Things rank and gross in nature
> Possess it merely.   (Act I, scene 2.)

It would require a long essay to argue properly that Leavis will not admit that life needs to be denied in order for it to be affirmed or to suggest that Lawrence knew this (in *The Crown*, for instance) and pursued a different, less health-ridden 'moral intensity' when he called Birkin and Ursula *fleurs du mal*. The submerged idealism behind Leavis's use of the word 'life' substitutes for experience a special way of looking at experience and it does this in the name of 'openness'. We do not expect such a writer to sympathise with Flaubert's kind of idealism or to see the tragic conflict it sets up between our need to see the world as it is with our need to see it as it might be. Leavis essentially says of Flaubert what James said: 'Why does the inevitable perpetually infuriate him, and why does he inveterately resent the ephemeral?'[15] Neither critic would have been satisfied with an answer which said that it was because the inevitable is inevitable and the ephemeral, ephemeral. Yet Flaubert's anger was an outlet for a desire to live as fully as he could imagine living, were it not that the conditions of life seemed to frustrate that desire. In the same way Hamlet felt bitter at the thought of Alexander's noble dust stopping a bung-hole, To say 'fie on't, ah, fie' may express not a denial of life so much as a protest against it, on behalf of human aspirations which life itself seems to deny. Flaubert's indignation, and need of it, was neither the product of fatigued sensibility nor a pose: it has the exhilarating aliveness of Emma's denunciation of Rodolphe.

I unexpectedly find common ground with *The Great Tradition* when Leavis describes the 'limiting characteristics' of the Jamesian 'genius':

> It was not, in short, D. H. Lawrence's or any thing like it. James had no such immediate sense of human solidarity, no such nourishing intuition of the unity of life, as could make up to him for the deficiencies of civilised intercourse: life for him must be humane or it was nothing. There was nowhere in his work that preoccupation with ultimate sanctions which we may call religious.[16]

I am puzzled to say whether I dissent from Leavis's view of James or whether I simply think that Leavis was wrong to place James in his 'great tradition' at all. For the absence of an 'immediate sense of human solidarity' in his 1902 essay on Flaubert prompts one to doubt whether James really wrote out of real 'reverent openness before life'. He perhaps pretended to do so, just as his Isabel misled Ralph Touchett into thinking that she wanted to live, but his concern for 'civilised intercourse' barred him from a religious sense of life and limited his interest in manners and culture to the social aspect of the 'unity of life'.[17] His characters are seldom men and women first and foremost, before they are Americans or Italians, French or English. As before, the *Study of Thomas Hardy* provides a focus on James. Lawrence is trying to argue that the 'real stuff of tragedy' in *The Return of the Native* is the 'primitive, primal earth'[18] of Egdon Heath:

> This is the wonder of Hardy's novels, and gives them their beauty. The vast, unexplored morality of life itself, what we call the immorality of nature, surrounds us in its eternal incomprehensibility, and in its midst goes on the little human morality play, with its queer frame of morality and its mechanised move-

ment; seriously, portentously, till some one of the protagonists chances to look out of the charmed circle, weary of the stage, to look into the wilderness raging round. Then he is lost, his little drama falls to pieces, or becomes mere repetition, but the stupendous theatre outside goes on enacting its own incomprehensible drama, untouched.[19]

James's characters do not look outside the circle of their social world and when they renounce that world it is by turning inwards to a world within, like Fleda Vetch in *The Spoils of Poynton*. Lawrence's sense of Hardy's view of nature may seem anachronistic but it does evoke those moments in Hardy (there are more with the wood in *The Woodlanders* than on Egdon Heath) which come nearest to the effect of the storm in *King Lear* which thrilled Flaubert. When Emma feels the music of her arteries filling the countryside we are given a similar apprehension of the 'immorality of nature'. It is not something which Leavis's reductive phrase about 'disgust or disdain or boredom' would credit Flaubert with but then, it is not perhaps something which his stress on 'marked moral intensity' always permits him to see in Lawrence either. There is good reason to be wary of letting Leavis's interpretation of Lawrence intrude into Lawrence's view of Flaubert.

IV

Flaubert conquers beauty through an act of contemplation which dissolves the world as it mirrors it.[20] Emma shares at least the negative side of this contemplativeness in her constant fondness for reviewing her own life rather than living it. Her inarticulacy is a price paid for Flaubert's finding a voice in his art and she is afflicted by the sense of an unbridgeable gap between the life she conceives and the life she actually lives. This makes her silent and at the mercy of words and Flaubert makes her suffer all the torment of his own despairing sense of the gap that must always exist between language and things, the self and the world. The perception of this gap makes Emma's mind turn passively in on itself to prey on its own conceptions. She has no way of putting what is buried inside herself into lived life. Her mistake is to try to live in spite of this, whereas Flaubert, by a more thorough-going passiveness, was able at special moments to make it appear unnecessary to try to bridge the gap which she can never cross. When she does seem to cross this gap it tends to be in silence and not in words – as in the scene when she first makes love with Rodolphe – and it is at moments like this that reading must be especially alert.

Emma's helplessness is often seen as the result of some outside control, devoid of any balancing inner resistance of a breeze from within herself. Action is not an expression of personality so much as an effort to dissolve it. For example, when she seeks help from the curé, Bournisien:

> Alors un attendrissement la saisit; elle se sentit molle et toute abandonnée, comme un duvet d'oiseau qui tournoit dans la tempête; et ce fut sans en avoir conscience qu'elle s'achemina vers l'église, disposée à n'importe quelle dévotion, pourvu qu'elle y absorbât son âme et que l'existence entière y disparût. (P. 154.)
>
> (Then a moved feeling took hold of her; she felt lifeless and utterly forsaken, like bird's down blown about in a storm, and it was without knowing what she did that she set off towards the church, ready for any form of worship whatsoever, so long as it would absorb her soul and her whole existence might be blotted out in it.)

It is the pathos of a radical lack of energy. She is so weighed down by the accumulated past that she can only sleep-walk will-lessly through her present. What she asks of life is, in reality, death. In the context of the whole chapter her plight may be tragicomic but here the prose acquires a lyrical, elegiac quality. It is out of such passivity that she creates the kind of energy that characterises her behaviour from her Rouen affair with Léon to the end of the novel.

Because Emma sees her life as a whole through memory she abjures seeing it as a process in action. Mere contingency takes on the character of necessity. The prose assumes something of the same immobility:

> Au fond de son âme, cependant, elle attendait un événement. Comme les matelots en détresse, elle promenait sur la solitude de sa vie des yeux désespérés, cherchant au loin quelque voile blanche dans les brumes de l'horizon. Elle ne savait pas quel serait ce hasard, le vent qui le pousserait jusqu'à elle, vers quel rivage il la mènerait, s'il était chaloupe où vaisseau à trois ponts, chargé d'angoisses ou plein de félicités jusqu'aux sabords. Mais, chaque matin, à son réveil, elle l'espérait pour la journée, et elle écoutait tous les bruits, se levait en sursaut, s'étonnait qu'il ne vînt pas, puis, au coucher du soleil, toujours plus triste, désirait être au lendemain. (Pp. 86–7.)
>
> (But in the depths of her soul she was waiting for something to happen. Like a sailor in distress, her desperate eyes scanned the loneliness of her life, seeking some white sail in the mists of the far-off horizon. She did not know what that chance would be or

on what wind it would be borne to her, nor what shore it would lead her to, whether in a longboat or a galleon, laden down with anguish or with happiness brimming out of the very port-holes. But each morning when she awoke she hoped it would come that day, and she rose with a start to listen to every noise, amazed at its not coming; then at sunset, feeling sadder still, she longed for it to be tomorrow.)

The greatness of the passage is that its poignancy subtly includes the reader. As Pascal says, 'nous ne vivons jamais mais nous espérons de vivre'. Yet the sadness does not include us completely: it makes life seem all outside Emma rather than within. We wonder if she is capable of creating feeling or only of responding to things coming to her from outside by chance.

The consequence of this is that Emma thinks that any amelioration of her lot must lie in transcending not the self but the world: her defiance is always a way of distinguishing herself from other people by acting in a way they find bizarre and imponderable:

Lorsqu'elle avait bien rudoyé sa servante, elle lui faisait des cadeaux ou l'envoyait se promener chez les voisines, de même qu'elle jetait parfois aux pauvres toutes les pièces blanches de sa bourse, quoiqu'elle ne fût guère tendre cependant, ni facilement accessible à l'émotion d'autrui. . . . (P. 92.)

(When she had given her servant a good ticking off she would give her presents or send her for a walk to the neighbours and, in the same way, she sometimes threw all the gold pieces in her purse to the poor, although she was hardly tender-hearted or easily accessible to the emotion of another person. . . .)

Her stategy of caprice misleads others as to her true self, so that she can take refuge in guarding it in secret with an enhanced feeling of superiority. This extends even to hiding from Léon the sexual desire she has for him:

Elle était amoureuse de Léon, et elle recherchait la solitude, afin de pouvoir plus à l'aise se délecter en son image. La vue de sa personne troublait la volupté de cette méditation. (P. 149.)

(She was in love with Léon and yet she sought solitude, so that she would be freer to picture him to herself with more relish. It disturbed the voluptuousness of these meditations if she saw him in the flesh.)

She is most real when most silent and unexpressive, happiest in treating her feeling for Léon as an end in itself, a consumer of her own emotions as their object dwindles into their mere occasion.[21]

It is appropriate that when Emma does break out of this vicious circle of self it should be in silence and in nature, beyond the banality of words and the claustrophobia of the town:

Le drap de sa robe s'accrochait au velours de l'habit. Elle renversa son cou blanc, qui se gonflait d'un soupir, et, défaillante, tout en pleurs, avec un long frémissement et se cachant la figure, elle s'abandonna.

Les ombres du soir descendaient; le soleil horizontal, passant entre les branches, lui éblouissait les yeux. Çà et là, tout autour d'elle dans les feuilles ou par terre, des taches lumineuses tremblaient, comme si des colibris, en volant, eussent éparpillé leurs plumes. Le silence était partout; quelque chose de doux semblait sortir des arbres; elle sentait son cœur, dont les battements recommençaient, et le sang circulait dans sa chair comme un fleuve de lait. Alors, elle entendit tout au loin, au delà du bois, sur les autres collines, un cri vague et prolongé, une voix qui se traînait, et elle l'écoutait silencieusement, se mêlant comme une musique aux dernières vibrations de ses nerfs émus. Rodolphe, le cigare aux dents, raccammodait avec son canif une des deux brides cassée.

Ils s'en revinrent à Yonville, par le même chemin. Ils revirent sur la boue les traces de leurs chevaux, côte à côte, et les mêmes buissons, les mêmes cailloux dans l'herbe. Rien autour d'eux n'avait changé; et pour elle, cependant, quelque chose était survenu de plus considérable que si les montagnes se fussent déplacés. Rodolphe, de temps à autre, se penchait et lui prenait sa main pour la baiser.

Elle était charmante, à cheval. Droite, avec sa taille mince, le genou plié sur la crinière de sa bête et un peu colorée par le grand air, dans la rougeur du soir.

En entrant dans Yonville, elle caracola sur les pavès. On la regardait des fenêtres. (Pp. 223-4.)

(The material of her dress was clinging to the velvet of his riding habit. She threw back her white neck, her throat swelled as she sighed, and, swooning, her eyes full of tears and hiding her face, in a long quivering movement she abandoned herself.

The evening shadows were falling; the sun, low on the horizon, dazzled her eyes as it passed between the trees. Here and there, all round her, in the leaves and on the ground, were bright patches of shimmering light, as if humming-birds in flying off had strewn their feathers about. The silence was everywhere and something mild seemed to be issuing from the trees. She felt her heart as it began to pound again, and the blood flowed in her flesh like a river of milk. Then she heard a voice fading away in a faint, drawn-out cry, far in the distance beyond the wood, on the other side of the valley, and she listened to it in silence as it blended like music with the last vibrations of her sensitive nerves. Rodolphe, a cigar between his teeth, was mending one of the broken bridles with his pocket-knife.

They came back to Yonville by the same track. They saw the same hoof-prints, side by side in the mud, the same bushes, the same stones in the grass. Nothing around them had changed, and yet, for her, something more momentous had come to pass than if the mountains had moved. Every now and then, Rodolphe woud lean over to take her hand and kiss it.

She was charming, on horse-back; straight-backed, slim-waisted, her knee folded over the animal's mane and looking a little flushed by the open air, in the redness of the evening.

Coming into Yonville, she clattered over the cobble-stones. People were watching her from their windows.)

The key words in this beautifully unified passage are 'silence' and 'silencieusement'. As Emma goes beyond self in love she also goes beyond words and imagination.[22] Her habitual passivity is still there but it is positive and sensual instead of negative and languid. The cadences are quietly joyful, no longer elegiac. As she succumbs to Rodolphe she hides her face, blotting out that persistent remembering which saddens her at other times. Nowhere in her relations with her baby daughter is there any image like the one which likens her blood to a river of milk in her flesh. She is absorbed into her surroundings without being nullified by them, their music harmonises with the music of her feelings. Though nothing has changed around her when she returns to Yonville, everything is changed; her high colour, the clatter of her horse on the cobble-stones, ring out her fulfilment. The neighbours may stare and think her impudent but they are no longer staring at an unhappy woman: she is too contented to be defiant. Flaubert does all this without glamourising Rodolphe in the slightest. We can see, by the way he holds the cigar in his teeth, why he attracts Emma; we never imagine that his experience is profound in the way hers is. Flaubert will need all the irony of the *fiacre* scene, all the deliberate resolve not to see Emma's feeling for Léon from within in this way, to make us forget what, at her best and happiest, she can be.

But mostly, when Emma tries to go beyond self, she remains self-absorbed. She always feels her rage against life, not as rage at the common lot but as rage at what life has done to *her*. This resentment only alienates her from others. This is how she feels about Charles, the person closest to her, after the fiasco of the operation on Hippolyte's club-foot:

Tout en lui l'irritait maintenant, sa figure, son costume, ce qu'il
ne disait pas, sa personne entière, son existence enfin. Elle se
repentit, comme d'un crime, de sa vertu passée, et ce qui en
restait encore s'écroulait sous les coups furieux de son orgueil. Elle
se délectait dans toutes les ironies mauvaises de l'adultère triomphant. Le souvenir de son amant revenait à elle avec des attrac-
tions vertigineuses; elle y jetait son âme, emportée vers cette image
par un enthousiasme nouveau; et Charles lui semblait aussi
détaché de sa vie, aussi absent pour toujours, aussi impossible et
anéanti, que s'il allait mourir et qu'il eût agonisé sous ses yeux.
(Pp. 256–7.)

(Everything about him irritated her now, his face, his dress,
the things he didn't say, his whole person – in short, his very
being. She repented her past virtue as if it were a crime and what
still remained of it caved in beneath the furious battery of her
pride. She savoured all the malign ironies of triumphant adultery.
The memory of her lover came back to her with a dizzying attrac-
tiveness, sweeping her with renewed eagerness towards his image,
until her soul was consumed in it; whilst Charles seemed as
remote from her life, as permanently absent, unthinkable and
blotted out, as if he were in his death-throes, about to die before
her eyes.)

Flaubert makes her thoughts lurid in a way foreign to the prose of
the scene with Rodolphe. Phrases like 'les ironies mauvaises de
l'adultère triomphant' are not really serious; they do not, and are
not meant to make us sympathetic to the notion that, for Emma,
there is a moral necessity for self-fulfilment in adultery. Her proud
indifference is the same emotion which spurs her to defiance:

Ses regards devinrent plus hardis, ses discours plus libres; elle eut
même l'inconvenance de se promener avec M. Rodolphe une
cigarette à la bouche, *comme pour narguer le monde*; enfin, ceux
qui doutaient encore ne doutèrent plus quand on la vit, un jour,
descendre de l'*Hirondelle*, la taille serrée dans un gilet, à la façon
d'un homme. . . . (P. 266.)

(Her looks grew bolder, her speech more free; she even had the
indelicacy to go walking with M. Rodolphe with a cigarette in
her mouth, *as if to flout people*. In the end, those who still had
doubts doubted no longer when, one day, she was seen getting
out of the *Hirondelle*, her figure pulled in tightly by a waistcoat
just like a man's.)

She tries to become her own self by asserting herself against others.
As a result, she is trapped by the comedy of the prying Yonvillais.

In her pride Emma becomes most independent of Flaubert by becoming most like him. She looks down on Charles just as he is often imagined to have looked down on her, partaking of the arrogant side of his 'impassibilité'. She not only stands for *bourgeois* values which he hates, she shares his own contempt for them. Flaubert once asked Louise Colet, 'When will people write the facts from the point-of-view of a *superior joke,* that is to say, as God sees them from on high?' (*Corr.,* III, p. 37.) This is how Emma tries to see life:

> Quelquefois, dans un écartement des nuées, sous un rayon de soleil, on apercevait au loin les toits de Yonville, avec les jardins au bord de l'eau, les cours, les murs, et le clocher de l'église. Emma fermait à demi les paupières pour reconnaître sa maison, et jamais ce pauvre village où elle vivait ne lui avait semblait si petit. De la hauteur où ils étaient, toute la vallée paraissait un immense lac pâle, s'évaporant à l'air. Les massifs d'arbres, de place en place, saillissaient comme des rochers noirs; et les hautes lignes des peupliers, qui dépassaient la brume, figuraient des grèves que le vent remuait. (Pp. 219–20.)
>
> (Sometimes, when a ray of sunlight shone through a parting in the clouds, the rooftops of Yonville could be glimpsed in the distance, with its river-side gardens and courtyards, its walls and the steeple of the church. Emma narrowed her eye-lids to make out her own house, and never had that sorry village where she lived seemed so tiny to her. From the height they were at, the whole valley appeared to be an immense, pale lake, evaporating into the air. Here and there, clumps of trees jutted out like black rocks, and the lofty lines of the poplars, rising above the mist, were whirling like the sand of a wind-swept beach.)

Emma is permitted to share in her creator's aerial perspective on Yonville. At other moments, such calmness resides only in *his* feeling for her. Her passivity brings out the savage comedy which is at the core of his tragic feeling for her plight.

One such moment is the great scene when she attempts suicide after hearing that Rodolphe has gone away. It combines more vividly than anywhere the twin movement of ascent and descent in which Flaubert symbolised his spiritual experience and his idea of art: the pyramid passage in *Souvenirs*, the description of the telegraph operator in *Par les Champs et les Grèves*, the account of Shakespeare, the letters about artistic creation, the apotheosis of St Julien. It is remarkable to see how Flaubert finds images of such a frightening *netteté* to include the physical suffering in her spiritual crisis:

Les ardoises laissaient tomber d'aplomb une chaleur, qui lui serrait les tempes et l'étouffait; elles se traîna jusqu'à la mansarde close, dont elle tira le verrou, et la lumière éblouissante jaillit d'un bond.

En face, par dessus les toits, la pleine campagne s'étalait à perte de vue. En bas, la place du village était vide; les cailloux du trottoir scintillaient, les girouettes des maisons se tenaient immobiles au coin de la rue, il partit d'un étage inférieur une sorte de ronflement à modulations stridentes. C'était Binet qui tournait.

Elle s'était appuyée contre l'embrasure de la mansarde et elle relisait la lettre avec des ricanements de colère. Mais plus elle y fixait d'attention, plus ses idées se confondaient. Elle le revoyait, elle l'entendait, elle l'entourait de ses deux bras; et des battements de cœur, qui la frappaient sous la poitrine comme à grands coups de bélier, s'accéléraient l'un après l'autre, à intermittences inégales. Elle jetait les yeux tout autour d'elle avec l'envie que la terre croulât. Pourquoi n'en pas finir? Qui la retenait donc? Elle était libre. Et elle s'avança, elle regarda les pavés en se disant:

'Allons! allons!'

Le rayon lumineux qui montait d'en bas directement tirait vers l'abîme le poids de son corps. Il lui semblait que le sol de de la place oscillant s'élevait le long des murs, et que le plancher s'inclinait par le bout, à la manière d'un vaisseau qui tangue. Elle se tenait tout au bord, presque suspendue, entourée d'un grand espace. Le bleu du ciel l'envahissait, l'air circulait dans sa tête creuse, elle n'avait qu'à céder, qu'à se laisser prendre; et le ronflement du tour ne discontinuait pas, comme une voix furieuse qui l'appelait.

– Ma femme! ma femme! cria Charles.

Elle s'arrêta.

– Où es-tu donc? Arrive!

L'idée qu'elle venait d'échapper à la mort faillit la faire s'évanouir de terreur; elle ferma les yeux; puis elle tressaillit au contact d'une main sur sa manche: c'était Félicité.

– Monsieur vous attend, Madame; la soupe est servie.

Et il fallut descendre! il fallut se mettre à table. (Pp. 284–5.)

(A stuffy heat descending from below the roof slates pressed on her temples and stifled her. She dragged herself to the attic window, drew back the bolt of the shuttter, and a dazzling light streamed in.

Opposite, above the rooftops, the open countryside stretched as far as the eye could see. Below was the empty village square; stones were glittering on the pavement and the weather-vanes on the housetops were motionless. A sort of whirring noise, uneven and piercing, came from a lower floor at the corner of the street. It was Binet at his lathe.

She lent against the window-frame, re-reading the letter, with angry, derisive laughter. But the more she concentrated upon it, the more muddled became her thoughts. She seemed to see and hear him, to be clasping him in her arms, and the thumping of her heart-beat came and went, getting faster and faster, as if she were being butted in the chest by a great ram. She cast her eyes all around her, wishing the earth would crumble in. Why not make an end of it? Who was holding her back? – she was free. She went forward and looked down at the cobbles, saying to herself:

'Go on! go on!'

A beam of light coming from directly beneath her drew the weight of her body towards the abyss. In the square the ground seemed to be tilting up against the walls, and the floor seemed to slope from side to side, tossing like a boat. She stood right at the edge, suspended almost, and surrounded by a great space. The blue of the sky was invading her, the air flowing round inside her hollow head, and she had only to give in and let herself be taken. The lathe droned on and on, like an angry voice summoning her.

'Emma dear!' called Charles.

She froze.

'Wherever are you? Come on!'

The thought that she had just escaped death almost made her faint from terror. She shut her eyes: then, at the touch of a hand on her sleeve, she shuddered: it was Félicité.

'Master's waiting for you, Madame; the soup's served.'

And down she had to go, and seat herself at the dinner-table!)

t is the irony of 'la soupe est servie' that makes Emma's imprisonment seem utterly inexorable. Yet the tragic comedy, so linked, as he presence of Binet implies, to the calm of 'impassibilité', does ot exclude a certain grandeur from Emma's resolution to commit uicide when she is at the end of her tether.[23] For once, she can see er own weak mortality for what it is. The moment she is really apped she begins to perceive a possible, if inverted, freedom of ction: 'Qui la retenait donc? Elle était libre.' Death offers a freeom that life denies – or, rather, the freedom has to entail death as s consequence. Hence, its oddly passive kind of action: 'elle n'avait u'à céder, qu'à se laisser prendre . . .'. Extinction offers a release om imprisonment, consummation rather than obliteration. At the und of Charles's voice from below and the touch of Félicité's hand she returns to the self as she is brought back to the physical. As she tries to eat her dinner she is again in the grip of the romantic obsession with self as seen by self, her freedom evaporated. But this scene has nonetheless been the first moment in which the thought of death takes on an inner significance for Emma and appears as more than just a blow from the dark. She glimpses that perfection of nothingness which is so perpetually the end of desire in Flaubert's work: she approaches her creator's own wish to be a brahmin.[24] To adapt the words of the Gymnosophiste in the final *Tentation*:

> J'abandonne la sale auberge de mon corps, maçonnée de chair, rougie de sang, couverte d'une peau hideuse, pleine d'immondices; – et, pour ma récompense, je vais enfin dormir, au plus profond de l'absolu, dans l'Anéantissement. (P. 87.)
>
> (I quit the filthy hostelry of my body, bodged with flesh, reddened with blood, covered in hideous skin and full of dirt; and my reward will be to sleep at last, in the deepest depth of the absolute, in nothingness.)

Emma had perhaps approached a similar state to this through sex, when she went riding with Rodolphe. Nothingness seems the price that has to be paid for crossing the gap between self and the world.

Many of the feelings given to Emma were Flaubert's own. His strange affair with Louise Colet – which paralleled the inception and composition of the first part of *Madame Bovary* – suggests as much. The way he spaced out his passionate encounters with Louise in the hotel at Mantes-la-Jolie, deferring them to the last moment because of pressure of work, suggests that he enjoyed love less as direct experience of the other than as material for his imagination.[25] His most memorable experience of love was the night he spent with Koutchouk Hanem, an *almée* in Upper Egypt: her sexual talent was for remaining immobile in pleasure. On one occasion the Goncourts report the kind of discussion in the *cénacle* which James must have heard:

> Then the talk moved to the state of soul after amatory satisfaction. Some spoke of sadness and others of relief. Flaubert said he would dance in front of a mirror. 'For me, curiously,' said Tourguéneff, 'afterwards, and only afterwards, I enter again into relation with the things which surround me . . . things take back the reality that they did not have a moment before . . . I feel my own self . . . and the table which is there becomes a table again.'[26]

It is true that Emma sometimes feels something of what Turgenev describes here but this only makes plain why the Flaubert who danced before a mirror should prefer to show her as swallowed up in a world of things which all threaten her ego. One has to look in *Madame Bovary* for the kind of feelings which he did not confess to the Goncourts.

Just after her abortive suicide Emma again feels a sense of freedom, this time in a religious experience. This movement from the sexual to the religious is, of course, typical of the whole rhythm of the novel and the two kinds of feeling are closely linked. During her nervous illness after the departure of Rodolphe Emma becomes so ill that Bournisien administers the rite of extreme unction to her:

Sa chair allégée ne pensait plus, une autre vie commençait; il lui sembla que son être, montant vers Dieu, allait s'anéantir dans cet amour comme un encens allumé qui se dissipe en vapeur. On aspergea d'eau bénite les draps du lit; le prêtre retira du saint ciboire la blanche hostie; et ce fut en défaillant d'une joie céleste qu'elle avança les lèvres pour accepter le corps du Sauveur qui se présentait. . . . Alors elle laissa retomber sa tête, croyant entendre dans les espaces le chant des harpes séraphiques et apercevoir en un ciel d'azur, sur un trône d'or, au milieu des saints tenant des palmes vertes, Dieu le Père tout éclatant de majesté, et qui d'un signe faisait descendre sur la terre des anges aux ailes de flamme pour l'emporter dans leurs bras.

Cette vision splendide demeura dans sa mémoire comme la chose la plus belle qu'il fût possible de rêver; si bien qu'à présent elle s'efforçait d'en resaisir la sensation, qui continuait cependant, mais d'une manière moins exclusive et avec une douceur aussi profonde. Son âme, courbatue d'orgueil, se reposait enfin dans l'humilité chrétienne; et, savourant le plaisir d'être faible, Emma contemplait en elle-même la destruction de sa volonté, qui devait faire aux envahissements de la grâce une large entrée. Il existait donc à la place du bonheur des félicités plus grandes, un autre amour au-dessus de tous les amours, sans intermittence ni fin, et qui s'accroîtrait éternellement! Elle entrevit, parmi les illusions de son espoir, un état de pureté flottant au-dessus de la terre, se confondant avec le ciel, et où elle aspira d'être. Elle voulut devenir une sainte. Elle acheta des chapelets, elle porta des amulettes; elle souhaitait avoir dans sa chambre, au chevet de sa couche, un reliquaire enchâssé d'émeraudes, pour le baiser tous les soirs. (Pp. 295–6.)

(Her flesh was soothed, thought-racked no longer, and another life was beginning; it seemed to her that her being, rising towards God, was going to drown itself in this love as burning incense is dispersed in fumes. The bed-sheets were sprinkled with holy water, the priest took the white wafer from the pyx, and, swoon-

ing with a celestial bliss, her lips parted to receive the offered
body of her Saviour . . . She let her head drop back, thinking
she could hear the music of seraphs' harps carried through the air,
and see, surrounded by His saints bearing green branches of
palm, where God the Father, refulgent in majesty on a golden
throne in an azure blue sky, by one gesture sent flame-winged
angels down to earth to take her up in their arms.

This glorious vision lodged in her memory as the most beautiful
dream that could ever be dreamt; so much so that, as it went on,
less intensely though with a sweetness just as deep, she strove
to recover the feeling of it. Her pride-deformed soul reposed at
last in Christian humility, and, savouring the pleasure of feeling
frail, Emma wondered inwardly at the destruction of her will,
which was opening wide the way to the ravishment of Grace.
So there did exist higher joys in place of earthly joy, another
love beyond all loves, with no intermittence nor end, which would
increase forever! Through her self-deluding hope, she glimpsed
a state of purity floating up above the earth and merging into
the sky, where she aspired to be. She wished to become a saint.
She bought rosaries, wore amulets and longed for a reliquary
mounted with emeralds to put in her room, at her bed-side, that
she might kiss it every evening.)

Religious joy in the thought of her own annihilation does not take
Emma out of her self. The experience is as transitory as her experience with Rodolphe (the word 'défaillant' is applied to both)
and as doomed. She takes pleasure in the 'destruction de sa volonté'
because she is still watching herself. Throughout the passage,
Flaubert's irony waits in ambush, in abeyance, but shedding a subtly
lurid light on her ecstasy, ready to pounce as her egoism is confirmed ('Elle voulut devenir une sainte') and she relapses into vain
desires for material things like the reliquary. Soon comes the inevitable descent back into the real and she is reading Bournisien's
religious tracts. Her ascent into wonder is forgotten save perhaps
as an ultimately spurious emotion. It is something on which one
is made afraid to put much weight.

This is not to say that Flaubert shows no moments when Emma
feels a more placid feeling of liberation than that promised by
elopement with Rodolphe or being a saint. The most beautiful is
perhaps the description of her looking down over Rouen as she
is on her way to see Léon:

Puis, d'un seul coup d'œil, la ville apparaissait.
    Descendant tout en amphithéâtre et noyée dans le brouillard,
elle s'élargissait au delà des ponts, confusément. La pleine cam-

pagne remontait ensuite d'un mouvement monotone, jusqu'à
toucher au loin la base indécise du ciel pâle. Ainsi vu d'en haut,
le paysage tout entier avait l'air immobile comme une peinture; les
navires à l'ancre se tassaient dans un coin; le fleuve arrondissait
sa courbe au pied des collines vertes, et les îles, de forme oblongue,
semblaient sur l'eau de grands poissons noirs arrêtés. Les
cheminées des usines poussaient d'immenses panaches bruns qui
s'envolaient par le bout. On entendait le ronflement des fonderies
avec le carillon clair des églises qui se dressaient dans la brume.
Les arbres des boulevards, sans feuilles, faisaient des broussailles
violettes au milieu des maisons, et les toits, tout reluisants de la
pluie, miroitaient inégalement, selon la hauteur des quartiers.
Parfois un coup de vent emportait les nuages vers la côte Saint-
Catherine, comme des flots aériens qui se brisaient en silence
contre une falaise.

Quelque chose de vertigineux se dégageait pour elle de ces
existences amassées, et son cœur s'en gonflait abondamment comme
si les cent vingt mille âmes qui palpitaient là lui eussent envoyé
toutes à la fois la vapeur des passions qu'elle leur supposait. Son
amour s'aggrandissait devant l'espace, et s'emplissait de tumulte
aux bourdonnements vagues qui montaient. Elle le renversait au
dehors, sur les places, sur les promenades, sur les rues, et la vieille
cité normande s'étalait à ses yeux comme une capitale
démesurée, comme une Babylone où elle entrait. (Pp. 363-4.)

(Then, in a flash, the town appeared.

Sloping down like an amphitheatre and submerged in mist, it
spread out confusedly beyond the bridges. The open countryside
rose up behind it in a monotonous sweep to touch the hazy rim of
pale sky in the distance. Seen from on high, the whole landscape
looked as still as a painting: in one corner, a cluster of ships
at anchor, the river rounding its curve at the foot of the green
hills, its oblong-shaped islands looking like great black fish
arrested on the water. The factory chimneys were sending forth
great plumes of brown smoke that drifted away into the sky. The
roar of foundries could be heard amid the clear pealing of bells
from churches that were rising up in the mist. On the boulevards,
violet clumps of leafless trees stood out in the midst of the houses,
and the shining, wet rooftops shimmered from high and low in
the town with uneven light. Occasionally, a gust of wind would
carry the clouds towards St. Catherine's Hill, like airy billows
breaking silently against a cliff.

The massed existences below evoked in her a feeling of dizziness,
and her heart swelled and swelled with it, as though all the one
hundred and twenty thousand souls throbbing down there had
each sent up to her at the self-same moment the fumes from the

passions that she attributed to them. Her love grew and grew at the prospect of space before her, filling with tumult at the vague hum that was rising up to her. She poured it forth, out onto the squares and the walks and the streets, and the old Norman city extended before her eyes like a boundless capital, a Babylon into which she was making her entrance.)

The play of Emma's ego is perfectly caught through the slowly unfolding view of the landscape as it takes her out of herself. Yet she only manages to feel in this way when things assume her own immobility, 'comme une peinture', tractable to imagination. This calm is succeeded in the second paragraph by the grandiose rhetorical description of her feelings of vertigo. Her sense of dominating Rouen and being succoured by the life in it measures the losing battle her will is fighting to hold onto her experience of calm. The lurid reference to Babylon marks an inevitable return to posing. The grandiloquent irony preserves for Flaubert the spiritual calm from which Emma has to descend. His freedom confirms her enslavement. When, later, she returns to Yonville to the waiting Charles, the narrative is still calm, like the landscape through which Emma travels so frantically.[27]

One may decide, in spite of Lawrence but with his help, that Emma is always teetering on the verge of finding her being and then falling back; that she does discover a small space of solitary unassertive freedom beyond the apparent necessity in which she is trapped. What matters is that Emma's freedom should be seen to exist, however briefly and flickeringly. The novel then escapes from the toils of its own flirtation with determinism. It is necessary to ask how far on the road to selfhood Flaubert is finally willing for Emma to travel. If her self is a flag, in Lawrence's image, will she be allowed to fly it?

5 Flaubert's Art: Beauty versus Tragedy?

If these had made one poem's period,
And all combined in beauty's worthiness,
Yet should there hover in their restless heads
One thought, one grace, one wonder, at the least,
Which into words no virtue can digest.[1]   (Marlowe)

I

An English critic who asks whether Flaubert allows Emma to fly the flag of herself needs to be on guard. It is so easy to look at her in terms of Anglo-Saxon notions of selfhood which are foreign to the tradition of French fiction. As Emma relapses into self from the high point of being she reaches with Rodolphe or in looking down on Rouen on her way to see Léon, a comparison with an English meditation on selfhood and egoism has often suggested itself to me: Leavis's fine essay on 'Tragedy and the "Medium" ' in *The Common Pursuit*. The crux of this subtle argument is the idea that, in tragedy, our self goes beyond its own ego to an awareness of its common place in a larger world. As the veil of ego is torn, awe and wonder pour through the rent to give a new and fuller sense of the world. This 'tragic experience' is 'incompatible' with any 'indulgence in the dramatisation of one's nobly-suffering self':[2]

> At any rate, it is an essential part of the definition of the tragic that it breaks down, or undermines and supersedes, such attitudes. It establishes below them a kind of profound impersonality in which experience matters, not because it is mine – because it is to me it belongs, or happens, or because it subserves or issues in purpose or will, but because it is what it is, the 'mine' mattering only in so far as the individual sentience is the indispensable focus of experience. (Ibid., p. 130.)

This 'profound impersonality' is related to the 'sense of enhanced vitality' (ibid., p. 127) that Leavis finds in tragedy:

> The sense of heightened life that goes with the tragic experience is conditioned by a transcending of the ego – an escape from all attitudes of self-assertion. 'Escape', perhaps, is not altogether a

good word, since it might suggest something negative and irresponsible (just as 'Dionysiac' carries unacceptable suggestions of the Dark Gods). Actually the experience is constructive or creative and involves a recognising positive value as in some way defined and vindicated by death. It is as if we were challenged at the profoundest level with the question, 'In what does the significance of life reside?', and found ourselves contemplating, for answer, a view of life, and of the things giving it value, that makes the valued appear unquestionably more important than the valuer, so that significance lies, clearly and inescapably, in the willing adhesion of the individual self to something other than itself. (Ibid., pp. 131–2.)

This can give us a way of looking at the end of *Madame Bovary*, as long as we recognise that Leavis is, here, an heir of the English version of the Romanticism against which Flaubert was in such ambiguous reaction. For example, his way of refining the word 'individual' is crucial. It might make us want to argue that, by keeping Emma on a leash of irony, Flaubert made it impossible for her ever to transcend her ego and, in consequence, never finally freed the general question, 'In what does the significance of life reside?', from the more relative one about the nature of Emma's 'individual self'. This, in turn, suggests that our resultant uncertainty would prevent us granting a 'willing adhesion' to the resolution of her tragic fate: our 'recognition' of it has to be ensured with the help of determinism (or irony or 'form').

Yet this would be going too far with Leavis. Part of what feels tragic in *Madame Bovary* is precisely the way Emma so unremittingly slips back from an impossible transcendence of her ego. Since there is clearly some relation between the tragic protagonist's experience and the tragic experience that it makes possible for us, one might also say that it is when Emma is most 'willing' to adhere to something greater than self (as when she takes the last rites) that she is furthest from seeing her life tragically and most vulnerable to irony. If this is obviously unfair to Leavis it does, I think, suggest the way in which the emotion of 'enhanced vitality' he describes is rather a religious than a tragic emotion. For the 'recognition' he speaks of in tragedy surely also comes to us *in spite of* our natural wish *not* to recognise how tragic life can be. In *King Lear*, part of us is with Cornwall when, at the end of Act II, he says to Regan, 'Come out o' the storm': there is a kind of folly in seeing life tragically. In his sonnet on reading *Lear*, Keats spoke of having to brace himself to 'burn through' the play. To know that Dr Johnson could not bear to re-read the end of *Lear* until he had to edit it perhaps tells us as much about tragic emotion as Leavis does. There can only be a tragic kind of 'willing adhesion' to life where it has been won out of *unwilling* resistance to it. It is in posing for us an acute opposition between how we want to see life and how we are obliged to see it that tragedy, pulling us in both ways at once, wrings from us its 'enhanced vitality', its painful, quizzical joy. I think it does so by showing us how the 'significance' of which Leavis speaks finally eludes us and is consumed in our (selfless) awe at something deeply familiar to us, yet unknown and all too unknowable.[3] To put it in another, less general, way: part of the tragic emotion is what Flaubert gives us in the comedy of Bouvard and Pécuchet's fruitless quest for knowledge and meaning. Therefore, though I shall try to take some of what Leavis says about tragedy to *Madame Bovary*, the way in which the end of that novel can, as it were, strike us dumb with a kind of tragic incomprehension, also helps to show how Leavis's emphasis on the 'creative', the 'constructive' and the 'positive' suggests a more welcome, fulfilling sense of life than the tragic, something that might be called more Wordsworthian than Shakespearian.

Reading Flaubert makes one question any account of tragedy in the half-disguised terms of a rational morality like George Eliot's analysis of 'egoism' in *Middlemarch*. How can the tragic experience of life be registered through a valuation from the discriminating (and therefore self-possessed?) spectator of the tragedy? It seems as if the final tragic emotion made possible by this 'sense of enhanced vitality' lies not so much in our being swept up in 'willing adhesion' to the universe, as in the consolation that the tragic hero's being so swept up offers *us* a significant moral resting place. How can any 'valuer' say where the 'significance of life' resides if he is overwhelmed by the sense that the 'valued' is so much greater than he is? Such valuing, by-passing pity and fear and, perhaps, death, is not felt as painful or cathartic, in any sense of that slippery word. To think either of Emma as she looks back at Rodolphe's 'impassible château' at the end of *Madame Bovary*, or of the storm scene in *Lear* which Flaubert so admired, is to feel that Leavis is reducing tragic awe to a more simply ethical kind of wonder which, though profound in itself, is profound as a way out of tragedy. What is 'valued', after all, is presumably not just the 'profound impersonality' of the 'individual sentience' but the world of which Edgar says, 'But that thy strange mutations make us hate thee, / Life would not yield to age'. Affliction becomes an avenue for that metaphysical reunion of the self and the world which Robbe-Grillet attacked.

Leavis's notion of creative selfhood helps to explain his antipathy to a writer like Flaubert, who sees the self not simply as something to be transcended but also as a terrifying abyss. This different

notion of self can be illustrated by referring to Leavis's discussion
of comedy in James, in which, I think, can be seen the same stress
on 'significance' as we find in his discussion of tragedy. James's
peculiar kind of imaginativeness, the gift for converting realism
into 'romance' that we first see clearly in *The American,* perhaps
finds its finest expression in delicately fabling, high-spirited comedy.
The most brilliant example of this is in the way the problem of
whether or not a young girl is 'out' is explored in *The Awkward
Age.* The light-hearted experiment of placing Felix Young in the
Wentworth family in *The Europeans* is an example of this kind
of comic fancy which Leavis greatly admires. Leavis finds that the
comic interractions of Europeans and Americans in that novel 'rivals
the admired and comparable things of Shakespeare and Molière.'[4]
I would argue that James's control of his 'fable' (to use Leavis's apt
but un-Shakespearian word) makes one employ one's intelligence in
a more excited and cerebral way than do the less self-conscious wit
and poetry of a *Twelfth Night* and more urbanely than the exhilarating and frightening comic insights of a play like *Tartufe.*
Leavis may be correct in saying that, 'When we elicit judgements
and valuations from the fable – which is perfectly dramatic and
perfectly a work of art – we don't think of them as coming from
the author.' (Ibid., p. 70.) Yet this 'self-sufficiency' of the drama
depends on the novel's sharpening in us a habit of 'discrimination'
and 'valuation' which is less imaginatively comic than Leavis claims:

> The Baroness and her brother, we shall have noted, are them-
> selves opposed in value to one another; as representative Europ-
> eans, they are complementary, and establish, in their difference,
> another essential discrimination for James. In fact, all the figures
> in the book play their parts in this business of discriminating
> attitudes and values, which is performed with remarkable pre-
> cision and economy; the total effect being an affirmation, made
> with the force of inspired art.[5]

This 'discrimination' seems to me a lesser thing than the resonant
openness of a less rational 'fable' like *Great Expectations* or, to take
a novel Leavis dislikes, *Bouvard et Pécuchet.* Leavis describes a
genuine quality in the James novel but it is essentially a critical
rather than an imaginative quality. The comedy is enlivening
because it makes us confident in the ability of our perceptions to
grasp a complex situation (if, at least, we see the book as Leavis
does). The comedy of Molière, which Flaubert thought plumbed
the human soul deeper than did the great tragedies, elicits not
'discrimination' of this kind, but an altogether more disturbing
sense of mystery. In even a relatively simple play like *Le Bourgeois*

Gentilhomme, we soon find ourselves forced to question the very
judgements the comedy tempts us to make. No sooner do we mock
the absurd snobbery of Monsieur Jourdain than we find that we
have fallen into the trap of seeing him as his aristocratic parasites
do; no sooner are we rebuked into sympathy with him than Molière
confronts us with what is inhuman as well as absurd in his
behaviour. At moments of the greatest hilarity we can be held in the
grip of a nearly intolerable tension because of the way the wit
makes our imagination probe our judgements. We are never allowed
the respite and repose of feeling assured. Leavis, speaking of James,
has used Molière's name in vain.

The kind of mystery we find in the hearts of Tartufe or Harpagon
(just as we find it in Goneril or Edmund) has enough in common
with the sense of hidden depths that we get either from Homais or
from Emma herself for one not to seek in *Madame Bovary* for the
kind of 'discrimination' found by Leavis in James. Though James
does have a deep sense of the mystery of personality, his intelligence
is habitually trying to keep it at bay, so that it is often elicited only
as the half-hidden underside of a rationalised psychological surface
which is the product of his need to discriminate and his adherence
to consciousness as a value in itself. Robert Acton, in *The
Europeans*, is a good example of a character whose real depths are
concealed by James's desire to utilise him as a moral touchstone;
Rowland Mallet, in *Roderick Hudson*, is another. (It is significant
that Leavis misses Acton's cold shrinkingness from life because he
does not see that it is precisely his faculty of discrimination which
kills the spontaneity in him.) When James explores the abysses of
personality he seeks to relate them through some value on which
he can rest. In this he is a true follower of the Jane Austen of
Emma: a Gilbert Osmond is as explicable as is Mr Elton. The
mystery of personality is couched as an ambiguity which we have
to fathom from over the shoulders of innocence; once seen through,
Osmond proves containable in a quite simple moral judgement, not
an abyss but a code which has been cracked. If Milly Theale remains
mysterious, she becomes a mystery in which we can participate, a
vantage point from which to look out on those she mystifies. James
always believes in the novelist's ability to 'go behind' the surface
of a character to reveal his or her 'soul'.[6] It is this notion of a seiz-
able soul which often results in a confusion between his impulse to
discriminate and his sense of human mystery. There is a similar
confusion in Leavis's notion of tragic character, in which the ego
is fathomed, defined and dissolved by tragic experience in a process
of self-liberation which focuses on a mystery in life *outside* the self.
Neither James nor Leavis provides an idea of selfhood which can
be taken to Flaubert to argue that his characters are un-tragic

because they never achieve such transcendence. In novels like *La Tentation* and *Bouvard et Pécuchet* mystery has two dimensions; it is as inherent in the deceptively simple characters as in the larger life revealed through them. There is a silence in them which neither they themselves, nor their creator, can ever fully express or define, let alone transcend.

With these reservations, Leavis can supply a context in which to examine Emma Bovary. 'Tragedy and the "Medium"' conveys a clear sense of the way tragic experience can mark the culmination of a life, and not simply its meaningless dissolution, and it is worth asking whether Emma is still fully alive when she is on the brink of death, whether suffering generates in her a resilience of spirit or whether her death simply leaves us feeling drained and reduced by the thought of how little resilience she can finally muster. To ask this is not necessarily to look in her for self-transcendence so much as to ask whether Flaubert is willing to show in her the whole extent of the self we feel to be there.

Writing to Louise Colet, Flaubert gave a graphic account of his own creative experience when describing Emma and Rodolphe's love-making in the forest:

> No matter, for good or ill it's a delicious thing to write, to be no longer *oneself*, but to circulate in the whole creation of which one speaks. Today for example, both man and woman together, lover and mistress at the same moment, I rode on horseback through a forest, on an autumn afternoon, under yellow leaves, and I was the horses, the leaves, the wind, the words they said to each other and the red sun which made their love-drenched eyelids close. Is this pride or piety, a foolish transport of exaggerated self-satisfaction or some vague and noble instinct of religion? (*Corr.*, III, p. 405.)

It is just this sort of experience that Emma is moving towards in the scene itself: 'elle entendit tout au loin, au delà du bois, sur les autres collines, un cri vague et prolongé, une voix qui se traînait, et elle l'écoutait silencieusement, se mêlant comme une musique aux dernières vibrations de ses nerfs émus.' (P. 224.) This is not written out of the tense, self-torturing empathy found in the *fiacre* scene but from a deep self-exploratory fellow-feeling with Emma. Why, then, was Flaubert unable to abandon the security of his pre-planned scenario for an Emma who might share his own emotions more creatively? For in the Emma of the *Troisième Partie* such emotions retain only a negative aspect of self-transcendence, not the positive, though vague, 'instinct de religion' of which the letter speaks. Flaubert was perhaps never more than half-convinced by such experiences. As Du Bos said, 'on all sides he bathes in rêverie, and yet he is not one of those who find in it their true homeland'.[7] The materialist in him always suspected the mystic of self-indulgence, a 'foolish transport of exaggerated self-satisfaction'. In *Madame Bovary*, therefore, Emma, with her 'commonplace soul', serves not only to express his predilection for rêverie but as a caution against it.

This may justify some of the things which James criticised in Emma, but it does not exonerate Flaubert from a subtler kind of duplicity. She is liable to appear as a safety-valve for his own self-doubts, as if the authenticity of the creative experience he described to Louise could only be preserved by isolating if from Emma's capacity for similar experiences in love. It is as if he were only able to be an Artist by casting doubt on the power of the imagination. He therefore rejected the alternative of putting Emma in a situation in which she had any real chance of self-fulfilment. How much he needed a Rodolphe as her lover; how little he could have afforded to have her meet, say, a Mâtho.[8] The final comment to make on his worship of Art may well be that it was essentially a retreat from the Shelleyan view of the artist as an 'unacknowledged legislator' to seeing him as a self-distrusting devotee of a sublime quixotism. Believing more in the beauty of art than in its power, he could not believe in the possibility of an Emma able to change as well as suffer her life. What he makes of Emma and the kind of artistic beauty he aspires to are indivisible. His notion of beauty is as passive as he tries to show Emma as being:

> I remember my heart beating with a sense of violent pleasure as I contemplated a wall of the Acropolis, a completely bare wall . . . I ask myself if a book, independently of what it says, can't produce the same effect? In the precision of the structure, the rarity of the elements, the polish of its surface, the harmony of the whole, isn't there an intrinsic virtue, a kind of divine force, something eternal like a principle? (I speak in the terms of a Platonist.) (*Corr.*, IV, pp. 252–3.)

He writes of a beauty that is finished and immobile, a beauty which would be counteracted by an Emma whose meaning, like that of a character in Lawrence or Stendhal, could remain half-completed, free to reverberate in our minds beyond the pages of the book.

II

One of the most striking differences between Emma's affair with Léon and her affair with Rodolphe is that, with Léon, she is nearly always seen indoors. There are no scenes between them like the nocturnal meetings with Rodolphe in her garden. This enables Flaubert to insinuate that the Rouen hotel room where they make love is an imaginary world which, despite all the elaborate descriptions of the furniture and the wallpaper, is more like the fantasy world to which Emma hopes to elope than the real world of Yonville in which she met Rodolphe:

> Emma pensait qu'il y avait quarante-huit heures à peine, ils étaient ensemble, loin du monde, tout en ivresse, et n'ayant pas assez d'yeux pour se contempler. Elle tâchait de ressaisir les plus imperceptibles détails de cette journée disparue. Mais la présence de la belle mère et du mari la gênait. Elle aurait voulu ne rien entendre, ne rien voir, afin de ne pas déranger le recueillement de son amour qui allait se perdant, quoi qu'elle fît, sous les sensations extérieures. (P. 348.)
>
> (Emma was thinking that barely forty-eight hours ago they were together far from the world, enraptured, needing more than the eyes they had to gaze at each other with. She tried to recapture the most imperceptible details of that vanished day, but the presence of her mother-in-law and her husband hindered her. She would have liked to hear nothing, see nothing, so as not to ruffle the composure of her love which, whatever she did, went on being undermined by external sensations.)

The false opposition of 'loin du monde' and 'sensations extérieures' disguises the fact that Emma's essential world is just as much in the Rouen hotel as in Yonville. In the hotel, we can imagine Emma and Léon responding to each other with real joy and gaiety but, even there, the terse flourishes of Flaubert's prose distract us from what they feel by wryly concentrating on the room itself:

> . . . ils se regardaient face à face, avec des rires de volupté et des appellations de tendresse.
>   Le lit était un grand lit d'acajou en forme de nacelle. Les rideaux de levantine rouge, qui descendaient du plafond, se cintraient trop bas près du chevet évasé; – et rien au monde n'était beau comme sa tête brune et sa peau blanche se détachant sur cette couleur pourpre, quand, par un geste de pudeur, elle fermait ses deux bras nus, en se cachant la figure dans les mains. . .
>   Comme ils aimaient cette bonne chambre pleine de gaieté, malgré sa splendeur un peu fanée! Ils retrouvaient toujours les meubles à leur place, et parfois des épingles à cheveux qu'elle avait oubliées, l'autre jeudi, sous le socle de la pendule. Ils déjeunaient au coin du feu, sur un petit guéridon incrusté de

palissandre. Emma découpait, lui mettait des morceaux dans son assiette, en débitant toutes sortes de chatteries; et elle riait d'un rire sonore et libertin quand la mousse du vin de Champagne débordait du verre léger sur les bagues de ses doigts. Ils étaient si complètement perdus en la possession d'eux-mêmes, qu'ils se croyaient là dans leur maison particulière. . . . (P. 366.)

(. . . they looked into each other's eyes, laughing voluptuously and calling themselves by tender names.

There was a big mahogany bed, curved like a small boat, with curtains of red levantine silk which swept down from the ceiling to flare out near the floor over the protruding bed-head. Nothing in the world was so beautiful as her dark head and white skin, set out against that crimson colour, when she folded her bare arms together in a gesture of modesty, hiding her face in her hands. . . .

How they loved that dear old room, so full of gaiety despite its slightly faded splendour! They always found the furniture arranged in the same way, and sometimes hair-pins she had forgotten the previous Thursday would turn up, under the clock-stand. They lunched by the fire-side, on a little pedestal table inlaid with rosewood. Emma would carve, coaxing him garrulously as she laid the meat on his plate, and her laughter was loud and wanton when the frothing champagne brimmed over her slender glass onto the rings on her fingers. They were so utterly absorbed in the possession of one another, that they imagined themselves to be in the privacy of their own home. . . .)

The descriptions of the room evoke their naiveté with detached pathos and the exactness of the prose (as in Emma's 'rire libertin et sonore') responds less to the experience it describes than incorporates it into its own undeviating momentum. Flaubert's cadences usurp Emma's own freedom of feeling and become virtual substitutes for her emotions. She is almost frozen in their lapidary melancholy. It is a rhythm more appropriate to *ennui* than desire, enclosing her emotion in itself, making it more state of mind than impulse. An aphorism in one of the letters sums up the effect: 'Continuity makes style, as constancy makes for virtue.' (*Corr.*, III, p. 401.) The language proceeds rather than grows.[9]

It is not, then, Emma's joy and gaiety which are explored but the desperate, self-abandoning frenzy she wills herself to as her real feeling for Léon burns itself out. Léon, we are told, is more like her mistress than she is a mistress to him, and she relishes the opportunities his inadequacy gives her as much as she resents it. At most he is a mere vehicle for the passion she tries to expend. Her energy is only interesting to Flaubert as an onanistic writhing on the hook.

Far from seeking again the kind of ecstasy she felt with Rodolphe in the forest her will urges her towards self-obliteration. She is a maenad who seeks to cancel the world out and not to commune with it. In the final fling of her desperation at the masked ball Léon takes her to, Flaubert again moves away from her emotions to the shabby, depressing scene which seals their futility:

> Elle sauta toute la nuit, au son furieux des trombones; on faisait cercle autour d'elle; et elle se trouva le matin sur le péristyle du théâtre parmi cinq ou six masques, débardeuses et matelots, des camarades de Léon, qui parlaient d'aller souper.
>
> Les cafés d'alentour étaient pleins. Ils avisèrent sur le port un restaurant des plus médiocres, dont le maître leur ouvrit, au quatrième étage, une petite chambre.
>
> Les hommes chuchotèrent dans un coin, sans doute se consultant sur la dépense. Il y avait un clerc, deux carabins et un commis: quelle société pour elle! Quant aux femmes, Emma s'aperçut vite, au timbre de leurs voix, qu'elles devaient être, presque toutes, du dernier rang. Elle eut peur alors, recula sa chaise et baissa les yeux.
>
> Les autres se mirent à manger. Elle ne mangea pas; elle avait le front en feu, des picotements aux paupières et un froid de glace à la peau. Elle sentait dans sa tête le plancher du bal rebondissant encore sous la pulsation rythmique des mille pieds qui dansaient. Puis l'odeur du punch avec la fumée des cigares l'étourdit. Elle s'évanouissait; on la porta devant la fenêtre.
>
> Le jour commençait à se lever, et une grande tâche de couleur pourpre s'élargissait dans le ciel pâle du côté de Sainte-Catherine. La rivière livide frissonnait au vent; il n'y avait personne sur les ponts; les réverbères s'éteignaient. (Pp. 402–3.)
>
> (All night she cavorted to the furious din of trombones, the other dancers making a ring round her, and in the morning she found herself on the steps of the theatre, with five or six of Léon's friends, in their fancy-dress of sailors or longshoremen, who were talking of going off for supper.
>
> The cafés near by were full. Down by the port, they spotted a third-rate restaurant, whose proprietor showed them up to a small room on the fourth floor.
>
> The men whispered in a corner, no doubt consulting each other over the expense. There was a clerk, two medical students and a shopman: what company for her to be in! As for the women, Emma quickly perceived from the tone of their voices, that they must nearly all be of the lowest order. At this she felt scared, drew back her chair and lowered her eyes.
>
> The others began to eat. She ate nothing: her forehead was

burning, her eyelids tingled, her skin felt ice-cold. Inside her head she could still feel the ball-room floor as it vibrated beneath the pulsating rhythm of a thousand dancing feet. Then the smell of punch and cigar-smoke made her head swim. She fainted, and was carried over to the window.

Day was just breaking, and a great crimson-coloured stain was spreading over the pale sky in the direction of St Catherine's. The livid river was shuddering in the wind; the bridges were deserted; the street-lamps were going out.)

Flaubert is too reticent for us to say how far this is a 'great kick at misery' and how far the dancing merely turns Emma into a piece of human clockwork. The devastating details – the men whispering over the price in the corner, the accents of the women – quench and incarcerate her vitality. She has no part in the day breaking over the river. If the dawn wind that makes the water shudder is tragic, that is a secret between Flaubert and his reader: there is no human counterweight to it. When Léon takes Emma's hand a few pages later it feels utterly lifeless: 'Emma no longer had the strength to feel anything.' (P. 412.)[10] Perhaps this is what is meant when we speak of the comedy of *Madame Bovary*.

A simplification which is encouraged by moralising about Emma is the view that she is unlucky in her lovers; part of the blame for her failure can be put on Léon's weakness. Yet Emma chooses Léon *because* of his malleability. She never convinces herself that she wants to fulfil her desires. Rather, she seems half-afraid of her passions and uses them more to annul Léon than to find him. She really wants to lose both him and herself. Flaubert was fond of telling his friends that one must try not to live in the self. For Emma too, the self is an embarrassment and a clog. Her dreamland has obvious affinities with Flaubert's own self-purging conception of art and is the expression of a similar self-absorption. For her, nothingness is not an opposite to self but its culmination. Despite his devotion to *Don Quixote*, Flaubert never consistently saw that nobility as well as folly co-exist in Emma's helpless yearnings. There is no Dulcinea in his world. The only conceivable ideal lies in the beauty of an art which defies all conclusions and mocks thought. This beauty fills the void created by his sense of metaphysical emptiness and silence. Just as Emma's desire to live out her life is really a desire to lose her life, to purge her own vitality by riding it to the point of exhaustion, so Flaubert's realism may be seen as a strategy for dissolving the material world into a beauty which will no longer be the prey of our inept and fruitless quest for meanings. It may be finally nearer to Buddhism and Plato than to the notion of mimesis Zola found in it. Emma's spent will and Flaubert's 'affres

du style' share a common purpose, as they share the same irate
energy.

Emma's suicide could be seen as her attempt to transfer the
mystical desire she has pursued in sex onto death itself. When
Bournisien administers the last rites, she kisses the crucifix with the
'longest kiss of love she had ever given'. (P. 446.) Death is her only
way out of her single self, but it is a way. It is a last refuge for
humanness in a world become inhuman, her defiant passionateness
all of humanity that can be salvaged from tragedy, just as indignation was often all that Flaubert himself could salvage from despair.
Her 'great kick at misery', when she wants to spit in the face of the
world, reminds us of Flaubert's:

> – Flaubert said today, rather picturesquely: 'No, indignation is
> the only thing that keeps me going. . . . For me, indignation is the
> skewer which dolls have stuffed up inside them to keep them
> standing upright. When I am no longer indignant I will fall flat
> on my face!' And with a gesture of his hand he described the
> silhouette of a puppet flopped on the floor.[11]

It is a minimally redemptive triumph, either for him or for Emma.
It is, then, in an extreme negative way, that she might be said to
fly the flag of herself. It is certainly then that Flaubert grudges her
for escaping from his clutches and begins inventing things like the
fiacre, to nullify our sense of her defiant liberty. And the main
nullifying agent, even deeper and more inexorable than his sense of
determinism, is his quest for beauty. Determinism, after all, is really
just form imposed from outside.

Beyond life, Emma finds nothing but physical decay, the dark
poison streaming over her white shroud. She escapes her condition
to find rest in a God who no longer exists, just as she tried
to escape Yonville for a love that did not exist. As he contemplates
her death with the exhilarated serenity of Sirius, Flaubert becomes
a surrogate for his non-existent God. Beauty has usurped His throne.
Emma's secret freedom was already charted in her creator's devotion
to Art. It is the kind of tragedy which occurs when man can still
conceive of God although God is absent: self-responsibility has not
yet taken His place as an ultimate value, as it is beginning to do
in English (Protestant) literature. For Flaubert is a kind of inverted
Voltairean: had God existed he would have found it spiritually
necessary to invent disbelief. It is a nineteenth-century tragedy,
the causes of which are further to seek than in the private neuroses
of Flaubert himself. A tragedy which nearly eschews tragic conflict,
by making the odds against man too great, was, perhaps, the truest
way for tragic thought to find expression in mid-nineteenth-century
France.

The doubt which must remain at the end of *Madame Bovary*, and the price paid for the classic beauty in it which James so admired, is that one hesitates as to how much general weight to put on Emma's poor selfhood. At several points, I have found myself arguing that tragic feeling is given with greater purity in Flaubert's vision of the Norman landscape. The poetic vision of nature is never quite reborn in an equally poetic vision of human emotion. This is not simply because Emma is usually passive but because Flaubert never invests her with his own sense of death. It comes back to the persistence of an old prejudice, the prejudice of a rather crabbed, rather innocent bachelor:

Women do not love death . . . the being who brings forth life is incensed that life is not eternal . . . don't tell them that you harbour an immense aspiration to return to the unknown and the infinite, like a water-drop that evaporates to fall back again into the ocean; don't tell them, pale-browed thinkers, to accompany you on your voyage or to scale the mountain with you, for their eyes are not keen enough to contemplate the precipices of thought, nor their lungs sufficiently deep to inhale the air of the high places.[12]

Emma is therefore excluded from that spiritual mountain air of which Flaubert talks so often. This is what Lawrence's reservations about *Madame Bovary* eventually came down to too:

. . . a great soul like Flaubert's has a pure satisfaction and joy in its own consciousness, even if the consciousness be only of ultimate tragedy or misery. But the very fact of being so marvellously and vividly *aware*, awake, as Flaubert's soul was, is in itself a refutation of the all-is-misery doctrine. Since the human soul has supreme joy in true, vivid consciousness. And Flaubert's soul has this joy. But Emma Bovary's soul does not, poor thing, because she was deliberately chosen because her soul was ordinary.[13]

It is part of her lack of this joy that, even after taking the last rites, Emma should ask for a mirror:

. . . elle regarda tout autour d'elle, lentement, comme quelqu'un qui se réveille d'un songe; puis, d'une voix distincte, elle demanda son miroir, et elle resta penchée dessus quelque temps, jusqu'au moment où de grosses larmes lui découlèrent des yeux. (Pp. 447–8.)
(. . . she looked all round her, slowly, like someone waking from a dream. Then, in a clear voice, she asked for her mirror, and

remained bent over it for some time, till big tears began to flow from her eyes.)

She relapses into her clinging reliance on self. Yet, for all that we can say about her limitations, she has known more of joy than Lawrence supposed and has, at least, enough spirit to know that she has lived more than the spiritual mediocrities amongst whom she dies. We do not feel just misery when she dies but, like Charles, 'the vague satisfaction of having done with it all'. (P. 467.) It is then that the book gives its most profound suggestions of human community, in the comic vigil of Homais and Bournisien and the gentle meditating on mortality of the funeral scene. For all its pessimism, the end of *Madame Bovary* is not a spiritual dead-end for Flaubert but a glimpse beyond the misery of day to day life. One thinks forward to a moving passage at the end of *Bouvard et Pécuchet*:

> L'idée de la mort les avait saisis. Ils en causèrent, en revenant.
>
> Après tout elle n'existe pas. On s'en va dans la rosée, dans la brise, dans les étoiles. On devient quelque chose de la sève des arbres, de l'éclat des pierres fines, du plumage des oiseaux. On redonne à la Nature ce qu'elle vous a prêté et le Néant qui est devant nous n'a rien de plus affreux que le Néant qui se trouve derrière.
>
> Ils táchaient de l'imaginer sous la forme d'une nuit intense, d'un trou sans fond, d'un évanouissement continu, n'importe quoi valait mieux que cette existence monotone, absurde, et sans espoir.[14]
>
> (They were gripped by the thought of death. Coming back, they chatted about it.
>
> After all, it does not exist. One departs into the dew and the breeze and the stars, becomes part of the sap of the trees, the lustre of precious stones and the plumage of birds, giving back to Nature what she has lent us, and the nothingness that lies before us is no more dreadful than the nothingness that lies behind.
>
> They tried to imagine it as an intensely black night, a bottomless hole or a continual fainting, anything was preferable to this existence: monotonous, absurd and without hope.)

When the melancholy farcicalness of Bouvard and Pécuchet themselves has been rightly understood, mocked only with the poignancy with which people mock themselves, there is a truthfulness and a dignity here which, claiming nothing for itself, is beyond mere depression or romantic histrionics.

III

The consequence of Flaubert's reluctance to explore Emma's spirituality as far as he might have done is the novel's classic form. Just as her tragedy consists in the frustration of her desire for beauty in life (a desire which was to typify the *fin de siècle* – Des Esseintes is an Emma who has his way), so Flaubert's disbelief in the imagination is expressed by his need for abstract form. Such form is imposed from outside the work of art, just as fate imposes itself on the rhythm of Emma's experience from outside it. Thus, it fits the book like a glove, since death is the final, perfect form. This brings me to my central reservation about *Madame Bovary*. It is also my main reservation about James's view of its 'crowned classicism'. The book's essential thought is more perfectly captured in shorter passages, like prose poems, than in the movement of the whole. This is the main difference between *Madame Bovary* and *L'Education Sentimentale*. In the later novel plot is sacrificed to rhythm, so that it becomes a seamless, unobstructed poetic flux in its movement, an agonisingly time-dominated tone-poem. In *Madame Bovary*, Flaubert had not yet spent the legacy of the Balzacian plot. In this connection, the representative episode of *Madame Bovary* is the Comices Agricoles. It has been overpraised by admirers of cinematic form. In fact, as Flaubert's difficulties in writing it suggest, it is a too obviously brilliant *tour de force* of formal patterning; form and meaning are imposed from outside by the over-precise definitions of the irony; the scene lacks mystery and shadow. A similarly central passage in the *Education*, such as the end of part two, where Frédéric's affair with Rosanette and his love for Mme Arnoux both come to a head as the 1848 revolution breaks out, has a more random and spontaneous surprisingness which, in its unstructured appearance, suggests the momentum of time rather than just the control of the author. Its rhythm insists on itself beneath its orchestration. Form, in this sense, the kind of movement and shape given to the action, is inseparable from tragic effect. For Emma, the artist's pursuit of formal beauty is itself a kind of fate.

Flaubert's prose often seems to be pouring Emma's emotions into a hard mould and watching them as they set. Its calm pressure derives from his twin sense of life as repetition and flux. Murry rightly thought that, 'the power of awakening in us a sense of the process of time was Flaubert's most individual achievement as a writer.'[15] One way in which *Madame Bovary* is made rounded and coherent is by showing the essence of the dead Emma's experience recapitulated in that of the mourning Charles. To have ended with Emma's own death and burial would have seemed too particular. So Charles repeats Emma after her death. Just as she discovered the

'pourriture instantanée des choses où elle s'appuyait', so his un-
realisable desire for her bears the same fruit:

> Une chose étrange, c'est que Bovary, tout en pensant à Emma
> continuellement, l'oubliait; et il se désespérait à sentir cette image
> lui échapper de la mémoire au milieu des efforts qu'il faisait
> pour la retenir. Chaque nuit pourtant, il la rêvait; c'était toujours
> le même rêve: il s'approchait d'elle; mais quand il venait à
> l'étreindre, elle tombait en pourriture dans ses bras. (P. 476.)

(What was odd was that, while constantly thinking of Emma,
Bovary was forgetting her, and it drove him to despair to feel
her image evading his memory in the midst of his struggle to
retain it. Yet each night he would dream about her. The dream
was always the same: he came up close to her, but, just as he
was hugging her, she began to putrefy in his arms.)

It is not easy to sort out what is creative from what is automatic
in such repetitions. They are acutely painful, possibly to the point
of oppressiveness.

What I am saying is that, in the last part of *Madame Bovary*, the
novel fails to burst through its own pre-established form just as
Emma fails to burst through her pre-established self. The last part
is therefore slightly redundant in spite of its power. Lawrence is
again helpful here, in his essay on Thomas Mann this time:

> And yet it seems to me, this craving for form is the outcome,
> not of artistic conscience, but of a certain attitude to life. For
> form is not a personal thing like style. It is impersonal like logic.
> And just as the school of Alexander Pope was logical in its ex-
> pressions, so it seems the school of Flaubert is, as it were, logical
> in its aesthetic form. 'Nothing outside the definite line of the
> book', is a maxim. But can the human mind fix absolutely the
> definite line of a book, any more than it can fix absolutely any
> definite line of action for a living being?'[16]

In fact, as the argument develops, Lawrence does find a personal
quality in 'form': it expresses a particular philosophy of life. Lawrence distrusts this philosophy but distrust does not blunt his insight
into the school of Flaubert:

> And even while he (Thomas Mann) has a rhythm in style, yet his
> work has none of the rhythm of a living thing, the rise of a
> poppy, then the after uplift of the bud, the shedding of the calyx
> and the spreading wide of the petals, the falling of the flower
> and the pride of the seed-head. There is an unexpectedness in

this such as does not come from their carefully plotted and arranged developments. Even *Madame Bovary* seems to me dead in respect of the living rhythm of the whole work. While it is there in *Macbeth* like life itself. (Ibid., p. 313.)

Lawrence does not seem to have read the *Education* (which I believe, does have this 'rhythm') and it is not so much true that *Madame Bovary* lacks a 'living rhythm' as that Emma is too seldom allowed to dance to it herself. The reason for quoting him here is that his criticisms were first made by Flaubert himself, in the *Correspondence*.

With his taste for self-inflicted *ennui*, for mysteries which stupefy the mind, Flaubert found the subject of *Madame Bovary* so anti-pathetic that he had to force himself to plan it. He saw the novel, very differently from James, as never perfectly melding style and subject:

> *Bovary* . . . will have been an unheard of *tour de force* but I alone will ever really understand this: the subject, the character, the effect, etc., all lie outside me. It should make me make a great step forward after it. In writing this book I am like a man playing the piano with balls of lead on each finger-tip. But when I know my own fingering well, and if a tune to my taste falls under my hand and I can play with my sleeves rolled up, it will perhaps be good. (*Corr.*, III, pp. 3–4.)

The novel seemed lacking in 'the rhythm of a living thing':

> This book is all so calculated, its style so cunning, it does not come from my blood, I don't carry it in my guts, I feel that on my part it is something willed and factitious. It will perhaps be a *tour de force* which some people will admire (and then only a few); others will find some truth of detail and observation in it. But for some air, some fresh air! (*Corr.*, III, pp. 201–2.)

'Mais de l'air! de l'air!' Flaubert only contradicted his feeling that the book was not of his blood by transferring this frustrated aspiration to Emma herself. What he found especially hard as he wrote was to knit one episode into the next episode in a natural way:

> Each paragraph is good in itself, and there are, I am sure, pages which are perfect. But precisely as a result of that, *it doesn't move forward*. It's a series of well-turned, arrested paragraphs which don't slot into each other. It will be necessary to unscrew them and loosen the joints, as one does with the masts of a ship when

one wants the sails to take up more wind. (*Corr.*, III, p. 92.)

One owes it to Flaubert to take such honest remarks seriously and not dismiss them as mere self-doubt.

If Flaubert presses too hard on his pen at the end of *Madame Bovary* such insistence also accounts for one of the greatest pleasures the book offers: the delight of a single paragraph so complete in itself that it seems more like a prose-poem than an extract from a developing fiction. Here, from the first chapter, is a random example of his flair for the clinching peroration, so much more a gift for endings than for beginnings:

> On lui avait bien dit qu'elle serait malheureuse; et elle finissait en lui demandant quelque sirop pour sa santé et un peu plus d'amour. (P. 14.)
>
> (They had certainly told her that she would be unhappy; and she ended up by asking him for some syrup or other for her health, and a little more love.)

The beautifully precise wit has a finality which directs us back to itself.[17] This means that it is not always at home in a long novel, that it offers more a chance to steep ourselves in the tone of the author's mind than any unravelling of the action. Flaubert himself saw his gift as analytic rather than dramatic. Hence his problems in making the jump in his narration from psychology to action. The chapter leading to Emma and Rodolphe's first kiss took him seven weeks. The best prose-poems in *Madame Bovary* describe either landscapes or else people seen from outside, often seen in landscapes too. Descriptions of what goes on in Emma's mind, the sort of thing more common in the novels of the period, show a strain and, at the end, even a luridity which makes it much harder for the reader to banish the sense of the author's presence. The last question *Madame Bovary* invites follows from this: did Flaubert's poetry ever find a narrative which could voice it consistently enough for the whole work to become a poem?

IV

One of the finest passages in *Madame Bovary* describes an old woman, Catherine Leroux, who is given a long-service medal at the Comices Agricoles. Its poetry comes from a fusing of realism, irony and unsentimental compassion. It portrays not just one woman but a whole class in its clear vision of her weather-beaten face and thin, muscular build. Perhaps the novel does not contain another instance of human dignity so moving. As always, comedy is near the surface and part of the woman's dignity exists in the very absurdity of her devotion to her callous masters. In another way, she is unfeeling as they are:

Alors on vit s'avancer sur l'estrade une petite vielle femme de maintien craintif, et qui paraissait se ratatiner dans ses pauvres vêtements. Elle avait aux pieds de grosses galoches de bois, et le long des hanches, un grand tablier bleu. Son visage maigre, entouré d'un béguin sans bordure, était plus plissé de rides qu'une pomme de reinette flétrie, et des manches de sa camisole rouge dépassaient deux longues mains, à articulations noueuses. La poussière des granges, la potasse des lessives et le suint des laines les avaient si bien encroûtées, éraillées, durcies, qu'elles semblaient sales quoiqu'elles fussent rincées d'eau claire; et à force d'avoir servi, elles restaient entr'ouvertes, comme pour présenter d'elles- mêmes l'humble témoignage de tant de souffran-ces subies. Quelque chose d'une rigidité monacale relevait l'expression de sa figure. Rein de triste ou d'attendri n'amollissait ce regard pâle. Dans la fréquentation des animaux, elle avait pris leur mutisme et leur placidité. C'était la première fois qu'elle se voyait au milieu d'une compagnie si nombreuse; et intérieure-ment effarouchée par les drapeaux, par les tambours, par les messieurs en habit noir et par la croix d'honneur du conseiller, elle demeurait tout immobile, ne sachant s'il fallait s'avancer ou s'enfuir, ni pourquoi la foule la poussait et pourquoi les ex-aminateurs lui souriaient. Ainsi se tenait devant ces bourgeois épanouis, ce demi-siècle de servitude. (Pp. 208–9.)

(Then a little, wizened old woman, who seemed to be dis-appearing into her threadbare clothes, walked timorously up to the platform. She wore great wooden clogs on her feet and a big blue apron round her hips. Her thin face, enclosed in a plain unbordered hood, was more wrinkled than a withered russet apple, and from the sleeves of her red camisole extended two long, knottily jointed hands, so caked and chafed and hardened by barn-dust, washing-soda and wool-grease that they seemed dirty though they had been well rinsed in fresh water. By dint of serving others, they remained opened out, as if to offer their own humble testimony to all the miseries they had borne. The expression of her face was heightened by a look of monastic stiffness, and nothing sad or tender softened its pallor. Living amongst animals, she had grown mute and placid as they were. This was the first time she had ever found herself in the midst of such a throng of people, and she stood without moving, scared out of her wits by the flags and the drums, by the gentlemen in their black frock-coats and the medals on the councillor's chest, not knowing whether to go forward or to flee, nor why the crowd was pushing her on or why the judges were smiling at her. Thus stood this half-century of servitude, before those flushed and beaming bourgeois.)

In its natural movement from tenderness to the savage, and perfect, conclusion the prose keeps us throughout on the brink of pathos and the brink of comedy at the same time. There is no search for 'objects of pity' and the tone is too firmly discreet to suggest comparisons with the nearly-overflowing tone used for the tragedy of humble life in *Adam Bede*. There is a profundity here which would make one wish that Emma were treated in the same way, were it not for the fact that Catherine Leroux represents just that endurance of life which it is Emma's strength to refuse. Why should such a life be endured? What the passage may suggest is that Flaubert's own sense of tragedy comes more spontaneously through this 'little person' than it often does through Emma herself. We think, of course, of *Un Cœur Simple*, a tale which has a good claim to be considered a sustained poem from beginning to end.

The greatness of *Un Cœur Simple* is that it has no need of psychological complexity to involve us in it. The expression, for all its impassive control, is essentially lyrical. Félicité has none of the self-pity which sometimes intrudes on our compassion for Emma. As Brombert puts it:

The suffering remains exclusively that of the omniscient and 'impassive' author. Félicité cannot view her own fate: she does not even know that her story is one of pathos, tenderness, devotion and naïve moral beauty.[18]

That, however, makes it sound as if Flaubert has conceived his tale condescendingly as if to draw a moral from her. It is not essential to the effect that she should be good; Flaubert is blunt about her when she is stupid or sentimental. There is some absurd comedy of a Beckettian kind when he evokes the metaphysical void in her world which makes her associate her parrot Loulou with the Holy Ghost. Pathos can be distilled from farce as well as tragedy and, in Flaubert, farce is often tragedy turned inside out. What the tale gives most of all is the shape of a whole life, its small events and upheavals made coherent within an enveloping sense of time passing:

Arrivé au sommet d'Ecquemauville, elle aperçut les lumières de Honfleur qui scintillaient dans la nuit comme une quantité d'étoiles; la mer, plus loin, s'étalait confusément. Alors, une faiblesse l'arrêta; et la misère de son enfance, la déception du premier amour, le départ de son neveu, la mort de Virginie, comme les flots d'une marée, revinrent à la fois, et, lui montant à la gorge, l'étouffaient.[19]

(When she reached the high point of Ecquemauville, she caught sight of the lights of Honfleur glittering in the night like a mass of stars. The sea stretched out indistinctly beyond. Then a feeling of weakness brought her to a halt, and the misery of her childhood, the disappointments of her first love, her nephew's departure, the death of Virginie, all came back to her together like a tidal wave, bringing a lump to her throat and choking her.)

This tidal wave of memory is even more moving than those moments when Emma looks back on her past: it evokes the events themselves, unaltered and unsentimentalised by the person remembering them. The feeling is more elegiac than tragic: *Trois Contes* is a work of middle age. Félicité's life evokes, in a little space, the increasingly large part played by loss and regret in any life approaching old age. It moves inexorably to the vacant house of Mme Aubain, for sale and unsold, the image of a heart vacant like a bare cupboard, just as *Madame Bovary* moves toward the moment when the bailiffs are called in and *L'Education* to the final auction of Mme Arnoux's possessions. Without its sense of time the tale would be of only minor interest, the slight chronicle of the existence of a servant, in a sleepy provincial town. The poetry lies in the absence of pressure from either pity or irony and in a tone of perfect seriousness. Félicité is simply a vehicle for that undramatic, incurable monotony of suffering to which Flaubert was so sensitive and which helped him, not to make life seem monotonous, but to illuminate it in its simplest, least eventful form.

When *Un Cœur Simple* was published most of the reviewers described Flaubert as a poet. Théodore de Banville, for example:

> I said a poet, and this word must be taken in its strictest sense; for the great writer of whom I speak here has known how to conquer an essential and definitive form, where every phrase and every word has its necessary and fatal reason for being there, and where it is as impossible to change anything as in an ode of Horace's or a fable of La Fontaine's.[20]

Flaubert would have been flattered by these comparisons but it seems to me that Banville's idea of a poet is too restricted. It is not just style which gives *Un Cœur Simple* a greater poetic depth and permanence than is normal in fiction. The prose is some of Flau-

bert's least flashy and its density comes from the way the narrative
is conducted, more than from its own intrinsic effects. The whole
tale has to be read to appreciate this – there is not a seam showing
– and I can only quote one passage to suggest some of its flavour,
the scene where Mme Aubain tells Félicité of the death of her
nephew Victor:

> – C'est un malheur . . . qu'on vous annonce, Votre neveu. . . .
> Il était mort. On n'en disait pas davantage.
> Félicité tomba sur une chaise, en s'appuyant la tête à la cloison,
> et ferma ses paupières qui devinrent roses tout à coup. Puis, le
> front baissé, les mains pendantes, l'œil fixe, elle répétait par
> intervalles:
> – Pauvre petit gars! pauvre petit gars!
> Liébard la considérait en exhalant des soupirs. Mme Aubain
> tremblait un peu.
> Elle lui proposa d'aller voir sa sœur, à Trouville.
> Félicité répondit, par un geste, qu'elle n'en avait pas besoin.
> Il y eut un silence. Le bonhomme Liébard jugea convenable
> de se retirer.
> Alors elle dit:
> – Ca ne leur fait rien, à eux!
> Sa tête retomba; et machinalement elle soulevait, de temps à
> autre, les longues aiguilles sur la table à ouvrage.
> Des femmes passèrent dans la cour avec un bard d'où dégout-
> telait du linge.
> En les apercevant par les carreaux, elle se rappela sa lessive;
> l'ayant coulée la veille, il fallait aujourd'hui la rincer; et elle
> sortit de l'apartement.
> Sa planche et son tonneau étaient au bord de la Toucques.
> Elle jeta sur la berge un tas de chemises, retroussa ses manches,
> prit son battoir; et les coups forts qu'elle donnait s'entendaient
> dans les autres jardins à côté. Les prairies étaient vides, le vent
> agitaient la rivière; au fond, de grandes herbes s'y penchaient,
> comme des chevelures de cadavres flottant dans l'eau. Elle retenait
> sa douleur, jusqu'au soir fut très brave; mais dans sa chambre, elle
> s'y abandonna, à plat ventre sur son matelas, le visage dans
> l'oreiller et les deux poings contre les tempes.
> Beaucoup plus tard, par le capitaine de Victor lui-même, elle
> connut les circonstances de sa fin.
> On l'avait trop saigné, à l'hôpital, pour la fièvre jaune. Quatre
> médecins le tenaient à la fois. Il était mort immédiatement, et le
> chef avait dit:
> – Bon! encore un!
> Ses parents l'avaient toujours traité avec barbarie. Elle aima

mieux ne pas les revoir; et ils ne firent aucune avance, par oubli, ou endurcissement des misérables.

Virginie s'affaiblissait.

Des oppressions, de la toux, une fièvre continuelle et des marbrures aux pommettes décelaient quelque affection profonde. M. Poupart avait conseillé un séjour en Provence. Mme Aubain s'y décida, et eût tout de suite repris sa fille à la maison, sans le climat de Pont-l'Evêque. (Pp. 33–5.)

('They've come to break some bad news to you. Your nephew. . . .'

He was dead. No more was said of it.

Félicité dropped into a chair, rested her head against the partition and shut her eyes. Her eyelids at once became red. Then, with her forehead bowed down, her hands hanging loose and staring fixedly, she kept on repeating at intervals:

'Poor little lad! poor little lad!'

Liébard, sighing noisily, was considering her. Mme Aubain was shaking a little.

She proposed that she go to visit her sister in Trouville.

Félicité replied, by a sign, that she had no need to do so.

There was a silence. The good-natured Liébard judged it proper to withdraw.

Then she said:

'It doesn't mean a thing to them!'

Her head dropped again and, from time to time, she would pick up the long needles on the work-table, mechanically.

Some women crossed in the yard with a hand-barrow of dripping washing.

Glimpsing them through the window-panes, she remembered her washing: she had soaked it the evening before and today it needed rinsing. She left the room.

Her board and tub were by the side of the Toucques. She threw a pile of shirts on the bank, rolled her sleeves and picked up her battledore. The hefty blows she gave could be heard in the next-door gardens. The fields were deserted and the wind was ruffling the river; on the other side, long grasses were inclining over its surface, like the hair of corpses floating in the water. Until evening, she was very brave and held back her grief, but, in her room, she gave way to it, flopped face-down on her mattress, her face in the pillow, her two fists pressing her temples.

She learnt the circumstances of his end much later, from Victor's captain himself.

He had been bled too much for yellow fever, in the hospital. Four doctors in all had held him down. He had died at once, and the doctor in charge had said:

'Well, there goes one more!'

His parents had always treated her inhumanly. She preferred not to see them again, and, out of forgetfulness or the callousness of the wretched, they made no advance to her.

Virginie was getting weaker.

Breathlessness, coughing, constant fever and mottlings on her cheeks disclosed some serious complaint. M. Poupart had advised a stay in Provence. Mme Aubain made up her mind to it and would have brought her daughter back home at once, but for the climate of Pont-l'Evêque.)

This is the continuity of *L'Education Sentimentale* rather than that of *Madame Bovary*. Nothing impedes the transitions from the bad news to the washing and from the story of Victor's parents to Virginie's illness, nothing is too fast or too slow and each event has the same importance without losing any of its particular tone. This is kept up in the description of Virginie's death and Mme Aubain's mourning which follows. Incidentally, it is wrong to think of the tale as just the pathetic story of Félicité: Mme Aubain – bourgeoise as she is – has a pathos just as real.

The one criticism that can be made of *Un Cœur Simple* is that it lacks Flaubert's usual intensity. It has been popular because it is less excruciating than the longer works. There is perhaps a shade too much sober acquiescence in its catalogue of suffering for it to have real vitality as a picture of life. Things are seen through the filter of serene despair, with a distance granted by memory, so that it can be hard not to feel that one is looking back on Félicité's life with sentiments akin to nostalgia. Whereas the elegiac feeling in *Madame Bovary* was made acute through Emma's passionate protest against life, Félicité makes Flaubert's tone too muted and undemanding for it to be fully alive. This is the price paid for the tale's harmoniousness. The quest for beauty has succeeded so well that it has perhaps made it slightly too easy to reconcile oneself to its theme of *lacrimae rerum*. Beauty is a solace but it is seldom free from deception. There is something left unexpressed because of the very perfection of the tale's expression, 'one wonder, at the least, / Which into words no virtue can digest.'

The paradox of *Trois Contes* is that they achieve such a contained harmony of tone that we put them down asking what lacunae their beauty issues from, what unfulfilled possibilities enable them to seem so locally fulfilled as art. The essential question about Flaubert emerges with more clarity than in the longer works, *because* of their perfection: is there a split, a hiatus, between their human truth and their formal beauty? If there is, it is one Flaubert would himself have perceived. Though he always, from the start of *Madame Bovary*, sacrificed to beauty, he did so knowingly, never allowing formal beauty to stand together with the greater 'creation and generalisation' of those artists, like Shakespeare, whom he most revered. Such beauty represented for him the pinnacle of art like Horace's – art which was classic without being of the greatest sort. His own classicism was *faute de mieux*, an acknowledgement of what he saw as his own limited abilities. His letters never praise a Shakespeare in the terms in which they describe either his own aspirations after beauty or the work of such favourite authors as Boileau. We therefore have his own sanction for asking what the achieved beauty of such things as *La Légende de St Julien l'Hospitalier* – which Proust thought 'the most perfect' of his works – had as its price. [21] There is a case for seeing the tale as the most perfectly tragic of all his works, but there is also a point in asking whether its very beauty does not override its own deepest implications, dissolving the horror of parricide and matricide into a strangely soothing and effortless dream. Is *St Julien* perhaps a little too attractive?

The tale unites the blessing of great economy with the blessing of great resonance, as befits something legendary and non-realistic. [22] The more precise its details are, the more luminous becomes their significance, and, given space, one might quote page upon page of marvellous descriptive poems, notably from the hunting scenes. This is partly because Julien, as a hero of legend, is quite outside us and acts as a conductor of the feelings his world prompts in him, without our sensing, as is usually the case in Flaubert, an ironic discrepancy between his vision of things and things as they really are, as Flaubert wants them to be seen. Irony is latent in the action as tragic irony, but not in the style. From the start, Julien's life is marked out by the prophecies of the angel and the hermit and, later, the terrible prediction of the great stag which he kills. The tale feels inevitable and we do not try to detect breaks in the chain that links its causes to its effects: it is as if there were no chain at all. Supernatural phenomena and destiny mould Julien's life into such a clear spiritual shape that he seems almost to sleep-walk his way through it. The tale is both limpidly static and in a state of constant, fluid change. Each image is fixed in the mind like the stained glass images from which the tale was drawn, and image flows on to image without our asking why. I do not mean it is just a naïve, mystical fairy-tale. Its resonance comes from its simple, natural confrontation of elemental human nature – parental love, filial feeling, violence, guilt, charity – through the lucid medium of an absolute necessity. If the action feels as if it has been dreamt it is because nothing is being rigged.

This beauty does not make Julien himself into a cypher, as might be expected. Because he always foreknows his fate (though not its final form) he can stand better than other Flaubert characters for the desire to make one's own fate. When he leaves home or becomes a beggar because of the stag's predictions, necessity forces him to find a shape for his own life. His murder of his parents is neither pure accident nor pure fate because it also stems from his irresistible need to hunt and the frustration of his desire to slay all the beasts in the forest. He is, on the other hand, as much the instrument as the initiator of his own deepest passions, so the relation between fate and freewill in his actions is as unfathomable as it is in *Macbeth*. It leaves us transfixed by the mysteriously inescapable facts of his legend. Yet, though the tale is too durable in significance to be dismissed as a beautiful anachronism, its legendary nature prevents us from participating in Julien's feelings as we can in a Macbeth's.[23] His inner soul is subordinate to the overall tragic feeling just as Emma's was; it is a vehicle, a mirror to reflect what happens to him back to the reader. No one could associate the beauty of the tale with a beauty and profoundity in Julien himself, as Bradley did with characters like Hamlet.

When Julien is destroyed by the appalling interweaving of his desires with necessity (the stag re-appears at the moment of the unintentional parricide) Flaubert tells us that 'henceforth he no longer existed'.[24] This emptiness is not quite that of Emma at her last meeting with Léon; his feelings are still hidden from him and he finds his own nature impenetrable:

> Le soleil, tous les soirs, étalait du sang dans les nuages; et chaque nuit, en rêve, son parricide recommençait.
> Il se fit un cilice avec des pointes de fer. Il monta sur les deux genoux toutes les collines ayant une chapelle à leur sommet. Mais l'impitoyable pensée obscurcissait la splendeur des tabernacles, le torturait à travers les macérations de la pénitence.
> Il ne se révoltait pas contre Dieu qui lui avait infligé cette action, et pourtant se désespérait de l'avoir pu commettre. (P. 117.)
> (Every evening the sun laid out blood over the clouds, and each night his parricide began again in dreams.
> He made himself a hair-shirt which had iron points. He climbed every hill which had a chapel at its top on his two knees. But his pitiless thoughts darkened the splendour of the tabernacles, torturing him through the mortifications of penitence.
> He did not rebel against God who had inflicted this action on him, yet he was driven to despair at having been able to commit it.)

He is not concerned to shift his guilt onto other shoulders and so, when he looks into a mirror as Emma does, unlike her he can recognise himself for what he really is:

... il vit paraître en face de lui un vieillard tout décharné, à barbe blanche et d'un aspect si lamentable qu'il lui fut impossible de retenir ses pleurs. L'autre, aussi, pleurait. Sans reconnaître son image, Julien se rappelait confusément une figure ressemblant à celle-là. Il poussa un cri; c'était son père; et il ne pensa plus à se tuer. (P. 118.)

(... he saw an emaciated old man appear before him, white-bearded and so pitiful-looking that it was impossible for him to hold back his tears. The other was weeping too. Without recognising his reflection, Julien had a confused memory of a face resembling that one. He let forth a cry; it was his father; he no longer thought of killing himself.)

A cycle begins over again in this terrible vision of a human bond and the bondage it exacts. Recognising himself in others, Julien dedicates himself to their service. When the leper comes for him his self-discovery is completed and, naked as when he was born, he achieves a transcendence of which Emma, who was never so stripped of self, could only dream:

Le toit s'envola, le firmament se déployait; – et Julien monta vers les espaces bleus, face à face avec Notre-Seigneur Jésus, qui l'emportait dans le ciel.

Et voilà l'histoire de saint Julien l'Hospitalier, telle à peu près qu'on la trouve, sur un vitrail d'église, dans mon pays. (Pp.124–5.)[25]

(The roof flew off, the firmament was unfurling – and Julien rose towards the blue spaces, face to face with Our Lord Jesus, who was carrying him into heaven.

And that is the story of Saint Julien the Hospitaller, more or less as it is to be found on a church window, in the place I come from.)

That is all: the tale ends with what is apparently the most naïve sentence in all Flaubert.

What, if the tale is as tragic as I have suggested, is to be made of this deliberately *faux naif* conclusion? Is this the one place where irony peeps out from a work in which it is otherwise suppressed? It seems as if the simplicity has been grafted onto the fable, rather than expressing the profound simplicity with which the legend has been imagined. The last sentence is one of those Flaubertian utterances we never get to the bottom of. It has the same blank profundity that the saint's soul seems to express. Does the tone suggest that Julien's apotheosis is an absurd, impossible transcendence only credible in legend? If so, it implies a final comment on the artist's own tragic quest for beauty, for the air of the high mountains he always longs to breathe. Yet Julien has transcended self and, in a poetic fable, it is natural for this to be symbolised. One's main doubt concerns the beauty of the ending. The allusion to the stained glass window perhaps casts a sheen of glamourous medieval poetry over Julien's tragedy, as if to imply that its ending is wishfully happy. In any other of Flaubert's works, he would have been conducted through all the hideous stages of leprosy, as Hannon is in *Salammbô*. The dream-like limpidity of the stained glass is only so beautiful if darker thoughts can be contained and resolved within it. The beauty may make us dream – as Flaubert always wanted his prose to do – but it does so by providing us with a detached image to contemplate, rather than a tragic experience we are forced to re-live. What is salvaged from life through art only fully flowers as art, as an end in itself. *L'Education Sentimentale* may be less beautiful than *St Julien* but it is infinitely more moving and nearer home. The tale which began from a work of art ends by suggesting the tragedy as well as the miracle of the pursuit of the beautiful, and this, though an increasingly prevalent, and even fashionable, version of tragedy in the later nineteenth century, is only Flaubert's own tragedy, not the wider tragedy of his two greatest novels. It is where he most expresses his own age and the words of a fellow victim may serve as its epitaph:

> Je suis belle, ô mortels! comme un rêve de pierre,
> Et mon sein, où chacun s'est meurtri tour à tour,
> Est fait pour inspirer au poète un amour
> Eternel et muet ainsi que la matière.[26]
> (O mortals, my beauty like a dream of stone,
> My breast, where you each bruised yourselves in turn,
> Are made to inspire in the poet a love
> Eternal and dumb just as matter is.)

Such words could not so well express the creative energy which lay behind *Madame Bovary*, dreaming not only of beauty, but of an ordinary life which was beauty's deepest source.

6 A Simple Young Woman from Albany

Really, universally, relations stop nowhere, and the exquisite problem of the artist is eternally but to draw, by a geometry of his own, the circle within which they shall happily *appear* to do so.[1]   (James)

With the Cold War, when a cultivated but detached liberalism was so inviting to American intellectuals, the reputation of Henry James reached a high point. Leon Edel's lavish biography, begun in 1950, epitomised the new note of deference and, even, unction which began to be sounded in writing on James. By the 1960s, criticism of the novels was tending to becloud them with incense. Critics of quite opposite persuasions, from formalist to Leavisite, collaborated in swinging this incense into all the corners of the Jamesian temple. There were, of course, dissenters but their dissent often seemed half-determined by the prevailing tone of eulogy. The best-known critique of James in the 1960s, Maxwell Geismar's *Henry James and his Cult*, was so impatient of the effusions of the 'Jacobites', so hopeless about resisting their influence, that it squandered its critical insights in the kind of wilfully vulgar diatribe which admirers of so subtle and polished a writer as James have always found it easy to dismiss.[2]

One consequence of the esteem in which James has been held since the War is that his word has often been taken as gospel as a guide both to the nature of his own fiction and to that of his predecessors and contemporaries. This is surprising when one considers the specialised nature of his gift as a novelist. Yet to cite just one example of this influence, there have been three books published since 1971 which discuss the novels in relation to the work of other great writers without ever seriously questioning James's own account of what those writers were trying to do and of how well they did it.[3] Similarly, his own prefaces to his novels have too often moulded the interpretation of them. Is James necessarily his own best advocate? In discussing *The Portrait of a Lady*, I shall suggest that, in crucial ways, his art shows a disparity between its intentional, surface meaning and its real imaginative drift. I see James as a novelist who, while constantly looking over his own shoulder in an effort to be relentlessly conscious of what he is doing, in fact expresses more of what he has to say when his imagination is, so to speak, making free behind his own back. It is, of course, dangerous to try to read a novel against its own grain but, with *The Portrait*, I have no better method to offer.

I

James's novel has enough in common with Flaubert's for one to see why he said of *Madame Bovary* that 'the reader himself seems to have lived in it all, more than in any other novel we can recall'.[4] Both works describe imaginative young women who make disastrous marriages and, as a result, fail to satisfy the demands which their imagination makes of life. That Isabel Archer is virtuous while Emma is not is less significant than the fact that they each believe themselves to be spiritually unfettered by life, only to discover they are mistaken. Not surprisingly, critics have taken up this similarity between them. Quentin Anderson thinks that 'James may very well have been intent on producing an American analogue to Emma Bovary, who likewise incorporates internal contradictions'.[5] Stallman, I think rightly, sees the following exchange between Isabel and her friend Henrietta Stackpole as an allusion to *Madame Bovary*:[6]

> 'Do you know where you're drifting?' Henrietta pursued, holding out her bonnet delicately.
> 'No, I haven't the least idea, and I find it very pleasant not to know. A swift carriage, of a dark night, rattling with four horses over roads that one can't see – that's my idea of happiness.'
> 'Mr Goodwood certainly didn't teach you to say such things as that – like the heroine of an immoral novel', said Miss Stackpole.[7]

This quickly alerts us to how different Isabel is from Flaubert's heroine. Emma does not enjoy 'drifting' and has no leisure for pert epigrams: she is a passionate risk-taker whereas Isabel seems here to be carrying on a cool, rather smug flirtation with life. It is characteristically unclear whether James is mocking her naïve irresponsibility or teasing Henrietta for taking too crude a view of Isabel's feelings; on either view, Isabel seems flippant. For Emma Bovary, the point of being whisked away in a carriage at dead of night would have been the man in the carriage with her; for Isabel, the point seems less the thought of any actual experience than her sensation of self as the seat of experience. This small example, then, gives us little cause for thinking, as James himself must have done, that Isabel Archer can show us more about 'life' than an Emma Bovary. Yet Isabel, like Cleopatra, is one of those characters whose destiny is more interesting to her acolytes than is their own. Critics have often corroborated James's obvious respect for her sensibility; for example, 'James's millionaires and heiresses have in his novels exactly the same dramatic function as the kings, queens and princes in Shakespeare's plays. They are "representatives" of all humanity in the modern world. . . .'[8] The difference between the head of a community and a Jamesian expatriate is passed over. So too is the fact that what makes a Shakespearian hero or heroine 'representative' is not simply character but the action in which that character is caught up. In a similar way, the fact that there may be some doubt about whether Isabel is ready to give herself to the life she encounters has not deterred another critic from assuming that *The Portrait* is 'sufficiently recognised as a tragic novel of the first order'.[9] It is true that James goes out of his way to set Isabel up as a tragedy queen but, with *Madame Bovary* in mind, *The Portrait* may be as likely to strike us as a subtle evasion of the tragic.

The impression James took from *Madame Bovary* resembled the one he took from *Daniel Deronda*: 'The universe forcing itself with a slow, inexorable pressure into a narrow, complacent, and yet after all extremely sensitive mind, and making it ache with the pain of the process.'[10] Does anything that could be described as 'the universe' force itself into Isabel's mind at the end of *The Portrait*? It is true that she often speaks about 'fate', but is it her tragic 'fate' which most interests James? His friend Howells thought not:

> There is no question, of course, but he could tell the story of Isabel in *The Portrait of a Lady* to the end, yet he does not tell it. We must agree, then, to take what seems a fragment instead of a whole, and to find, when we can, a name for this new kind of fiction. Evidently it is the character, not the fate, of his people which occupies him; when he has fully developed their character he leaves them to what destiny the reader pleases.[11]

Nothing in James's preface to the novel suggests that he would not have agreed that the novel began and ended with its heroine's character. The reader, however, is likely to ask how Isabel's character can be 'fully developed' when her 'fate' is left up in the air: is James palming us off with the liberty to speculate about her character rather than fully exploring it in action? I would explain this putativeness in the novel in terms of the quotation at the head of this chapter: James refrains from extending our knowledge of Isabel in the interests of his 'geometry'; he draws his 'circle' around her in such a way as to prevent the other characters from weighing the action in the way she is allowed to, making their behaviour a means to the end of showing her in the light in which he wishes her to be seen. He is too personally involved in her to become sufficiently involved with his other characters as people in their own right. For there is no one in *The Portrait* who has the kind of independent life that is to be found in Homais or Lheureux or Catherine Leroux, characters who are not there just because Emma Bovary is the kind of woman she is. Because Isabel is so much the cynosure of *The Portrait* – for the author, the reader, the other characters and for herself – one doubts whether she is at odds with 'the universe' in the way James felt Gwendolen Harleth was. Emma and Gwendolen submit to the world and renounce happiness because life makes happiness unattainable for them, but Isabel's renunciation is very different. At the end of the novel she seems rather to renounce the life inside her than to submit to such pressure from 'the universe' as the by then shadowy Osmond can be felt to represent. Why she should do this is, perhaps, the main question that *The Portrait* leaves with its readers.

II

The more light James sheds on Isabel the less confident of understanding her I become. This feeling has been a common one. Most of the novel's early reviewers echoed R. H. Hutton's blunt reaction to its title: 'She is the lady of whom no portrait is given, though she is studied till the reader is weary of the study.'[12] Leavis has said that:

> James's marvellous art is devoted to contenting us with very little in the way of inward realisation of Isabel, and to keeping us interested, instead, in a kind of psychological detective work – keeping us intently wondering from the outside, and constructing, on a strict economy of evidence, what is going on inside.[13]

This is very perceptive but it does not decide whether James is trying to expose Isabel inwardly or just to keep his readers guessing about her. It is true that James's sense of her has to be putative because the sense she has of herself is also putative, yet one of the central purposes of his art was to get right inside the consciousness of his protagonists. A passage from *The Lesson of Balzac* will give a good idea of what James is usually thought of as doing with Isabel. He is discussing Taine's opinion that Balzac loved Valérie Marneffe as Thackeray was unable to love Becky Sharp:

> He [Balzac] at all events robustly loved the sense of another explored, assumed, assimilated identity – enjoyed it as the hand enjoys the glove when the glove ideally fits. My image indeed is

loose; for what he liked was absolutely to get into the constituted consciousness. . . . How do we know given persons, for any purpose of demonstration, unless we see it [life] from their point of vision, that is, from their point of pressing consciousness or sensation? – without our allowing for which there is no appreciation. Balzac loved his Valérie then as Thackeray did not love his Becky. . . .

Was this how James loved his Isabel?[14]

A passage from chapter 6 of *The Portrait* will show at least, how much he enjoyed elaborating on his heroine's nature:

. . . she only had a general idea that people were right when they treated her as if she were rather superior. Whether or not she were superior, people were right in admiring her if they thought her so; for it seemed to her often that her mind moved more quickly than theirs, and this encouraged an impatience that might easily be confounded with superiority. It may be affirmed without delay that Isabel was probably very liable to the sin of self-esteem; she often surveyed with complacency the field of her own nature; she was in the habit of taking for granted, on scanty evidence, that she was right; she treated herself to occasions of homage. Meanwhile her errors and delusions were frequently such as a biographer interested in preserving the dignity of his subject must shrink from specifying. Her thoughts were a tangle of vague outlines which had never been corrected by the judgement of people speaking with authority. In matters of opinion she had had her own way, and it had led her into a thousand ridiculous zigzags. At moments she discovered she was grotesquely wrong, and then she treated herself to a week of passionate humility. After this she held her head higher than ever again; for it was of no use, she had an unquenchable desire to think well of herself. She had a theory that it was only under this provision life was worth living; that one should be one of the best, should be conscious of a fine organisation (she couldn't help knowing her organisation was fine), should move in a realm of light, of natural wisdom, of happy impulse, of inspiration gracefully chronic. It was almost as unnecessary to cultivate doubt of one's self as to cultivate doubt of one's best friend: one should try to be one's own best friend and to give one's self, in this manner, distinguished company. The girl had a certain nobleness of imagination which rendered her a good many services and played her a great many tricks. She spent half her time in thinking of beauty and bravery and magnanimity; she had a fixed determination to regard the world as a place of brightness, of free expansion, of

irresistible action: she held it must be detestable to be afraid
or ashamed. She had an infinite hope that she should never do
anything wrong. (I, pp. 59–60.)

It is a brilliantly disingenuous passage in which the author seems
to take himself in as much as he does his reader. He seems unaware
of how priggish he is making Isabel seem. The irony is that of a
fond parent who seeks to skim over his child's faults; its playful
tone enhances Isabel's dignity under the guise of candid criticism.
'Whether or not she were superior' insinuates a doubt that one cannot believe James really feels. The frankness of 'It may be affirmed
without delay' is dissolved by the word 'probably', so that the phrase
'the sin of self-esteem' loses its sting and feels merely urbane and
whimsical: there is no Balzacian dive into the depths of the character. It is perhaps a certain condescension to Isabel which determines the tone of James's affection for her; the phrase 'a biographer
interested in preserving the dignity of his subject' keeps her at a
distance by being both coy and sly. Yet one also feels that James
can't distance himself enough from Isabel for her to be taken as a
character to whom one can respond freely. Balzac's relish for
Valérie's energy is compatible with his making it plain that she is
evil; it is impossible to separate Isabel's sense of the fineness of her
'organisation' from James's own sense of it. We are tempted to adopt
her own 'theory' of her 'natural wisdom', and her 'desire to think
well of herself' comes across as simply charming. She has been
criticised to disarm criticism. The searching observations at the end
of the passage come to seem generalised and lacking in sharpness,
despite the irony which the development of the novel gives them.

At the end of the passage quoted from chapter 6 James comes out
in the open:

. . . her determination to see, to try, to know, her combination of
the delicate, desultory, flame-like spirit and the eager and personal creature of condition: she would be an easy victim of
scientific criticism if she were not intended to awaken on the
reader's part an impulse more tender and more purely expectant.
(I, p. 61.)

This seems fair – a novel reader is not a prosecuting counsel – until
one reflects that the 'scientific criticism' James smiles at need not
be the only alternative to the pseudo-ironical tenderness he has
given us. Jane Austen can enlist us on a character's side by being
straightforward about his or her shortcomings. The frank spirit of
her treatment of Emma gives no temptation to the kind of irritated
quibbling that the reserves in James's irony provoke in the case of

Isabel. Isabel, alas, did not have the blessing of a Mr Knightley.

There is a distinct resemblance between Isabel's reticent self-esteem and the reserved kind of affection which James himself feels for her; it is as if his effort to fathom her is also an effort to fathom his own nature. She cultivates the same aura of aloofness and mystery towards her friends as we find in his own teasing irony. She withholds things from her friends just as he withholds things from the reader. Neither Madame Merle nor Ralph nor her sisters are told of the progress of her courtship with Osmond, and neither are we. She also shares with James that facility which self-conscious people have for seeing the self as if it were other, just as he could be curiously objective when discussing his own creations. The scene when Lord Warburton proposes to her is typical:

> It suddenly came upon her that her situation was one which a few weeks ago she would have deemed deeply romantic: the park of an old English country house, with the foreground embellished by a 'great' (as she supposed) nobleman in the act of making love to a young lady who, on careful inspection, should be found to present remarkable analogies with herself. But if she was now the heroine of the situation she succeeded scarcely the less in looking at it from the outside. (I, p. 129.)

The lack of spontaneity implied by that 'on careful inspection' is rather frightening. Because she is at one remove from her own self she thinks of Warburton as a 'great opportunity' (I, p. 137), not as a man who is deeply in love. She has difficulty in understanding that people may have something to give her or that she may have something to offer them; this makes her see Warburton as a threat to her freedom. It is the same with Osmond's proposal. Here is her reply when he tells her, 'I'm absolutely in love with you': (II, p. 16):

> 'Oh, don't say that, please', she answered with an intensity that expressed the dread of having, in this case too, to choose and decide. What made her dread great was precisely the force which, as it would seem, ought to have banished all dread – the sense of something within herself, deep down, that she supposed to be inspired and trustful passion. It was there like a large sum stored in a bank – which there was a terror in having to begin to spend. If she touched it, it would all come out. (II, p. 16.)

Love seems subject to the same laws as capital and her 'passion' is imagined as an inert deposit deep inside her. The implication is that, if it should 'come out', it might be exhausted. Perhaps the main reason that Osmond wins her in spite of this fear is that he gives the impression of not wanting to take her. They seem to conspire to keep at a distance by loving in each other more the impressions they give of themselves than what they really, secretly, are. In an early chapter James remarks that 'Isabel's chief dread in life . . . was that she should appear narrow-minded; what she feared next afterwards was that she should really be so'. (I, pp. 72–3.) One might say that what Osmond wanted most was to be thought 'the man with the best taste in the world' (II, p. 169), and what he wanted next was really to be that man.

The measure of James's personal stake in Isabel is that her own ideas about herself form the core of his tragic feeling for her. In the mental blueprint she has of her life at the start she is already the tragedy queen:

> It appeared to Isabel that the unpleasant had even been too absent from her knowledge, for she had gathered from her acquaintance with literature that it was often a source of interest and even of instruction. (I, p. 37.)

She almost feels obliged to suffer and uses this feeling to turn down her chances of life. She spells this out to Warburton:

> 'I'm not bent on a life of misery', said Isabel. 'I've always been intensely determined to be happy, and I've often believed I should be. I've told people that; you can ask them. But it comes over me every now and then that I can never be happy in any extraordinary way; not by turning away, by separating myself.'
> 'By separating yourself from what?'
> 'From life.' (I. p. 165.)

It might seem as if 'life' is precisely what Isabel is separating herself from. To reject happiness is, after all, to minimise the hold that suffering can have on her too. What is beginning to emerge is the strange Jamesian celebration of renunciation which is to end the novel. The narrator and his heroine constantly peddle a series of ideas, which are liberally spread over the novel's surface like the catch-phrases of a critic, to validate a renunciation of life: 'The finer natures were those that shone at the larger times' (I. p. 214); 'The more you know the more unhappy you are.' (I. p. 325.) It is as though James deliberately planned Isabel's tragedy to demonstrate her noble nature and that, in doing so, his own instincts and hers went hand in hand. Often, only the comic veneer of the prose hides this from the reader:

Smile not, however, I venture to repeat, at this simple young woman from Albany who debated whether she should accept an English peer before he had offered himself and who was disposed to believe that on the whole she could do better. She was a person of great good faith, and if there was a great deal of folly in her wisdom those who judge her severely may have the satisfaction of finding that, later, she became consistently wise only at the cost of an amount of folly, which will constitute almost a direct appeal to charity. (I, p. 127.)

This not only begs several questions, it tries to pre-arrange the reader's response. Later, more is said about Isabel's 'good faith' but James has surely compromised his own already: did any reader ever imagine Isabel as a 'simple young woman'? Does James really want us to feel for her such a patronising 'charity'? The appeal to our better feelings – those who 'judge her severely' are presumed to be vindictive – is a debating tactic.

This passage raises one of the main problems for the reader of *The Portrait*: how to penetrate beneath James's admiration for Isabel and the veil of polite irony he draws over it, to a sense of the deepest springs of her selfhood. One of the more curious aspects of James's world is that people seek relationships with people who seem perplexing and inaccessible to them. It is this which makes Isabel so popular and the same quality attracts her to others. Ralph sees her as a closed door:

He surveyed the edifice from the outside and admired it greatly; he looked in at the windows and received an impression of proportions equally fair. But he felt that he saw it only by glimpses and that he had not yet stood under the roof. The door was fastened, and though he had keys in his pocket he had a conviction that none of them would fit. (I, p. 76.)

Ralph too has a screen, which he describes as a 'band of music in my ante-room':

Isabel often found herself irritated by this perpetual fiddling; she would have liked to pass through the ante-room, as her cousin called it, and enter the private apartments. (I, p. 72.)

As Isabel and Ralph are, so too is Osmond. When he first appears he is symbolised by his screen, which is his Florentine villa: 'It was the mask, not the face of the house. It had heavy lids, but no eyes; the house in reality looked another way. . . .' (I, p. 286.) Such tantalising glimpses are the basis of the novel's psychological method

and the main-spring of its peculiar suspense. Like the irony, they
are signs that the conscious art of the book is extremely manipu-
lative.

III

A good place from which to explore Isabel's central position in *The
Portrait* is the preface James wrote for the New York edition of
the book. This tells us of more than just the hindsight of the older
artist, because James is as intent on recapturing the sense of his
former inspiration as on detached criticism.[15] He tries to re-possess
his novel, to bridge the past and not just to look back on it. This
makes one take seriously the wistfully romantic patina he likes to
give to his own past. The preface begins with a nostalgic description of the Venice in which much of *The Portrait* was written and
this helps bring back the first gleams he had had of his subject:

> Trying to recover here, for recognition, the germ of my idea, I
> see that it must have consisted not at all in any conceit of a
> 'plot', nefarious name, in any flash, upon the fancy, of a set of
> relations, or in any one of those situations that, by a logic of their
> own, immediately fall, for the fabulist, into movement, into a
> march or a rush, a patter of quick steps; but altogether in the
> sense of a single character, the character and aspect of a par-
> ticular engaging young woman, to which all the usual elements
> of a 'subject', certainly of a setting, were to need to be super-
> added. (*The Art of the Novel*, p. 42.)

Isabel was not a character or a motive but one of the 'lurking forces
of expansion' (p. 42) in James's imagination, and, as such, she
appeared to him as a mystery which was part of the mystery of his
own mind, still to be fathomed:

> Thus I had my vivid individual – vivid, so strangely, in spite of
> being still at large, not confined by the conditions, not engaged
> in the tangle, to which we look for much of the impress that
> constitutes an identity. If the apparition was still all to be placed
> how came it to be vivid? – since we puzzle such quantities out,
> mostly, just by the business of placing them. One could answer
> such a question beautifully, doubtless, if one could do so subtle,
> if not so monstrous, a thing as to write the history of the growth
> of one's imagination. (P. 47.)

Isabel remains for most of the time an inaccessible 'apparition' to

the little ring of Isabel-watchers in the novel, but one wonders
whether James continued to feel her in that way: he often seems
to hold himself more remote from her than she does from him.[16]
The preface confirms the idea that he was manipulating her. It
goes on to see her as a 'precious object' that is 'curiously at my
disposal' (p. 48), moving, as it were, from Ralph's sense of her to
Osmond's. In the memory of the older James she had changed from
a fleeting 'apparition' to a genie at his beck and call, a 'figure' that
is:

> . . . placed in the imagination that detains it, preserves, protects,
> enjoys it, conscious of its presence in the dusky, crowded, hetero-
> geneous back-shop of the mind very much as a wary dealer in
> precious odds and ends, competent to make an 'advance' on the
> rare object confided to him, is conscious of the rare little 'piece'
> left in deposit by the reduced, mysterious lady of title or the
> speculative amateur, and which is already there to disclose its
> merit afresh as soon as a key shall have clicked in a cupboard
> door. (Pp. 47–8.)

As the metaphor grows Isabel is changed from something unfathomable in the 'back-shop' of James's mind to something that
can be displayed by the turning of a key: the novelist changes from
a 'speculative amateur' to a 'wary dealer'. This suggests that James
is really talking about two kinds of creativity and that, as he wrote
the novel, he was concentrating as much on the effect that Isabel
would have on the reader as on trying to explore her. At all events,
it is at this point in the preface that he turns to his need for a
plot: 'my pious desire but to place my treasure right' (p. 48.)
    There is only one mention of Osmond in the preface and that
is just a reminiscence of the way his name, along with the names
of the other minor characters, came to James suddenly one morning
as part of 'the definite array of contributions to Isabel Archer's
history' (p. 53). It was in organising these 'contributions' that he
became preoccupied with his novel's 'structure':

> . . . this single small corner-stone, the conception of a certain young
> woman affronting her destiny, had begun with being all my
> outfit for the large building of 'The Portrait of a Lady'. It came
> to be a square and spacious house – or has at least seemed so to me
> in this going over it again; but, such as it is, it had to be put up
> round my young woman while she stood there in perfect isolation.
> (P. 48.)

What interests James as he looks back is the fact that 'what one

was in for' was 'positively organising an ado about Isabel Archer'
(p. 48). The implication is that the 'ado' was interesting, not in its
own right, but for the way in which Isabel would see it. This is not,
as one might at first think, an inevitable consequence of James's
devotion to the notion of the finer consciousness. He also claims
to measure the fineness of a consciousness by its capacity to see as
much as possible of life as it is. He thinks of Isabel as embarking
on a 'free exploration of life' (I, p. 137) – just what he aspires to
do as a novelist – and it therefore becomes unclear why, for Isabel
'life' should have been represented by an 'ado' which was primarily
directed to the illumination of her own character. In saying this, I
am applying to the novel's action a criterion which is offered by
the preface itself: 'There is, I think, no more nutritive or suggestive
truth . . . than that of the perfect dependence of the "moral" sense
of a work of art on the amount of felt life concerned in producing
it.' (P. 45.)

James himself thought that to dwell on Isabel's 'relation to those
surrounding her' was too easy a way out of his difficulties, 'a bridge
for evasion, for retreat and flight' (p. 51):

> 'Place the centre of the subject in the young woman's own con-
> sciousness', I said to myself, and you get as interesting and as
> beautiful a difficulty as you could wish. Stick to that for the
> centre; put the heaviest weight into *that* scale, which will be so
> largely the scale of her relation to herself. Make her only inter-
> ested enough, at the same time, in the things that are not herself,
> and this relation needn't fear to be too limited. Place meanwhile
> in the other scale the lighter weight (which is usually the one
> that tips the balance of interest): press least hard, in short, on
> the consciousness of your heroine's satellites, especially the male;
> make it an interest contributive only to the greater one. See, at
> all events, what can be done in this way. What better field could
> there be for a due ingenuity? The girl hovers, inextinguishable,
> as a charming creature, and the job will be to translate her into
> the highest terms of that formula, and as nearly as possible more-
> over into *all* of them. (Pp. 51–2.)

For James, this means that certain elements in any work are of
the essence . . . others are only of the form' (p. 53). Yet why should
the 'lighter weight' be seen as merely a formal quantity when, to
Isabel, it is simply the weight of all the world she goes out to
encounter? Flaubert studied Emma's 'relation to herself' but, in
Madame Bovary, the look of a landscape or the way Charles eats
his soup are as essential to the 'felt life' of that study as are Emma's
own emotions. The effect of the comparison – it makes us see that

Charles Bovary is in no way Emma's 'satellite' – is to suggest that James permits Isabel a degree of immunity from the world's pressure which Emma is denied. By limiting the humanity of the people she is in conflict with, he was cushioning her against them. Their 'contributive' rôle is not calculated to make us take their views and feelings about her as seriously as her views and feelings about them.

In *Antony and Cleopatra*, which studies the little world its hero and heroine make for themselves, it is possible for Enobarbus to carry us completely with him for a moment when he rejects their love as a dishonourable evasion of the larger world. In *Timon of Athens*, the humble steward Flavius forces his misanthropic master to admit against his will that there is as least 'one honest man' in the world. (Act IV, scene 3.) Enobarbus and Flavius are allowed to be distinct from their masters; they are not *ficelles*.[17] In *The Portrait*, we never really discover what Osmond's feelings about Isabel's shortcomings actually are. Instead, we are given her grievances against him in the overpraised chapter 42 – the fire-side vigil which the James of the preface saw as 'searching criticism' – and they add up to an equivalent of Timon's tirades presented as the *whole* picture. There is a revealing remark in the entry on *The Portrait* in James's *Notebooks*: 'After a year or two of marriage the antagonism between her nature and Osmond's comes out – the opposition of a noble character and a narrow one.' (P. 15.) In making Isabel so much the *raison d'être* of the novel James was planning melodrama rather than tragedy.

There is a great deal to admire in James's picture of Osmond, especially the way his peculiar deadliness is caught in his tone of voice, but he remains abstract in proportion to the extent to which Isabel's sufferings are used to prevent us from entering into his. It may seem unfair to illustrate this point by reference to Shakespeare so I will invoke *Middlemarch* instead.[18] There too an attractive and idealistic young woman marries an older man who is deeply egotistic, but George Eliot's sympathies can shift from Dorothea to Casaubon – 'why always Dorothea? Was her point of view the only possible one with regard to this marriage?' we are asked. This feeling in no way softens the criticism of Casaubon's egoism:

Mr Casaubon had never had a strong bodily frame, and his soul was sensitive without being enthusiastic; it was too languid to thrill out of self-consciousness into passionate delight; it went on fluttering in the swampy ground where it was hatched, thinking of its wings and never flying. His experience was of that pitiable kind which shrinks from pity, and fears most of all that it should be known: it was that proud narrow sensitiveness which has not mass enough to spare for transformation into sympathy, and

quivers thread-like in small currents of self preoccupation or at
best of an egotistic scrupulosity.[19]

This is enough to suggest that James does not really ask himself
what it is that makes Osmond the man he is. Here, now, is part
of chapter 42 of *The Portrait*:

> She could come and go; she had her liberty; her husband was
> perfectly polite. He took himself so seriously; it was something
> appalling. Under all his culture, his cleverness, his amenity,
> under his good-nature, his facility, his knowledge of life, his
> egotism lay hidden like a serpent in a bank of flowers. She had
> taken him seriously, but she had not taken him so seriously as
> that. How could she – especially when she had known him better?
> She was to think of him as he thought of himself – as the first
> gentleman in Europe. So it was that she had thought of him
> at first, and that indeed was the reason she had married him.
> But when she began to see what it implied she drew back. . . .
> (II, p. 172.)

This serpent-like Osmond is slightly absurd because neither James
nor Isabel can take even his 'egotism' really 'seriously'. Comparisons
are odious (there would be small point in expecting George Eliot's
kind of sympathy for a fortune-hunter like Osmond) but one is
entitled to ask why James cannot spare a thought from the seriousness with which Isabel takes herself to see how pathetic Osmond's
seriousness is. It seems that both he and his heroine share with Mr
Casaubon 'that proud narrow sensitiveness which has not mass
enough to spare for transformation into sympathy'. Whereas
Casaubon is a human being who is also an egotist, Osmond becomes
a rather theatrical symbol of egoism in general. His static quality
is demonstrated by James's telling us that Isabel 'had not read him
right' (II, p. 168), as if there were only one thing about him which
needs understanding. The upshot is that Isabel's marriage does not
force her into real spiritual growth. He is a disastrous husband
and next to nothing in chapter 42 suggests she is anything but a
model wife. James can enjoy her self-pity unperturbed.

IV

To see why *The Portrait* is a more profound and fascinating novel
than the melodrama of victimised innocence which James tries to
make his reader believe in one has to look below its emotional
surface, taking up undeveloped insights which have been obscured

by subterfuge. In chapter 6 we are given the following remarks about Isabel:

> Deep in her soul – it was the deepest thing there – lay a belief that if a certain light should dawn she could give herself completely; but this image, on the whole, was too formidable to be attractive. Isabel's thoughts hovered about it, but they seldom rested on it long; after a little while it ended in alarms. It often seemed to her that she thought too much about herself. . . . (I, p. 63.)

I shall be arguing that to 'give herself completely' is not 'the deepest thing about her'. (Even this passage, in fact, is not so sure that it is as it at first seems to be.) My immediate object is, therefore, to question the common view that, in Mattheissen's words, when Isabel marries 'she proceeds to do the wrong thing for the right reasons'.[20]

Isabel regards life with the kind of mixture of fascination and distrust with which a virtuous person might look at sin. James implies this from the start when he describes her girlhood in Albany:

> She knew that this silent, motionless portal opened into the street; if the sidelights had not been filled with green paper she might have looked out upon the little brown stoop and the well-worn brick pavement. But she had no wish to look out, for this would have interfered with her theory that there was a strange, unseen place on the other side – a place which became to the child's imagination, according to its different moods, a region of delight or of terror. (I, pp. 26–7.)

The mind is most susceptible to romance at a distance from experience, which is why fairy stories are told to children. Isabel's inner sanctum was not like Fanny Price's East Room in *Mansfield Park*, a spiritual retreat for pondering on the pressures of living, but a vantage point from which living could be imagined. One can therefore see why the kind of life offered by an intensely private man like Gilbert Osmond would be so inviting to someone with Isabel's sense of inner freedom. But it is not this part of her which James chooses to stress:

> . . . she had an immense curiosity about life and was constantly staring and wondering. She carried within herself a great fund of life, and her deepest enjoyment was to feel the continuity between the movements of her own soul and the agitations of the world. (I, p. 39.)

'Curiosity *about* life' – some strange reserve in her overrules the
'continuity' of which James speaks. It is important that the way the
word 'life' is used here should not be mistaken. Marius Bewley has
written that, 'Henry James is the first great American novelist to
have been consciously and explicitly concerned with 'life' in the
way that D. H. Lawrence, for example, was concerned with it.'[21] If
this were true it is difficult to see why James should have provided
Isabel with Ralph Touchett's life-style as a touchstone for the
cultivation of her 'curiosity about life':

> His outward conformity to the manners that surrounded him
> was none the less the mask of a mind that greatly enjoyed its
> independence, on which nothing long imposed itself, and which,
> naturally inclined to adventure and irony, indulged in a bound-
> less liberty of appreciation. (I, p. 43.)

The effect Ralph has on Isabel is, as this suggests it would be, to
encourage her tendencies to flirt with life, to become priggish and
to patronise other people. The fact that James has a soft spot for
Ralph ought not to lead us into taking his 'boundless liberty of
appreciation' as spiritual richness.

Isabel's response to Gardencourt, the home of Ralph and his
father, calls forth some of the novel's finest passages; for instance,
the following one which concentrates many of James's ideas about
Isabel:

> It often seemed to her that she thought to much about herself;
> you could have made her colour, any day in the year, by calling
> her a rank egoist. She was always planning out her development,
> desiring her perfection, observing her progress. Her nature had, in
> her conceit, a certain garden like quality, a suggestion of perfume
> and murmuring boughs, of shady bowers and lengthening vistas,
> which made her feel that introspection was, after all, an exercise
> in the open air, and that a visit to the recesses of one's spirit was
> harmless when one returned from it with a lapful of roses. But
> she was often reminded that there were other gardens in the
> world than those of her remarkable soul, and that there were
> moreover a great many places which were not gardens at all –
> only dusky pestiferous tracts, planted thick with ugliness and
> misery. In the current of that repaid curiosity on which she had
> lately been floating, which had conveyed her to this beautiful
> old England and might carry her much further still, she often
> checked herself with the thought of thousands of people who
> were less happy than herself – a thought which for the moment
> made her fine, full consciousness appear a kind of immodesty.
> What should one do with the misery of the world in a scheme

of the agreeable for one's self? It must be confessed that this
question never held her long. She was too young, too impatient
to live, too unacquainted with pain. She always returned to her
theory that a young woman whom after all everyone thought clever
should begin by getting a general impression of life. This impression was necessary to prevent mistakes, and after it should be
secured she might make the unfortunate condition of others a
subject of special attention.

England was a revelation to her, and she found herself as
diverted as a child at a pantomime. (I, pp. 63–4.)

The most striking impression this leaves is of Isabel's 'remarkable
soul' as a garden, full of innocence and creativeness. There is also
a rather precious irony about overblown phrases such as 'shady
bowers and lengthening vistas' – that is, if this is not meant as a
straight description of how James sees her. Yet the passage really
leaves us with little idea of how Isabel will develop her soul. Not,
evidently, through self-knowledge, if the show of carefully doctored
self-analysis here is felt as characteristic. She appears unaware, as
does James, that her main reason for thinking that 'thousands of
other people' are less happy than she is, is that they lack her own
kind of 'fine, full consciousness'. One does not feel that 'curiosity
about life' really spurs her on in the way phrases like 'impatient to
live' suggest. It seems as if she regards 'misery' as something a superior
spirit should see, rather like the Louvre or St Peter's, and, though
she is interested in life, she does not seem interested in participating
in it. What she wants is a general impression of life that will
enable her to go on basking in the self. Her real interest is for the
garden of her own mind and England, however beautiful, is a
'pantomime'. It is typical of the novel that one can never be quite
sure whether James means to say this or not.

The Portrait proceeds as a series of such tantalising glimpses
into the recesses of Isabel's nature, rather than as a sustained and
developing study, though often these glimpses are very profound
ones. The scene between her and Lord Warburton in chapter 12 is
a good example. It is not pushed far enough because James, like
his heroine, cannot take Warburton completely seriously; he is there
to strike sparks from Isabel and not to entangle her in any really
deep way. Just as Caspar Goodwood has the job of standing for
American energy, so Warburton's relevance is more as an English
lord than as a man in love. His unfailing good manners are used
to prevent his feelings from vying in importance with Isabel's and
he is always the touching minor character:

She would have given her little finger at that moment to feel strongly and simply the impulse to answer: 'Lord Warburton, it's impossible for me to do better in this wonderful world, I think, than commit myself, very gratefully, to your loyalty.' But though she was lost in admiration of her opportunity she managed to move back into the deepest shade of it, even as some wild, caught creature in a vast cage. The splendid security so offered her was *not* the greatest she could conceive. What she finally bethought herself of saying was something very different – something that deferred the need of really facing her crisis. 'Don't think me unkind if I ask you to say no more about this today.'

'Certainly, certainly!' her companion cried. 'I wouldn't bore you for the world.'

'You've given me a great deal to think about, and I promise you to do it justice.'

'That's all I ask of you, of course – and that you'll remember how absolutely your happiness is in my hands.'

Isabel listened with extreme respect to this admonition, but she said after a minute: 'I must tell you that what I shall think about is some way of letting you know that what you ask is impossible – letting you know it without making you miserable.'

'There's no way to do that, Miss Archer. I won't say that if you refuse me you'll kill me, I shall not die of it. But I shall do worse; I shall live to no purpose.'

'You'll live to marry a better woman than I.'

'Don't say that, please', said Lord Warburton very gravely. 'That's fair to neither of us.'

'To marry a worse one then.' (I, pp. 134–5.)

Her witticism nervously liberates her feeling of being a 'wild, caught creature in a vast cage'. She is desperately, though inexplicably, in need of 'security':

'Do you know I'm very much afraid of it – of that remarkable mind of yours?'

Our heroine's biographer can scarcely tell why, but the question made her start and brought a conscious blush to her cheek. She returned his look a moment, and then with a note in her voice that might almost have appealed to his compassion, 'So am I, my Lord!' she oddly exclaimed. (I, pp. 135–6.)

Why should she be afraid of a mind from which she is in the habit of gathering 'a lapful of roses'?

Isabel at once rationalises her fears by telling herself that marriage to Warburton would impede 'the free exploration of life that she had hitherto entertained' (I. p. 137) but her self-doubts are not so easily dismissed. In the moving paragraph at the end of the chapter she thinks of her self as something she hardly dares to look into:

> Poor Isabel found ground to remind herself from time to time that she must not be too proud, and nothing could be more sincere than her prayer to be delivered from such a danger: the isolation and loneliness of pride had for her mind the horror of a desert place. If it had been pride that interfered with her accepting Lord Warburton such a *bêtise* was singularly misplaced; and she was so conscious of liking him that she ventured to assure herself it was the very softness, and the fine intelligence, of sympathy. She liked him too much to marry him, that was the truth; something assured her there was a fallacy somewhere in the glowing logic of the proposition – as *she* saw it – even though she mightn't put her very finest finger-point on it; and to inflict upon a man who offered so much a wife with a tendency to criticise would be a peculiarly discreditable act. She had promised him she would consider his question, and when, after he had left her, she wandered back to the bench where he had found her and lost herself in meditation, it might have seemed that she was keeping her vow. But this was not the case; she was wondering if she were not a cold, hard, priggish person, and, on her at last getting up and going rather quickly back to the house, felt, as she had said to her friend, really frightened at herself. (I, pp. 137–8.)

This is deeper self-examination than we have yet seen from her and James is less evasive in describing it. The problem is that one cannot quite assess the nature of her fear – it is surely not just a fear of being a prig – because its occasion here is rather factitious. She is not in love with Warburton and the fact that James makes her out as feeling almost obliged to be in love with him makes her emotion seem in excess of its cause. One might speculate that what she is considering is the idea of marriage in general, not just marriage to Lord Warburton, and that she is afraid to 'give herself completely', but this would be to be more precise than the prose actually is. James's irony seems to be hinting at how we should analyse Isabel's behaviour yet dissuading us from doing so. Despite the deeper notes that are sounded here, she still emerges from the chapter as the one young woman in twenty capable of turning down an English peer.

Like Warburton, Caspar Goodwood threatens Isabel with a 'diminished liberty' (I, p. 143). She always seems to be struggling to preserve her spiritual virginity from his clutches when they meet. His power over her seems much more a power to frighten than to attract but she can never bring herself to get rid of him for good. It is a pity that James is prevented from exploring this because he secretly thinks Goodwood's devotion to Isabel rather wooden and silly; she is permitted to place her suitor in her usual patronising way:

> . . . 'The strong man in pain' was one of the categories of the human appeal, little charm as he might exert in the given case. 'Why do you make me say such things to you?' she cried in a trembling voice. 'I only want to be gentle – to be thoroughly kind. It's not delightful to me to feel people care for me and yet to have to try and reason them out of it. I think others also ought to be considerate; we have each to judge for ourselves. I know you're considerate, as much as you can be; you've good reasons for what you do. But I really don't want to marry, or to talk about it at all now. I shall probably never do it – no, never. I've a perfect right to feel that way, and it's no kindness to a woman to press her so hard, to urge her against her will. If I give you pain I can only say I'm very sorry. It's not my fault; I can't marry you simply to please you. I won't say that I shall always remain your friend, because when women say that, in these situations, it passes, I believe, for a sort of mockery. But try me some day.' (I, p. 196.)

Behind Isabel's aloof defensiveness there is a good deal of well-intentioned teasing and patronising kindness. Goodwood is not being met on his own level of seriousness, and James, as so often, enjoys frustrating a person with strong desires. The dogged suitor does, however, turn the tables on the independence-loving Isabel for one brief moment:

> 'Who would wish less to curtail your liberty than I? What can give me greater pleasure than to see you perfectly independent – doing whatever you like? It's to make you independent that I want to marry you!' (I, p. 201.)

Isabel disguises her shrinkingness by again proclaiming her wish to choose her own fate (though it is choice she seems really afraid of) and James continues to assist her by doing nothing to make Goodwood seem like a possible husband for her.

Isabel, then, is put in a situation where she seems unable either to accept or refuse love and, not unnaturally, it makes her lose her poise so that her usual wit becomes a gross lack of tact:

> '. . . I don't need the aid of a clever man to teach me how to live.

I can find it out for myself.'

'Find out how to live alone? I wish that, when you have, you'd teach *me*!'

She looked at him a moment; then with a quick smile, 'Oh, *you* ought to marry!' she said.

He might be pardoned if for an instant this exclamation seemed to him to sound the infernal note, and it is not on record that her motive for discharging such a shaft had been of the clearest. He oughtn't to stride about lean and hungry, however, – she certainly felt *that* for him. 'God forgive you!' he murmured between his teeth as he turned away.

Her accent had put her slightly in the wrong, and after a moment she felt the need to right herself. The easiest way to do it was to place him where she had been. 'You do me great in-justice – you say what you don't know!' she broke out. 'I shouldn't be an easy victim – I've proved it.'

'Oh, to me, perfectly.'

'I've proved it to others as well.' And she paused a moment. 'I refused a proposal of marriage last week. . . .' (I, pp. 197–8.)[22]

James knows her well here but he seems not to see how repugnant it is for her to try to retrieve her gaffe by boasting of refusing War-burton. She only feels 'slightly in the wrong'. At the end of the chapter, when she breaks into tears, her tears are a kind of self-escape, tears of vexation rather than tears of remorse; she retreats from their incoherence into delight at her power over men:

She leaned back with that low, soft, aspiring murmur with which she often uttered her response to accidents of which the brighter side was not superficially obvious, and yielded to the satisfaction of having refused two ardent suitors in a fortnight. That love of liberty of which she had given Caspar Goodwood so bold a sketch was as yet almost exclusively theoretic; she had not been able to indulge it on a large scale. But it appeared to her she had done something; she had tasted of the delight, if not of battle, at least of victory; she had done what was truest to her plan. (I, pp. 205–6.)

This is one of the very few satisfactions to which she ever yields. The idea it is part of a 'plan' helps her to disguise from herself that she is living from the nerves, without inner directedness. What we have been asked to value as 'the free exploration of life' is turning out to be spiritually hand-to-mouth.

Ralph admires Isabel's plan because it chimes with his own pursuit of 'appreciation'. What she learns from him is not unlike what she learns from Madame Merle, who represents to her 'a woman of strong impulses kept in admirable order', something she sees as 'an ideal combination'. (I, p. 220.) The value of this comes home to Isabel when she sees Madame Merle's prowess in placing Henrietta so quickly:

> 'That's the great thing', Isabel solemnly pondered; 'that's the supreme good fortune: to be in a better position for appreciating people than they are for appreciating you.' And she added that such, when one considered it, was simply the essence of the aristocratic situation. In this light, if in none other, one should aim at the aristocratic situation. (I, pp. 238–9.)

In this sense of the word, James allows Isabel to be an aristocrat for the rest of the novel. Ralph, of course, does not see what he has in common with Madame Merle, or, indeed, with Osmond, though Madame Merle herself does.[23] He needs to romanticise Isabel's attitude, which is really a fear of being caught out by life, into a desire for life. She tries to make him see that he is mistaken, though to what extent James wants us to take her literally in the following conversation between them remains uncertain:

> 'You want to see life – you'll be hanged if you don't, as the young men say.'
> 'I don't think I want to see it as the young men want to see it. But I do want to look about me.'
> 'You want to drain the cup of experience.'
> 'No, I don't wish to touch the cup of experience. It's a poisoned drink! I only want to see for myself.'
> 'You want to see, but not to feel', Ralph remarked.
> 'I don't think that if one's a sentient being one can make the distinction.' (I, pp. 187–8.)

She may seem more fastidious than innocent in her last reply but she goes on working to undeceive Ralph and tells him not to 'fasten' ideas on her which she does not have. At this point in the novel one can readily say that, in Isabel's character, James has found a mysterious and engaging *donnée* for extensive study. It is a real loss, then, that for so much of the rest of the book he labours to suggest that it is Ralph and not Isabel who has given the truest account of her attitude to life. When she meets Osmond he is unafraid for her because, 'She'll please herself, of course; but she'll do so by studying human nature at close quarters and yet retaining her liberty.' (I, p. 350) Though his idea of her adventurous spirit boils down to much the same thing as her own feeling about experience as a 'poisoned drink' he fails to see that she will marry Osmond precisely because she hopes in doing so to study human nature and still retain her 'liberty'. For Osmond is the quintessential aristocrat who gives nothing away and yet seems to make no claims. It is no noble and innocent mistake that makes her marry him: with her own self-doubt such a trial to her, she clearly needs his consuming self-confidence. The tragedy is that he turns out not to be as aristocratic as she had thought; some of her saddest reflections in chapter 42 are over this disappointment:

> Her notion of the aristocratic life was simply the union of great knowledge with great liberty; the knowledge would give one a sense of duty and the liberty a sense of enjoyment. But for Osmond it was altogether a thing of forms, a conscious, calculated attitude. (II. p. 174.)

Her marriage does not make her question the value or meaning of what she calls 'liberty': she still has the idea off pat.

V

The central problem for the reader of *The Portrait of a Lady* is, then, that it shows Isabel suffering from an inner sickness which is never clearly divulged to our compassion: sometimes we are expected to pity her anxious self-consciousness and, at others, to admire it. James is always clearest when exposing her intellectual fallacies and the novel seems most coherent when read as a critique of transcendentalism. Lionel Trilling has said of Americans that, 'Somewhere in our mental constitution is the demand for life as pure spirit' and it is as an expression of this demand that Isabel's career has its most general meaning.[24]

One of the novel's key passages is the conversation about selfhood which Isabel has with Madame Merle. It is like a debate between Emerson and Balzac, the American and the European sympathies of James's mind that were in such fertile tension in his book on Hawthorne. It begins with Isabel's telling her friend about her 'inevitable young man', Caspar Goodwood:

> 'If you've had the identical young man you dreamed of, then that was success, and I congratulate you with all my heart. Only in that case why didn't you fly with him to his castle in the Apennines?'
> 'He has no castle in the Apennines.'
> 'What has he? An ugly brick house in Fortieth Street? Don't tell me that; I refuse to recognise that as an ideal.'

'I don't care anything about his house', said Isabel.

'That's very crude of you. When you've lived as long as I you'll see that every human being has his shell and that you must take the shell into account. By the shell I mean the whole envelope of circumstances. There's no such thing as an isolated man or woman; we're each of us made up of some cluster of appurtenances. What shall we call our 'self'? Where does it begin? where does it end? It overflows into everything that belongs to us – and then it flows back again. I know a large part of myself is in the clothes I choose to wear. I've a great respect for *things*! One's self – for other people – is one's expression of one's self; and one's house, one's furniture, one's garments, the books one reads, the company one keeps – these things are all expressive.'

This was very metaphysical; not more so, however, than several observations Madame Merle had already made. Isabel was fond of metaphysics, but was unable to accompany her friend into this bold analysis of the human personality. 'I don't agree with you. I think just the other way. I don't know whether I succeed in expressing myself, but I know that nothing else expresses me. Nothing that belongs to me is any measure of me; everything's on the contrary a limit, a barrier, and a perfectly arbitrary one. Certainly the clothes which, as you say, I choose to wear, don't express me; and heaven forbid they should!'

'You dress very well', Madame Merle lightly interposed.

'Possibly; but I don't care to be judged by that. My clothes may express the dressmaker, but they don't express me. To begin with, it's not my own choice that I wear them; they're imposed upon me by society.'

'Should you prefer to go without them?' Madame Merle inquired in a tone which virtually terminated the discussion. (I, pp. 252-3.)

This is one of the most dramatic pieces of comedy in the novel and it is surprising that more in the way of creative thinking is not generated by it. On the surface, Madame Merle has a good case and what seems crude and overweening in Isabel's tone of voice is subtly brought out, without obscuring her sincerity. The older woman's philosophy is socially more civilised and at least makes room for other people; do Isabel's friends in no way express her? But for the passage to work in the novel as a whole we would need to see Isabel coming to revise the position she assumes here and this, I think, is what James does not give us. Her passage from innocence to experience somehow bypasses such questions as whether there is a sense in which Osmond, or her sterile existence in

Rome, can be said to express her self. Another name for the kind of value she attaches to spirit – 'Nothing that belongs to me is any measure of me' – might be *bovarysme*. Despite her more ringing confidence she shares Emma's fear of the way the world beyond the self can intrude upon her selfhood and undermine it. If these implications of the passage are not pursued, but just deposited for us as nagging, unresolved doubts about Isabel's zest for life, it is, I think, because James presents his reader with a choice between untenable extremes rather than a genuine intellectual complexity. Neither Isabel nor Madame Merle describes any real 'continuity' between the self and the world of the kind that Isabel was seeking at the start of the novel. Tony Tanner assumes that the upshot of their exchange is that we feel Isabel's philosophy is superior to Madame Merle's substitution of appearance for inner spirit, but this does not explain why she is shown to be in many ways the sillier of the two.[23] It is safer to read the conversation as brilliantly providing us with a philosophical non-choice, probably because James is not sure which side he would come down on. His comedy is a way of brushing aside his need to find some common ground between the two theories.

James does not often allow anyone to disagree with Isabel as cogently as Madame Merle does, even though he often gives the impression that he considers her ideas fair game for satire. Osmond, for example, is never given an opportunity to put his objections to the way she looks at life; Ralph places everyone except for his cousin. But the comic Henrietta is permitted to give Isabel a few home-truths which carry Madame Merle's criticisms further:

'. . . you think you can lead a romantic life, that you can live by pleasing yourself and pleasing others. You'll find you're mistaken. Whatever life you lead you must put your soul in it – to make any sort of success of it; and from the moment you do that it ceases to be romance, I assure you: it becomes grim reality! And you can't always please yourself; you must sometimes please other people. That, I admit, you're very ready to do; but there's another thing that's still more important – you must often *displease* others. You must always be ready for that – you must never shrink from it. That doesn't suit you at all – you're too fond of admiration, you like to be thought well of. You think we can escape disagreeable duties by taking romantic views – that's your great illusion, my dear. But we can't. You must be prepared on many occasions in life to please no one at all – not even yourself.'

Isabel shook her head sadly; she looked troubled and frightened. 'This, for you, Henrietta', she said, 'must be one of those occasions!' (I, pp. 273–4.)

Isabel can only afford to notice Henrietta's advice-column tone.
James catches beautifully the flippant wit which is her only resource
when she is morally scared. For Henrietta has hit the nail on the
head: Isabel is given to the sort of self-criticism which makes
criticism from others so intolerable that she needs to be kind to
them for her own sake. She has as deep a need of the good opinion
of others as Osmond has. This is why other people, especially
rejected suitors, are such sources of fear for her. Henrietta's words
enable us to see that the self-division created by Isabel's 'curiosity
about life' being coupled with a fear of 'grim reality' may eventually
result in her becoming disillusioned with life. But James does not
want to push Henrietta's thought too far and its force is dissipated
by one of those distasteful comic passages about her *amours* with
Mr Bantling. Only for a moment do we get the kind of drama, so
basic in Molière, in which common sense punctuates sensibility.[26]

Isabel shows herself to know the truth of Henrietta's remarks a
little later in a scene where Ralph is telling her to forget her
'conscience' and 'rise above the ground':

> 'I try to care more about the world than about myself – but I
> always come back to myself. It's because I'm afraid.' She stopped;
> her voice had trembled a little. 'Yes, I'm afraid; I can't tell you.
> A large fortune means freedom, and I'm afraid of that. It's such
> a fine thing and one should make such a good use of it. If one
> shouldn't one would be ashamed. And one must keep thinking;
> it's a constant effort. I'm not sure it's not a greater happiness to
> be powerless.'
> 'For weak people I've no doubt it's a greater happiness. For
> weak people the effort not to be contemptible must be great.'
> 'And how do you know I'm not weak?' Isabel asked.
> 'Ah,' Ralph answered with a flush that the girl noticed, 'if you
> are I'm awfully sold!'
> The charm of the Mediterranean coast only deepened for our
> heroine on acquaintance, for it was the threshold of Italy, the gate
> of admirations. Italy, as yet imperfectly seen and felt, stretched
> before her as a land of promise, a land in which a love of the
> beautiful might be comforted by endless knowledge. (I, pp. 281–2.)

'I'm not sure it's not a greater happiness to be powerless.' The
moral numbness of this confession has a ring of truth. One reads
James for the way such psychological shocks can disturb the urbane,
unruffled surface of his prose and let a real, even if impoverished
and helpless, humanity peep through. Yet how quickly the surface
can become smooth again! The familiar Jamesian unction where
Italy is in question seems to appeal, on Isabel's behalf, for the

Osmond who is a connoisseur of the beautiful. The passage raises a doubt which becomes more insistent in the second half of the novel: will the Italian world in which James now places Isabel's 'remarkable soul' give him sufficient opportunities to continue examining her as he has begun to do?

Isabel's fears are, of course, alluded to in the rest of the novel but they are increasingly kept away from the centre of its meaning instead of becoming the main subject. From her marriage on, James seems unsure what to do with Isabel except to make an 'ado' about her. The turning point can perhaps be located at her most important attack of fear, when Osmond proposes:

> Her agitation – for it had not diminished – was very still, very deep. What had happened was something that for a week past her imagination had been going forward to meet; but here, when it came, she stopped – that sublime principle somehow broke down. The working of this young lady's spirit was strange, and I can only give it to you as I see it, not hoping to make it seem altogether natural. Her imagination, as I say, now hung back; there was a last vague space it couldn't cross – a dusky, uncertain tract which looked ambiguous and even slightly treacherous, like a moorland seen in the winter twilight. But she was to cross it yet. (II, p. 19.)

Is this 'last vague space' in Isabel or in Osmond? The muted sarcasm with which words like 'sublime' and 'strange' caress Isabel suggests that the 'ambiguous and slightly treacherous' moorland could refer to that 'spirit' in her which James cannot hope to make 'altogether natural'. The uncandid candour of 'I can only give it to you as I see it' is one with the deliberate poetic fuzziness of that moorland image: James offers to share our smiling, admiring bemusement while enjoying keeping us guessing. He enjoys keeping Isabel guessing too, for the suspense of 'But she was to cross it yet' clearly turns the sinister moorland into a symbol for the Osmond whom the trusting and undaunted heroine will be taken in by. If this is how the passage should be read, the word 'cross' could refer either to her marrying him (it hints that that will be her next step) or to her 'imagination' finally seeing through him and negotiating the 'winter twilight'. Perhaps is sees these two things as one and the same thing? At any rate, it seems too simple to say that we share an irony at Isabel's expense whilst James enjoys one at our's. This is not a Swiftian irony where only the reader is run aground on the ironist's quicksands. James is too much of a novelist and story-teller to give us the pleasure of knowing that we have been fooled. Under his prevailing tone of romantic sympathy for Isabel, he is canvassing more meanings than he knows what to do with. Should we see both Isabel and Osmond – both her 'imagination' and what it is imagining – as marrying and becoming like each other in his own moorland image and his own 'dusky' prose? Or has he forced us into a position where we have, like him, no real recourse but speculation? It is as if his art consisted in inviting us to imagine something which his own imagination is only half-prepared to divulge. For, as well as being sly, the phrase 'I can only give it to you as I see it' may be confessional.

Having gone out on a limb like this, I ought to propose my own version of what the real 'space' is that Isabel has to cross. It is, I conjecture, that 'fear' which prevents her getting beyond self to a relationship in which she will at last put her cards on the table. For that to happen, Osmond too would have to seek a two-way relationship though, and this is just what he is resolved not to do. He wants to correct Isabel's ideas and force her to adopt his own. Yet this process is what we never really see. In other words, Osmond's main function is to draw the most tantalising of all the veils James draws over his 'portrait', keeping our sympathy for Isabel within the bounds of a plangent and vicarious guesswork, saving James from taking his 'portrait' down from the wall for a closer look. It might be suggested that, in having his Isabel marry an egotist, James robbed her nature of its chance to express itself, just as Flaubert perhaps robbed Emma of that chance when he had her marry a Charles Bovary. Marriage to Warburton or Goodwood (though implausible) might have forced him to consider more deeply what he had implied about his heroine's soul. It would, though, have thrown away her opportunity of becoming a tragedy queen.

7 Isabel's Romance of Tragedy

When Isabel arrives in Italy James intends us to feel that her soul is blossoming in the presence of all the beauty that the country brings her; Italy is to be her deepest link with the world beyond herself and her own private life. How, then, does she respond to it? How substantially does James render it for her to respond to?

Isabel's first visit to Florence is made under the joint tutelage of Ralph and Madame Merle. In the following passage Madame Merle has just been telling her that she should see as many men as possible so that she will be better placed for despising most of them:

'You'll pick out, for your society, the few whom you don't despise.'
This was a note of cynicism that Madame Merle didn't often allow herself to sound; but Isabel was not alarmed, for she had never supposed that as one saw more of the world the sentiment of respect became the most active of one's emotions. It was excited, none the less, by the beautiful city of Florence, which pleased her not less than Madame Merle had promised; and if her unassisted perception had not been able to gauge its charms she had clever companions as priests to the mystery. She was in no want indeed of aesthetic illumination, for Ralph found it a joy that renewed his own early passion to act as cicerone to his eager young kinswoman. Madame Merle remained at home; she had seen the treasures of Florence again and again and had always something else to do. But she talked of all things with remarkable vividness of memory – she recalled the right-hand corner of the large Perugino and the position of the hands of the Saint Elizabeth in the picture next to it. She had her opinions as to the character of many famous works of art, differing often from Ralph with great sharpness and defending her interpretations with as much ingenuity as good-humour. Isabel listened to the discussions taking place between the two with a sense that she might derive much benefit from them and that they were among the advantages she couldn't have enjoyed for instance in Albany. In the clear May mornings before the formal break-fast – this repast at Mrs Touchett's was served at twelve o'clock – she wandered with her cousin through the narrow and sombre

Florentine streets, resting awhile in the thicker dusk of some
historic church or the vaulted chambers of some dispeopled
convent. She went to the galleries and palaces; she looked at the
pictures and statues that had hitherto been great names to her,
and exchanged for a knowledge which was sometimes a limitation
a presentiment which proved usually to have been a blank. She
performed all those acts of mental prostration in which, on a first
visit to Italy, youth and enthusiasm so freely indulge; she felt her
heart beat in the presence of immortal genius and knew the sweetness of rising tears in eyes to which faded fresco and darkened
marble grew dim. But the return, every day, was even pleasanter
than the going forth; the return into the wide, monumental
court of the great house in which Mrs Touchett, many years
before, had established herself, and into the high, cool rooms
where the carven rafters and pompous frescos of the sixteenth
century looked down on the familiar commodities of the age of
advertisement. Mrs Touchett inhabited an historic building in a
narrow street whose very name recalled the strife of medieval
factions; and found compensations for the darkness of her front-
age in the modicity of her rent and the brightness of a garden
where nature itself looked as archaic as the rugged architecture
of the palace and which cleared and scented the rooms in regular
use. To live in such a place was, for Isabel, to hold to her ear all
day a shell of the sea of the past. This vague eternal rumour kept
her imagination awake. (I, pp. 311–12.)

We are rather told than shown how the superior young lady of the
start of this passage comes to go into such raptures. Despite the
fine writing, very little of what Isabel is said to respond to feels
seen. The glow of tremulous emotion – 'the sweetness of rising tears
in eyes to which faded fresco and darkened marble grew dim' and
so on – only makes a sentimental, second-hand kind of experience
grand in a generalised way. This is not because James is describing
a general impression Isabel gets rather than specific responses; he
is all the time gesturing towards some experience he hopes we will
imagine for ourselves – 'all those acts of mental prostration in
which . . . youth and enthusiasm so freely indulge'. An unsurprising,
picture-postcard Florence is the result. The one emotion Isabel has
which rings true and is not an attempt to inflate our admiration
for her sensibility is her feeling of how much good Florence is doing
her – 'the advantages she couldn't have enjoyed . . . in Albany'. She
appears to have just an acquisitive, finishing-school culture in
which art is a backdrop to her emotions, a provider of easy spiritual
thrills. She is an irredeemable tourist and wants only an aroma of
history. Yet James does not appear to see that he has given her only

a cruder version of Osmond's aestheticism as evidence of the 'fund of life' she is supposed to possess. The irrelevance of this experience to the real growth of her soul is shown. I think, by the fact that very little is said about her response to Italy later in the novel. Yet, apart from her relationships with Osmond and Pansy, she is to be given very little else in the way of new experience at all.

In the passage just quoted there are occasional echoes of Ruskin's way of writing about Italy – 'the vaulted chambers of some dis-peopled convent', for example – and it is therefore appropriate to try to understand James's failure to bring Isabel's Italy to life with the help of a passage from *Modern Painters*. Ruskin is trying to illustrate the difference between what he calls the 'higher' and 'lower' picturesque by comparing a windmill drawn by Turner ('higher', of course) with a windmill by Stanfield. The criticisms he has to make of Stanfield's need to poeticise the past provide a a good means of characterising the same kind of 'lower picturesque' in *The Portrait*:

> For, in a certain sense, the lower picturesque ideal is eminently a heartless one; the lover of it seems to go forth into the world in a temper as merciless as its rocks. All other men feel some regret at the sight of disorder and ruin. He alone delights in both; it matters not of what. Fallen cottage – desolate villa – deserted village – blasted heath – mouldering castle – to him, so that they do but show jagged angles of stone and timber, all are sights equally joyful. Poverty, and darkness, and guilt, bring in their several contributions to his treasury of pleasant thoughts. . . .
>
> Yet, for all this, I do not say the lover of the lower picturesque is a monster in human form. He is by no means this, though truly we might at first thing so, if we came across him unawares, and had not met with any such sort of person before. Generally speaking he is kind-hearted, innocent of evil, but not broad in thought; somewhat selfish, and incapable of acute sympathy with others; gifted at the same time with strong artistic instincts . . . he is simple-minded and capable of unostentatious and economical delights, which, if not very helpful to other people, are at all events not utterly injurious, even to the victims or subjects of his picturesque fancies; while to many others his work is entertaining and useful. And, more than all this, even that delight which he *seems* to take in misery is not altogether unvirtuous. Through all his enjoyment there runs a certain undercurrent of tragical passion, – a real vein of human sympathy; – it lies at the root of all those strange morbid hauntings of his; a sad excitement, such as other people feel at a tragedy, only less in degree, just enough, indeed, to give a deeper tone to his pleasure,

and to make him choose for his subject the broken stones of a cottage wall rather than of a roadside bank, the picturesque beauty of form in each being supposed precisely the same; and, together with this slight tragical feeling, there is also a humble and romantic sympathy. . . .[1]

Not much needs to be changed in this to make it serve as a description of the way Isabel thinks of the murkily romantic Italian past and of the way she feels gratified by the burden of suffering that Italian architecture evokes for her. Ruskin's analysis of Stanfield helps one to see that the Florence of her enthusiasm is empty of people and divorced from the nineteenth century in which she and its natives have to live. Florence's picturesque appeal is, in short, the perfect setting for what, in the continuation of his argument Ruskin calls 'the light sensation of luxurious tragedy'.[2] (Incidentally, one of the words James changed most often in his revision of the text of *The Portrait* was the word 'picturesque'.)

James put too great a premium on urbanity in criticism to take Ruskin very seriously. In an essay in *Portraits of Places,* he makes fun of him for turning art into 'a sort of assize-court, in perpetual session' when, he says, it should really be 'the one corner of human life in which we may take our ease'.[3] It is, in fact, a desire to put the reader at 'ease' which accounts for many of the thinnest parts of *The Portrait,* particularly when art is the topic. The lyricism of the following passage may serve as an example of how much more easily James's reader is allowed to feel inward with art than Ruskin's reader ever is. Isabel is taking a rest from the solicitations of Osmond and Warburton (who pursue her alternately) in the sculpture gallery of the Capitol:

. . . in the glorious room, among the shining antique marbles. She sat down in the centre of the circle of these presences, regarding them vaguely, resting her eyes on their beautiful blank faces; listening, as it were, to their eternal silence. It is impossible, in Rome at least, to look long at a great company of Greek sculptures without feeling the effect of their noble quietude, which, as with a high door closed for the ceremony, slowly drops on the spirit the large white mantle of peace. I say in Rome especially, because the Roman air is such an exquisite medium for such impressions. The golden sunshine mingles with them, the deep stillness of the past, so vivid yet, though it is nothing but a void full of names, seems to throw a solemn spell upon them. The blinds were partly closed in the windows of the Capitol, and a clear, warm shadow rested on the figures and made them more mildly human. Isabel sat there a long time, under the charm of their motionless grace, wondering to what, of their experience, their absent eyes were open, and how, to our ears, their alien lips would sound. The dark red walls of the room threw them into relief; the polished marble floor reflected their beauty. (II, p. 7.)

The sculpture is used to decorate Isabel's meditations. The hushed tones of the prose suggest the loftiness of her thoughts without revealing them. The 'solemn spell' is exposed for the aesthetic day-dreaming it really is, not just by the banality of Isabel's fancies about 'absent eyes' and 'alien lips', but by the fact that James quite unironically describes this romantic past as 'nothing but a void full of names'. The 'spell' is, in fact, a bonus for the lover of the 'lower picturesque' – someone, perhaps, who has never visited Rome and wants the feeling of being drawn into its magic circle as if he had been familiar with it for a lifetime. The 'charm' of the description of the statues recalls the kind of film director who likes to lace emotional scenes with a few bars of Mozart or Mahler. Since it is by the illumination which such moments give that Isabel has to be felt as growing in maturity one cannot set the passage aside as an isolated piece of purple prose.

The same hedgingly poetic rhetoric occurs when Isabel's love for Osmond is being described. Again, it gives us only the illusion of entering into her feelings and does little to explain how the young lady who rejected Warburton and Goodwood comes to 'give herself completely':

It was in Italy that they had met, Italy had been a party to their first impressions of each other, and Italy should be a party to their happiness. Osmond had the attachment of old acquaintance and Isabel the stimulus of new, which seemed to assure her a future at a high level of consciousness of the beautiful. The desire for unlimited expansion had been succeeded in her soul by the sense that life was vacant without some private duty that might gather one's energies to a point. She had told Ralph she had 'seen life' in a year or two and that she was already tired, not of the act of living, but of that of observing. What had become of all her ardours, her aspirations, her theories, her high estimate of her independence and her incipient conviction that she should never marry? These things had been absorbed in a more primitive need – a need the answer to which brushed away numberless questions, yet gratified infinite desires. It simplified the situation at a stroke, it came down from above like the light of the stars, and it needed no explanation. There was explanation in the fact that he was her lover, her own, and that she should be able to be of use to him. She could surrender to him with a kind of humility, she could marry him with a kind of pride; she was not only taking, she was giving. (II, pp. 71–2.)

The 'primitive need' itself may need no explanation; what does is how Isabel should have come to feel it. The 'numberless questions' and 'infinite desires' boil down to very little. There is a vestige of former insights in the suggestion that Isabel finds it easier to marry a man with no money when she has a fortune, but this feeling is hardly 'primitive'. What is she really 'taking' and 'giving'? In the first part of the novel James was always making a bigger effort to understand Isabel; here, he is trying to fob us off with a figure of romance.

II

The way Isabel tends to be romanticised as the novel goes on is one indication of the fact that James, in his commitment to point-of-view, finds its increasingly unnecessary to distinguish Isabel's response to her sufferings from the response the reader is meant to have to them. As the irony is drained out of the book, so its objectivity – we saw it in Isabel's conversations with Madame Merle and Henrietta – drains away too.

Isabel thinks of the 'gulf' that opens up between herself and Osmond after their marriage in affectingly black and white terms:

It was a strange opposition, of the like of which she had never dreamed – an opposition in which the vital principle of the one was a thing of contempt to the other. It was not her fault – she had practised no deception, she had only admired and believed. She had taken all the first steps in the purest confidence, and then she had suddenly found the infinite vista of a multiplied life to be a dark, narrow alley with a dead wall at the end. (II, pp. 165–6.)

'It was not her fault . . .' and, we are told, 'she was, after all, herself – she couldn't help that'. (II, p. 167) How different a picture it is from the soul-destroying meals which Emma Bovary takes with Charles (whose own innocence is so essential to the general sadness of their lack of communication). James is seeking an easy pity for an innocent victim who cries pathetically over spilt milk. Isabel may attribute her sorrows to 'the eternal mystery of things' (II, p. 138) but to the reader the mystery is all too contrived. We are only required to participate in half of the drama, Isabel's half. To suggest that the sympathy needed to do this is not of a tragic kind I cannot do better than quote from Karl Jaspers' excellent little book, *Tragedy is not Enough*:

> The spectator partakes only through identification. What might befall him, too, he experiences as if it had befallen him in fact. For he has merged his own identity with that larger self of man which unites him with every one else. I am myself inside the human beings represented in the tragedy. To me the suffering addresses its message: 'This is you'. 'Sympathy' makes man human – sympathy, not in the sense of vague regrets, but as felt personal involvement: hence the atmosphere of humaneness found in great tragedy.[4]

Chapter 42 tries to preclude this 'sympathy' which relates the reader to all the characters. The result is that one feels that Isabel is not face to face with the 'mystery of things' but absorbed in the limited personality of an Osmond whose own inner life is largely a blank.

In James's novels the people credited with unusual capacity for living are never really given the chance to live. His idea of living is expressed through Ralph and not Henrietta, Hyacinth Robinson and not Millicent Henning, Milly Theale and not Kate Croy. It is almost as if what interests him in the desire to live is the way it can be frustrated. One way in which Isabel is made out to feel this desire is that the other characters are all habitually frustrated: Warburton, Goodwood, Ralph, Rosier, Pansy, Madame Merle and Osmond too. Frustration is the main ingredient of the 'ado' of the end of the novel and it is used with strange repetitiveness. This is the context in which one has to place Isabel's attempts to live after Osmond proposes to her. At first James works by omissions. Her courtship, her decision to marry, the early months of marriage – all these things are left out and saved for later, when Isabel can think of them in ways that suit James. At one point, Madame Merle divulges that Isabel 'had a poor little boy, who died two years ago, six months after his birth'. (II, p. 84.) It is unclear if he is an emblem of the marriage's sterility or just a gratuitous note of morbidity. He is never mentioned again, though the death of a son in a tense and otherwise childless marriage, particularly when the husband is middle-aged, might normally be thought of as a watershed in the relationship.[5] All we learn though, again from Madame Merle, is that Isabel and Osmond 'think quite differently'. (II, p. 82.) James has a strong desire to help Isabel construct a haughty and diffident façade round the feelings she has for Osmond. It might be said that such omissions are in the interest of formal economy, but what kind of form is it that requires, in the study of a marriage, the omission of love, marriage, childbirth, parenthood and death? In the few sentences in which Isabel's travels with Madame Merle before her marriage are described she is said to be like 'a thirsty person draining cup after cup' – does she finally taste the 'cup of experience'?

The conversation in which Ralph tries to persuade Isabel not to marry Osmond is one of the most revealing in the whole novel:

'You were the last person I expected to see caught.'
'I don't know why you call it caught.'
'Because you're going to be put in a cage.'
'If I like my cage, that needn't trouble you', she answered.
'That's what I wonder at. That's what I've been thinking of.'
'If you've been thinking you may imagine how I've thought! I'm satisfied that I'm doing well.'
'You must have changed immensely. A year ago you valued your liberty beyond everything. You wanted only to see life.'
'I've seen it', said Isabel. 'It doesn't look to me now, I admit, such an inviting expanse.' (II, pp. 56–7.)

One wonders where she has seen 'life' since she went off to the Middle East; there is no real suggestion that it is Osmond himself who has changed her way of thinking, since it is precisely her 'ideas' that he never does change. Her attitude does, however, have a clear affinity with what she takes to be Osmond's own view of things:

'He's not important – no, he's not important; he's a man to whom importance is supremely indifferent. If that's what you mean when you call him 'small', then he's as small as you please. I call that large – it's the largest thing I know.' (II, p. 63.)

Ralph, who has been Isabel's tutor in the 'aristocratic situation', should not be as surprised as he is by this. Even in chapter 42, when James wants her to seem most unlike her husband, the similarity of her ideas and his still comes out:

. . . there was more in the bond than she had meant to put her name to. It implied a sovereign contempt for everyone but some three or four exalted people whom he envied, and for everything in the world but half a dozen ideas of his own. That was very well; she would have gone with him even there a long distance; for he pointed out to her so much of the baseness and shabbiness of life, opened her eyes so wide to the stupidity, the depravity, the ignorance of mankind, that she had been properly impressed with the infinite vulgarity of things and of the virtue of keeping one's self unspotted by it. (II, pp. 172–3.)

Why was the ideal Isabel of James's fancy prepared to go so far with him? The most plausible explanation is that this 'virtue of keeping one's self unspotted' is really just another name for what, in the first half of the novel, was diagnosed as 'fear'.

The reason that Isabel fails to get on with Osmond is that he is not Osmond-like enough, not true to his own ideas:

> But this base, ignoble world, it appeared, was after all what one was to live for; one was to keep it for ever in one's eye, in order not to enlighten or convert or redeem it, but to extract from it some recognition of one's own superiority. On the one hand it was despicable, but on the other it afforded a standard. Osmond had talked to Isabel about his renunciation, his indifference, the ease with which he dispensed with the usual aids to success; and all this had seemed to her admirable. She had thought it a grand indifference, an exquisite independence. But indifference was really the last of his qualities; she had never seen anyone who thought so much of others. For herself, avowedly, the world had always interested her and the study of her fellow creatures had been her constant passion. She would have been willing, however, to renounce all her curiosities and sympathies for the sake of a personal life, if the person concerned had only been able to make her believe it was a gain. (II, p. 173.)

Who is it, in this novel, whose 'superiority' gets recognised by others and who deeply needs it to be? Osmond seems to have stolen all the colours from Isabel's palette, all the catch-words from her box of tricks. Her ideal life seems alarmingly close to the complete indifference he can only fake. It is on the recoil from this perception that one wishes for a more inward picture of his feelings as well as Isabel's. If he is as vile as James makes out, it becomes increasingly difficult to admire Isabel as much as we are asked to.

Isabel goes a long way to meeting the demands Osmond makes of her in the Pansy/Warburton affair, so that he will have no grounds for complaint against her. She needs his approval that she is in the right even when it is his right she is in and she suspects it of being wrong:

> Covert observation had become a habit with her; an instinct of which it is not an exaggeration to say that it was allied to that of self-defence, had made it habitual. She wished as much as possible to know his thoughts, to know what he would say, beforehand, so that she might prepare her answer. (II, p. 157.)

Osmond becomes a kind of parody of her conscience and self-doubt.

What is hardest for her to bear is not the death of love, nor even that she has been cheated of her chance to look down on life 'with a sense of exaltation and advantage, and judge and choose and pity' (II, p. 167) – it is his hatred, the withdrawal of approval which mockingly echoes her own deep dissatisfaction with her self. This is why she can afford none of her sympathy for him. James's own main interest in Osmond is in the effect he has on Isabel: his hostility to her is best understood as a kind of extension of her own addiction to moods of self-criticism. Osmond's malignancy, as far as his own character goes, is largely unexplained and, though Isabel thinks him neither 'violent' not 'cruel' (II, p. 167), he has to be imagined as a sadist for us to see why it should be assumed that he wishes to prolong the marriage.[6] As Yvor Winters saw, 'the species of terror which Isabel comes to feel in regard to him is absolutely unexplained by any of his actions or by any characteristic described'.[7] The undoubted pathos of chapter 42 seems another way of avoiding a real analysis of Isabel's fear. We are denied the kind of understanding of her which would evoke compassion and given a disingenuous pity instead.

III

James's method for arresting his own growing insight into Isabel is to impose on the novel a special kind of formal coherence. Despite the rather fulsome compliments he himself paid to *The Portrait's* 'architecture', it is, I think, precisely that quality in the novel which most makes one feel short-changed at the end.

There is almost as much suspense in James as in Dickens (both *The Wings of the Dove* and *The Ambassadors* have plots which hinge on it) but it is a different kind of suspense. Dickensian coincidence may often be crude but, at its best, in the later novels, it appears, not as a manipulation of the reader's emotions, but as a way which the whole novel has of pointing towards something mysterious and surprising in experience, a kind of meaning in disorder which is yet neither providence nor destiny. The co-incidences of *Great Expectations* are the means by which the chance events and momentary impulses of Pip's life are fused together into the incalculable unity of a human character and a human life. In *The Portrait* coincidence refers us less to life than to the skilful way in which the author has organised his fiction. This makes such things as the connection between Osmond, Madame Merle and Pansy seem schematic rather than mysterious. On a second reading there is nothing left to be pondered. Osmond, especially, is so theatrically presented that he is never again as convincing as on a first reading. The description of his villa, in chapter 22, is intended as an emblem for him more than as a place in itself, as it would be in Dickens. It figures as a kind of allegorical notation in James's gradual revealing of a known quantity. Osmond must remain fixed so that the reader can be put in the know, and this means that symmetry is more important than growth in the way he is perceived. This may, perhaps, be an apt way of representing a world which the heroine at first takes only at face value and fathoms out much later, but it still means that the reader must settle for the thin satisfaction of seeing an unfathomable world turning into one that is all too *known*. Suspense places us in the position of predicting the consequences of Isabel's actions before she can do so herself. It is the irony of the 'aristocratic situation': 'to be in a better position for appreciating people than they are for appreciating you'.

James's manipulation of Osmond and Madame Merle can be easily pointed out. They talk, in chapter 49, as if they themselves were unaware of what their real relationship is! The following exchange comes before we learn that Pansy is Madame Merle's daughter:

> 'It appears that I'm to be severely taught the disadvantages of a false position.'
> 'You express yourself like a sentence in a copy-book. We must look for our comfort where we can find it. If my wife doesn't like me, at least my child does. I shall look for compensations in Pansy. Fortunately I haven't a fault to find with her.'
> 'Ah', she said softly, 'if I had a child . . . !'
> Osmond waited, and then, with a little formal air, 'The children of others may be a great interest!' he announced.
> 'You're more like a copy-book than I. There's something after all that holds us together.'
> 'Is it the idea of the harm I may do you?' Osmond asked.
> 'No; it's the idea of the good I may do for you.' (II, p. 296.)

This teasing of the reader imputes to him the kind of curiosity and need for knowledge that James so often gives to his characters. In happily drawing a veil over Madame Merle's wrecked life – form admitting no irrelevant largesse of sympathy – James is reducing evil and remorse to the status of links in his fictional chain.[8] This is why Osmond never gives us any real sense of the hard fact of an evil nature. Though he has all the mannerisms of evil-ness, he stays functional. L. P. Hartley has an intelligent passage on this aspect of James's art in his Clark lectures on Hawthorne:

But though Henry James was so sensitive to evil that even in the

case of his minor characters he keeps a sort of chart of their
moral temperatures, evil is only one aspect of his multiple awareness. He uses it mainly for aesthetic purposes, to enrich the
texture of his books, to induce suspense, to make us take sides
with this character against that, to engage our feelings ever more
deeply with the plot he is unfolding. He seldom makes it the
dominant characteristic of any of his personages, he socialised it,
and only once does he show it, as it were, in isolation. The nearest he gets to doing this is in *The Turn of the Screw*. . . .
    But with Hawthorne evil was always a thing in itself. . . .'

If these remarks describe the impression Osmond makes, as I think
they do, they can help us to see just how limited James makes the
experience of life with which Isabel has to cope.
    The plotting which keeps Osmond and Madame Merle in care-
fully subordinate rôles can be seen in the rest of the second volume
of the novel. Chapter 43 comes at a crucial point but it is devoted
to Warburton's odd attentions to Pansy Osmond and the latter's
love for Rosier, not to Isabel herself. Warburton and Pansy are,
in this, both *ficelles* – characters of a limitedly interesting humanity.
They supply the place of any more intimate source of conflict
between Isabel and her husband. To do so, Warburton has to
change from an upstanding Briton to a man cultivating an immature and affected interest in unnaturally young girls. This is not
because James has much interest in his feelings but because he
wants him to go on being frustratedly in love with his heroine.
Warburton becomes a kind of devoted spaniel tagging on to its
mistress. At one point Isabel hopes that 'British politics had cured
him' (II, p. 114)! It is hard to say whether Pansy's story is touching
or precious because one cannot take Rosier, her suitor, very seriously.
Pansy becomes so prominent to provide the evidence of Osmond's
malignity which has not been supplied from his relations with
Isabel. Her fabricated misfortunes have serious consequences though,
for part of the reason for Isabel's return to Rome at the end
of the novel is that she has promised Pansy that she will return.
The forlorn Pansy seems more like a pretext than a sufficient motive
for the most important decision Isabel makes in the entire book.
    The most revealing plotting in the last parts of the novel is the
way the successive re-appearances of Warburton and Goodwood are
contrived as a build-up to Isabel's reconciliation with Ralph on his
death-bed. What is the justification for James's bringing them back
for an encore of 'the strong man in pain' scenes of the earlier
chapters? It is, surely, that they help to fill Isabel's Roman life up
and provide matter for her otherwise blank 'Thursdays', when she
receives those members of Roman society to whom Osmond is

prepared to condescend. James is thereby saved from having to indicate that there was any fresh life in Rome for Isabel after her marriage. In this way, the 'narrow alley' of her life becomes a more plausible dead-end for a young woman in her twenties. The onus for her failure to 'see life is put elsewhere: there is no new life for her to see. This strategy telescopes the novel to its conclusion with a polished symmetry:

> It seemed to Isabel that she had been very clever; she had artfully disposed of the superfluous Caspar. She had given him an occupation; she had converted him into a caretaker of Ralph. She had a plan of making him travel northward with her cousin as soon as the first mild weather should allow it. Lord Warburton had brought Ralph to Rome and Mr Goodwood should take him away. There seemed a happy symmetry in this, and she was now intensely eager that Ralph should depart. (II, pp. 259–60.)

All the loose ends are tied up and forgotten and the scene is set for the emotional diapason of her visit to the dying Ralph who, of course, dies at just the right time and in just the right place:

> She had a constant fear that he would die there before her eyes and a horror of the occurrence of this event at an inn, by her door, which he had so rarely entered. Ralph must sink to his last rest in his own dear house, in one of those deep, dim chambers of Gardencourt where the dark ivy would cluster round the edges of the glimmering windows. (II, p. 260.)

After several chapters of James's (and Isabel's) shrewd 'architecture', the novel can give way to its strain of sub-Tennysonian sentiment.

IV

When Isabel returns to Gardencourt, having vainly sought for an image of her self by which she might live, it is as if she still wishes to protect some pure selfhood which she has never managed to find. She seeks the sanctuary of the peaceful scene which saw her first entry into the world, as if she too, like Ralph, were facing not life but death:

> I have mentioned how passionately she needed to feel that her unhappiness should not have come to her through her own fault. She had no near prospect of dying, and yet she wished to make her peace with the world – to put her spiritual affairs in order. (II, p. 247.)

Death seems idyllic, as 'liberty' had done before, and James suggests that it is a desire for death which Isabel's desire to live has finally led her to:

> Nothing seemed of use to her today. All purpose, all intention was suspended; all desire too save the single desire to reach her much-embracing refuge. Gardencourt had been her starting-point, and to those muffled chambers it was at least a temporary solution to return. She had gone forth in her strength; she would come back in her weakness, and if the place had been a rest to her before, it would be a sanctuary now. She envied Ralph his dying, for if one were thinking of rest that was the most perfect of all. To cease utterly, to give it all up and not know anything more – this idea was as sweet as the vision of a cool bath in a marble tank, in a darkened chamber, in a hot land. (II, p. 342.)

This is moving as well as mannered; Isabel's feelings seem real and sensuous, less abstract than her feelings on her first visit to Gardencourt. The thought of 'dying' offers her a wistful dream of luxurious stoicism as solace for her sufferings. She experiences a gentle desire to slough off her anxious need to 'know'. If the sadness of the prose does not release any general, tragic thought for the reader this is, perhaps, because death is imagined only as the haven from unhappiness that Isabel herself feels it would be. Its mystery seems subordinated to her mood. Both heroine and author seem to seek shelter in an easeful, rather cloying lyricism.[10]

This lyricism ushers in one of the most intense passages of the latter half of the novel, one of the few to set beside the best things in the earlier chapters:

> She had moments indeed in her journey from Rome which were almost as good as being dead. She sat in her corner, so motionless, so passive, simply with the sense of being carried, so detached from hope and regret, that she recalled to herself one of those Etruscan figures couched upon the receptacle of their ashes. There was nothing to regret now – that was all over. Not only the time of her folly, but the time of her repentance was far. The only thing to regret was that Madame Merle had been so – well, so unimaginable. Just here her intelligence dropped, from literal inability to say what it was that Madame Merle had been. Whatever it was it was for Madame Merle herself to regret it; and doubtless she would do so in America, where she had announced she was going. It concerned Isabel no more; she had only had an impression that she should never again see Madame Merle. This impression carried her into the future, of which from time to

time she had a mutilated glimpse. She saw herself, in the distant years, still in the attitude of a woman who had her life to live, and these intimations contradicted the spirit of the present hour. It might be desirable to get quite away, really away, further away than little grey-green England, but this privilege was evidently to be denied her. Deep in her soul – deeper than any appetite for renunciation – was the sense that life would be her business for a long time to come. And at moments there was something inspiring, almost enlivening, in the conviction. It was a proof of strength – it was a proof she should some day be happy again. It couldn't be she was to live only to suffer; she was still young, after all, and a great many things might happen to her yet. To live only to suffer – only to feel the injury of life repeated and enlarged – it seemed to her that she was too valuable, too capable, for that. Then she wondered if it were vain and stupid to think so well of herself. When had it ever been a guarantee to be valuable? Wasn't all history full of the destruction of precious things? Wasn't it much more probable that if one were fine one would suffer? It involved then perhaps an admission that one had a certain grossness; but Isabel recognised, as it passed before her eyes, the quick vague shadow of a long future. She should never escape; she should last to the end. Then the middle years wrapped her about again and the grey curtain of her indifference closed her in. (II, pp. 342-3.)

Ruskin's phrase about the 'light sensation of luxurious tragedy' comes back to mind. Isabel is not so much confronted by reality as by her own fancies about the future. She is conspiring at her own fate and, to do this, James allows her a period of respite from it in which misery can be made self-conscious. Her imagination is itself courting the most tragic eventualities, possibly because she sees suffering as a means of retrieving her sense of spiritual distinction. She likes to dwell on the bleakness of her future life, so when we are told that her will to live is 'deeper than any appetite for renunciation' we surmise that an 'appetite for renunciation' is precisely what her will to live amounts to. The 'grey curtain of her indifference' (to what?) is all that James feels it necessary to posit about the nature of the 'life' to which she feels herself so bound. He has found Isabel a way of being an Etruscan figure at her own grave without her actually dying.

The inescapable quotation at this point is from Ralph's death-bed scene with Isabel, which, to make her 'suffering' real, ought to have been one of the central moments of the novel. It shows both of them at last happy in 'the knowledge that they were looking at the truth together' (II, p. 362):

'I don't want to think – I needn't think. I don't care for anything but you, and that's enough for the present. It will last a little yet. Here on my knees, with you dying in my arms, I'm happier than I have been for a long time. And I want you to be happy – not to think of anything sad; only to feel that I'm near you and I love you. Why should there be pain? In such hours as this what have we to do with pain? That's not the deepest thing; there's something deeper.'

Ralph evidently found from moment to moment greater difficulty in speaking; he had to wait longer to collect himself. At first he appeared to make no response to these last words; he let a long time elapse. Then he murmured simply: 'You must stay here.'

'I should like to stay – as long as seems right.'

'As seems right – as seems right?' he repeated her words. 'Yes, you think a great deal about that.'

'Of course one must. You're very tired', said Isabel.

'I'm very tired. You said just now that pain's not the deepest thing. No – no. But it's very deep. If I could stay – .'

'For me you'll always be here', she softly interrupted. It was easy to interrupt him.

But he went on, after a moment: 'It passes, after all; it's passing now. But love remains. I don't know why we should suffer so much. Perhaps I shall find out. There are many things in life. You're very young.'

'I feel very old', said Isabel.

'You'll grow young again. That's how I see you. I don't believe – ' But he stopped again; his strength failed him.

She begged him to be quiet now. 'We needn't speak to understand each other', she said.

'I don't believe that such a generous mistake as yours can hurt you for more than a little.'

'Oh, Ralph, I'm very happy now', she cried through her tears.

'And remember this', he continued, 'that if you've been hated you've also been loved. Ah but, Isabel – *adored*!' he just audibly and lingeringly breathed.

'Oh my brother!' she cried with a movement of still deeper protestation. (II, pp. 363–4.)

The large-sounding 'pain' and 'love' that swell this maudlin anaesthetising of Ralph's death have no vital relation to the novel's deepest concerns. The emotion operates at a level which leaves the reader relatively untouched by what is described. James is giving us an 'aesthetic tragedy', one in which we partake only as spectators. I take this term from another passage of Karl Jaspers':

It is essential that I not only watch and derive 'aesthetic' edifica-
tion from the tragedy, but also participate in it with my innermost self and act out its insight because of its direct importance
to me. The whole content is lost if I think myself safe, or if I
look upon the tragic as something alien to myself, or as something
that might have involved me but that I have now escaped for
good. I would then be looking at the world from the safety of
a harbor, as if I were no longer risking body and soul on its
troubled seas in search of my destiny. I would see the world in
terms of grandiose and tragic interpretations: the world is so
made that everything great in it is doomed to perish, and it is
so made for the delight of the unconcerned spectator. . . . As a
spectator I share the sensations, I derive self-satisfaction from the
presumed nobility of my emotions, I take sides, pass judgement,
allow myself to be shocked – and in reality I stay at a safe
distance.[11]

This, I believe, is what Isabel does and what the kind of pity James
curries on her behalf asks us to do.

Isabel's suffering comes more from inside her self than from any
clash between the impulses of her own soul with the conditions of
existence itself. We are moved by it, no doubt, in proportion to
how far James's interpretation of her soul strikes us as believable.
Osmond comes to seem almost accidental to her tragedy and no more
reflects anything universal for James than he is felt to share any
common condition with his wife. *The Portrait* spotlights an individual tragedy so brightly that all other suffering in the book
comes to seem like a back-drop to it. In this way, Isabel is felt as
almost beyond mere accident, guaranteed a leisure to contemplate
her sufferings which confirms their special, private nature. I can
perhaps put this more clearly by quoting a passage of Montaigne. It
is from his essay 'De la Tristesse' and he is writing about the feeling of Niobe on the death of her sons:

. . . cette morne, muette et sourde stupidité qui nous transit, lors
que les accidens nous accablent surpassans nostre portée.
  De Vray, l'effort d'un desplaisir, pour estre extreme, doit
estonner toute l'ame, et lui empescher la liberté de ses actions:
comme il nous advient à la chaude alarme d'un bien mauvaise
nouvelle, de nous sentir saisis, transis, et comme perclus de tous
mouvemens, de façon que l'ame se relaschant après aux larmes
et aux plaintes, semble se desprendre, se demesler et se mettre
plus au large, et à son aise,
      Et via vix tandem voci laxata dolore est.[12]

(. . . that bleak, mute and blank stupidity which pierces us through when we are overwhelmed by disasters beyond our capacity for endurance.

In truth, when the impact of affliction is really extreme it will utterly dumbfound the soul and curb its freedom of action, and when we experience that stinging alarm on hearing really bad news, we feel gripped, pierced and, as it were, stiff-jointed in all our movements, so that, as our soul is afterwards released in tears and lamentations, it seems to extricate and free itself, to open itself up, until, expressing itself freely,

At last sorrow gave passage to his voice.)

Isabel is not pierced through by the world in this way and knows neither the numbness nor the release of which Montaigne speaks: James turns the pain of existence into a tragical décor in which she can lament more picturesquely. Just after she realises that Madame Merle has married her, she goes off to be alone in a Rome whose history reminds her of the sufferings of the past:

> She had long before this taken old Rome into her confidence, for in a world of ruins the ruin of her happiness seemed a less un-natural catastrophe. She rested her weariness upon things that had crumbled for centuries and yet still were upright; she dropped her secret sadness into the silence of lonely places, where its very modern quality detached itself and grew objective, so that as she sat in a sun-warmed angle on a winter's day, or stood in a mouldy church to which no one came, she could almost smile at it and think of its smallness. Small it was, in the large Roman record, and her haunting sense of the continuity of the human lot easily carried her from the less to the greater. She had become deeply, tenderly acquainted with Rome; it interfused and moder-ated her passion. But she had grown to think of it chiefly as the place where people had suffered. This was what came to her in the starved churches, where the marble columns, transferred from pagan ruins, seemed to offer her a companionship in en-durance and the musty incense to be a compound of long-unanswered prayers. There was no gentler nor less consistent heretic than Isabel; the firmest of worshippers, gazing at dark altar-pictures or clustered candles, could not have felt more in-timately the suggestiveness of these objects nor have been more liable at such moments to a spiritual visitation. (II, pp. 286–7.)[13]

This seductively melancholy picture adapts the outside world to Isabel's mood: art, history and religion all assist her need for 'a spiritual visitation'. There could be no more typical example of Ruskin's 'lover of the lower picturesque'.

V

If Isabel's suffering seems not to join up with any larger suffering in the world of *The Portrait* this is, perhaps, because she inhabits no larger human world than the picturesque one of Rome. What the thinly poetical quality of much of the writing about Italy reveals is the difficulty James has in conceiving any actual community for her to live in. He never really sees that civilisation is also community, that it is in this sense that it might have figured as essential to the 'life' Isabel sets off to discover. He is too intent on thinking of her expatriation as a liberation of the free spirit from its social conditions. R. P. Blackmur, in an essay on American literary expatriates, once remarked that, 'Because of the loss of the cultural establishment we have put a tremendous burden on the pure individual consciousness'.[14] The poverty of experience of Isabel and her circle is first seen when the question of Lord Warburton's politics comes up. To Isabel (and James) Warburton is a 'magnate' who represents a class without ever seeming a member of a community. No English novelist between Jane Austen and Lawrence would have seen him in this way. His house at Lockleigh, like Gardencourt, seems to exist in an idyllic social limbo. His main interest for James is that his radical politics make him a kind of expatriate from his own class and it is from the unattached Ralph that we gather how we are meant to view them: with kindly amusement. He is just 'a man with a great position who's playing all sorts of tricks with it'. (I, p. 86.) Ralph admires his status rather as Osmond admires the Pope's: 'For me, in his place, I could be as solemn as a statue of Buddha.' (I, p. 87.) Later Warburton drifts in and out of the novel as an illustrious statesman who is the *bête noire* of *The Times* but it is even harder to imagine him involved in foreign policy than in Pansy Osmond. To Isabel, he is almost too picturesque to be human, a figure in her aesthetic view of society. The only person who takes his position seriously is Henrietta. Isabel, who laughs at Henrietta, is really only interested in places which are 'full of life' (I, p. 30) and not in places where things are happening.

This blank spot in the novel is more important than is often realised. For Isabel, pure individual though she is, is yet deeply preoccupied with the way society thinks of her. Her decision to return to Osmond at the end is presented as a cleaving to her sense of social responsibilities. Given the vagueness of the society in which she lives, her decision inevitably seems contrived:

> It seemed to her that only now she fully measured the great undertaking of matrimony. Marriage meant that in such a case as this, when one had to choose, one chose as a matter of course

for one's husband. . . . What he thought of her she knew, what
he was capable of saying to her she had felt; yet they were
married, for all that, and marriage meant that a woman should
cleave to the man with whom, uttering tremendous vows, she
had stood at the altar. (II, pp. 315–6.)

The sudden announcement of the sanctity of marriage comes as a
surprise, until we realise that James is simply draping Isabel in a
ready-to-wear convention that allows him to explore her fear and
her pride while giving them a noble appearance. It may be that
Isabel is so adamant here because she has so little real sense of
community that, like her husband, she clings all the more to its
forms:

'One must accept one's deeds. I married him before all the world;
I was perfectly free; it was impossible to do anything more
deliberate. One can't change that way', Isabel repeated.
    'You *have* changed, in spite of the impossibility. I hope you
don't mean to say you like him.'
    Isabel debated. 'No, I don't like him. I can tell you, because
I'm weary of my secret. But that's enough; I can't announce it
on the housetops.'
    Henrietta gave a laugh. 'Don't you think you're rather too
considerate?'
    'It's not of him that I'm considerate – it's of myself!' Isabel
answered. (II, p. 250.)

Osmond himself could not have regarded 'convention' with more
awe and respect.
    It is telling that the last scene of the novel should show Isabel
virtually playing Osmond to Caspar Goodwood's Isabel. She refuses
to accompany Caspar to the 'high places of happiness'. He comes
upon her as she is sitting in the garden at Gardencourt (on the very
bench where Warburton had proposed!). He is appalled at the
idea of her returning to Rome, thinking it a renunciation of life,
and has come to urge her not to go on playing a part. He offers
her the dream Osmond failed to bring true and a love more intense
than any she has yet known.

'You must save what you can of your life; you mustn't lose it all
simply because you've lost a part. It would be an insult to you
to assume that you care for the look of the thing, for what people
will say, for the bottomless idiocy of the world. We've nothing
to do with all that; we're quite out of it; we look at things as they
are. You took the great step in coming away; the next is nothing;

it's the natural one. I swear, as I stand here, that a woman deliberately made to suffer is justified in anything in life – in going down into the streets if that will help her! I know how you suffer, and that's why I'm here. We can do absolutely as we please; to whom under the sun do we owe anything? What is it that holds us, what is it that has the smallest right to interfere in such a question as this? Such a question is between ourselves – and to say that is to settle it! Were we born to rot in our misery – were we born to be afraid? I never knew *you* afraid! If you'll only trust me, how little you will be disappointed! The world's all before us – and the world's very big. I know something about that.'

Isabel gave a long murmur, like a creature in pain; it was as if he were pressing something that hurt her. 'The world's very small', she said at random; she had an immense desire to appear to resist. She said it at random, to hear herself say something; but it was not what she meant. The world, in truth, had never seemed so large; it seemed to open out, all round her, to take the form of a mighty sea, where she floated in fathomless waters. She had wanted help, and here was help; it had come in a rushing torrent. I know not whether she believed everything he said; *but she believed just then that to let him take her in his arms would be the next best thing to her dying.* This belief, for a moment, was a kind of rapture, in which she felt herself sink and sink. In the movement she seemed to beat with her feet in order to catch herself, to feel something to rest on. (II, pp. 379–80. My italics.)

When they kiss she feels as if she is drowning, for sex, it seems, is like death to her, an abdication of consciousness. It is this which impresses her in Caspar's appeal and it attracts her far more deeply than does his exhortation to be true to her free spirit. We now see how truthful she was when she told Ralph, before her marriage, that 'the world' no longer seemed to her 'an inviting expanse', how consistent she is after Caspar's kiss in seeing a 'very straight path' (II, p. 381) back to Gilbert Osmond.

Some readers may feel that James succeeds in conveying his final understanding of Isabel through the deep-seated symbolic images which well up into her mind in this last, remarkable passage. Certainly they have the power to radiate back through the novel and they go deeper than his more theoretical versions of her soul. Yet, even so, this scene is partly just a dramatic exorcism of instincts in Isabel which have never been truly sounded. We turn back on the brink of discovering more about her towards the contrived moral dilemma of why she should choose to go back to Rome. James finds safety in making us speculate. The scene, despite its force, is deeply factitious. There is nothing in Caspar to make him seem a possible partner for Isabel. Most of what he says he has no right to say; we were long ago convinced once and for all that she had no wish to marry him. Perhaps what the scene really does is to divert us from considering the much more credible alternative of her leaving Osmond and remaining single? When Caspar comes in from the wings at the end he does so to throw another veil over James's 'portrait'. The novel is not the less fascinating because of this, nor because a coherent interpretation of it seems impossible.

The final impression left by *The Portrait of a Lady* is that a certain intellectual duplicity is necessary to James if he is to bring his most personal feelings into the sphere of art, an impression of half-articulated depths which he is as bent on concealing as confronting. It is not an art which shows us a deep imaginative intelligence face to face with its true subject. In a way, *The Portrait* is constantly trying to elucidate its own true subject without ever quite doing so. William James had a keen sense of the pathos of this when he conjectured that his brother 'had taken an oath not to let himself out to more than half his humanhood in order to keep the other half from suffering'.[15] It is, above all, because of this holding back from the self that James's portrait of Isabel never quite achieves true generality or detachment. This holding back was, I believe, the real spring of James's concern for the 'architecture' of his novels. A fear of the subject, of the unknown, undetermined suggestions of the blank sheet of paper, resulted in a need to dominate that subject by defining it.

Once, late in his life, Morton Fullerton asked James what had been his '*point de départ*' and he replied, acknowledging some disjunction between the form of his works and their real meaning, in the following terms:

> The port from which I set out was, I think, from that of the essential *loneliness of my life* – and it seems to be the port also, in sooth, to which my course again finally directs itself! This loneliness (since I mention it!) what is it still but the deepest thing about one? Deeper about me, at any rate, than anything else; deeper than my 'genius', deeper than my 'discipline', deeper than my pride, deeper, above all, than the deep counterminings of art.[16]

There is an honesty and dignity in these words which dissuade one from seeing *The Portrait* as the work that its own preface makes it out to be. Both for the author and his heroine it is a genuine, groping exploration of the nature of selfhood. This would have been beyond the James whom André Gide dismissed as a mere

'maître-cuisinier' among novelists.[17] The 'form' of his novels always
does recede, if only briefly, so that we can hear through the darkness
the sound of a human voice speaking from a dim, twilight world
which it has resolved never to leave.

8 Some Afterthoughts

I

The flourish with which the last chapter concluded was, of course, too condescending to James. In criticism, the only conclusions that are useful are those – like the ending of *Rasselas* – in which 'nothing is concluded'. Pound once said that the critic 'must spend some of his time asking questions – which perhaps no-one can answer. It is much more his business to "stir up curiosity" than to insist on acceptances'.[1] Perhaps this book has tried too much for 'acceptances'? In this last chapter, I want to consider a question to which I can offer no definite 'answer': 'What are the qualities in James's art in which he goes beyond what Flaubert's art could have taught him?'

James himself addressed this question most directly in what he had to say about *L'Education Sentimentale*. His main complaint is against the book's hero, Frédéric Moreau:

> We meet Frédéric first, we remain with him long, as a *moyen*, a provincial bourgeois of the mid-century, educated and not without fortune, thereby with freedom, in whom the life of his day reflects itself. Yet the life of his day, on Frédéric's showing, hangs together with the poverty of Frédéric's own inward or for that matter outward life; so that, the whole thing being, for scale, intention and extension, a sort of epic of the usual (with the Revolution of 1848 introduced as an episode), it affects us as an epic without air, without wings to lift it; reminds us in fact more than anything else of a huge balloon, all of silk pieces strongly sewn together and patiently blown up, but that absolutely refuses to leave the ground. . . . Frédéric enjoys his position not only without the aid of a single 'sympathetic' character of consequence, but even without the aid of one with whom we can directly communicate. Can we communicate with the central personage? or would we really if we could? A hundred times no, and if he himself can communicate with the people shown us as surrounding him this only proves him of their kind.[2]

It will be simplest to begin from my reservations about this and then work towards what seems just in its description of the novel as an 'epic without air'.

Why does James resist the novel's satire? Flaubert clearly means to berate the spiritual 'poverty' of the age and, in another sense of the phrase, this is because Frédéric himself is 'without wings' to transcend his own 'epic of the usual'. James's recourse to the cant word 'sympathetic' is revealing. Is the communication of which he speaks only authentic when it takes the form of a consoling discovery of like-mindedness? Should we *want* to 'communicate' with Frédéric any more than we want to see ourselves in Gulliver? James's contempt for him is an insulation against Flaubert's irony, just as his pity for Emma was an insulation against his sense of tragedy. Yet he is perhaps less offended by Frédéric's mediocrity than by the fact that Flaubert's fiercest irony is reserved for those qualities which make him the most sensitive character in the book, a character whom Edmund Wilson has called a 'perfect Henry James character: he is sensitive, cautious, afraid of life; he lives on a little income and considers himself superior to the common run.'[3] Hence the grumpiness of that 'only proves him of their kind', which brushes our compassion for him aside, just as the word 'usual' brushes aside the book's sense of the quotidian. The phrase 'epic without air' reminds one of the enthusiastic letters in which Flaubert described turning to work on *Salammbô*, after his long immersion in the world of *Madame Bovary*. The 'balloon' image, of course, recalls the discussion of 'romance' in the preface to *The American*.

Yet one can see why James felt the novel is too intent on not leaving 'the ground' and that Flaubert is 'ironic to a tune that makes his final accepted state, his present literary dignity and "classic" peace, superficially anomalous'. (P. 66.) He took it as axiomatic that the greatest art goes beyond the 'ironic'. *L'Education Sentimentale*, like *Bouvard et Pécuchet*, often seems uncongenial on a first reading because its irony appears too like a demonstration of an *a priori* distrust of life. We wonder if a novelist can really render life when he seems to have made up his mind about it. In a short philosophic satire like *Candide* (which Flaubert greatly admired) the author's position is part of the fun; in a novel in which Flaubert aspired to give 'the moral history of the men of my generation' (*Corr.*, V, p. 158) a feeling that the irony is too predictable stops it from biting: our first impulse is to dismiss it as a safety valve for the author's own anger and *ennui*. If Frédéric is discredited too soon then his love for Madame Arnoux – the one thing that gives meaning to Flaubert's chronicle of meaningless events – will be discredited too. The novel will come to seem even more 'usual' than it was meant to be. It is perhaps because of the strength of such a first impression that one way of praising the novel has always been to praise its usualness. To Maupassant, it was,

. . . the perfect image of what goes on every day, the exact diary of existence. Its philosophy remains so completely latent, so completely hidden behind the facts, its psychology so completely bound-up in the acts and attitudes and words of the characters, that the mass public, used to underlined effects and obvious teachings, has not understood the value of this incomparable novel.[4]

Unquestionable, beautiful, pointless: all we can do, which so irked James, is to take it as it is. Its triumph is to pre-empt the reader's imagination. To Rémy de Gourmont, it was only accessible to stoics, 'le livre pour les forts'.[5] Both critics are too knowing. Is reading the novel no more than an exercise in how much our own toughness will stand? That would imply that both reader and author are trapped in its irony, in the self-protective, untragic notion that the book only speaks to those who already know the worst.

I have been trying to describe what a first reading of *L'Education* may feel like. Each time I have re-read it I have felt more convinced that its author is not a moral tough guy.[6] There may be moments when we are invited to congratulate ourselves on our strong stomachs – like the over-morbid death of Frédéric's and Rosanette's little boy – but they are not seriously troubling and stand out from the whole as being more reminiscent of the kind of tragic farce we sometimes get in Hardy than of its own best passages. The core of the novel is an unresolveable sense of pain. Its irony simply tricks us into an illusory detachment which we are increasingly unable to sustain as we become steeped in Flaubert's unique feeling for the passing of time. First reading cannot hope to pick up fully the way the novel's aimless. unremitting sequentiality sets our sensibility quivering, like an open wound which something is rubbing against. Yet the real source of the irony is this sense of transience.

Many readers besides James have thought *L'Education* monotonous but it is meant to be monotonous. From the passage of the steamer down the Seine at the start, we are in a world of liquid flux and the inconsecutive narrative winds on with the even, interminable, circuitous flow of a river. Like the river's ripples, no event is more important than any other. The revolution is as much an episode in time as one of Arnoux's dinner-parties. Almost no vestiges of the Balzac-like plotting of *Madame Bovary* remain. Perhaps this is why one does not find perfect, nearly self-contained prose poems in the book? To try through quotation to give a sense of what George Moore finely calls its 'philosophic tide of incident', its unifying rhythm, would be like unstitching a fine tapestry – how could one stop without taking everything out?[7] I can only urge the reader to turn back to even one of the more clearly orchestrated passages to see what I mean. Take the close of the *Deuxième Partie* (pp. 398–408), which counterpoints the outbreak of the revolution with Frédéric's long wait for Madame Arnoux in the rue Tronchet, her failure to turn up because of her vigil over her sick child and Frédéric's desperate profanation of her image by seducing Rosanette in the room he had prepared for his 'grand amour'. Much of the novel's essential vision – the vanity of trying to rescue something permanent from time when it is time's very impermanence that makes us suffer – is contained in these pages, but they are too integral to the movement of the whole to be taken as an epitome for it. Their resonance depends on their bringing to a point the cumulative effect of all the preceding chapters. The movement of the prose may seem superficially the same movement as on the book's first page but it is the ability of this unvarying prose to go on incorporating fresh experiences into its own momentum that makes for the deeper rhythm of the book as a whole.

This deep sense of the pain of living in time releases the compassion that Flaubert's irony at first conceals. It is something fundamental to the condition of all the characters – whatever we think of them – in which we can share. When we feel it the novel no longer seems limited to a lofty survey of the baseness of a particular society. The danger is rather that, when our compassion does begin to flow, it will never stop. Witness the way George Moore, with a typical mixture of sense and enthusiasm, discusses Rosanette, a character to whom James is indifferent:

> By no adventitious aids does Flaubert strive to engage our sympathy. He merely helps us to understand. When we do not understand we do not sympathise; pity is the corollary of knowledge, and all living things are pitiful: the saint as well as the courtesan. . . . We see her living as she was born to live; there have always been courtesans, and presumably there always will be, and she works out her destiny instinctively, as you and I do. Pity the poor little Maréchale and poor Mlle Vatnaz, her friend, pity them all, even Arnoux, the ever faithful husband; everything that lives is to be pitied.[8]

A sermon from Moore is an unsettling experience but this one does help us to see that the poetry of *L'Education* is 'in the pity', even if Moore's pity is too soft for the book. His note of fellow-feeling – 'as you and I do' – is just what James's moral judgement of Frédéric refuses. Yet Flaubert does not indulge in individual hostilities against his characters. Arnoux, for all his faults, is still the only man present at the dinner Monsieur Dambreuse gives, during the revolution, whose sentiments are honest, and his wife and Frédéric are forced to admit it. Frédéric would like only too well to be able to hate him but he would be despicable if he did. Such moments reveal a reverence for life which is beyond ordinary satire: we enjoy sharing Arnoux's humanity, his love of life, so we see that it is ourselves, and not just Jacques Arnoux, who is being satirised. A Jamesian rascal – Selah Tarrant in *The Bostonians*, for instance – is never relished for his very rascality in this way: we always look down on him from a height, rather as Olive Chancellor does only more amused.

It is, I think, to help Flaubert evoke an almost monumental feeling of transience that Frédéric has to be average and lightweight. He floats down the river of his life without ever really trying to swim against its current. His passivity contributes to the novel's unrelenting pathos, the way it gives an emotional equivalent to having one's arm twisted up behind one's back for a long time. Yet, in another way, it is his very passivity that makes Frédéric much more than the drab and spineless version of *l'homme moyen sensuel* he at first seems. His weakness springs from his forlorn, dogged impulse of spirituality, the radical innocence he nurtures in himself in nurturing for so long his adolescent love for Madame Arnoux, and it is this that makes him refuse to settle for the second-best life his world offers him and disqualifies him from trying to make it better. Had he been more like Arnoux, James could not have called him an 'abject human specimen' (p. 64). For all his disillusion, part of him remains, like the heroine of *Novembre*, virgin from life.

In a way, Frédéric wants Madame Arnoux to seem vague and inaccessible because he is afraid to test his ideal and find out whether it is an illusion or not. It suits him to be her husband's friend since it enables him to go on seeing her *and* go on keeping her on a pedestal. The pathos of *L'Education* is very different from that of Balzac's *Les Illusions Perdues* because Frédéric, unlike Lucien de Rubempré, becomes disillusioned while protecting his main illusion by taking no risks for it. Madame Arnoux is to him a beautiful pretext for not living, as Art perhaps was to his creator. This is why he only deserts her for more worldly, rather soul-less women like Rosanette and Madame Dambreuse: he never expects to get from them what he hoped (but hardly tried) to get from her and so he is never really disappointed by them. It is as if his unfulfilled love for Madame Arnoux spares him from suffering the real pain of love. His dreams dissolve as much with his own connivence as from the impact of reality. This is what makes him so different from Emma Bovary. If we compare him with George Eliot's Lydgate, who helps illustrate similar bleak truths about growing older, it seems as if Flaubert's irony for his hero is a way of pulling his hardest punches: we can always console ourselves with the thought that

Frédéric's failure can be put down to Frédéric's mediocrity. This is, I believe, one way in which James was right to complain that we cannot 'directly communicate' with him.

Flaubert, moreover, conspires to save Frédéric from having to confront his dream in real experience. Madame Arnoux fails to turn up on the one occasion when she looks like giving herself to Frédéric, though she does turn up in his rooms for a bitter-sweet lovers' tryst when he is middle-aged and she is grey. The possibility of happiness is presented as being impossible. Thus does this bleakest of novels salvage from its own disillusion a remnant of youthful romance. It is this romance which gives *L'Education* that irreducible pathos which we can never get beyond. It is a tragedy in which there is no tragedy; it lacks that quality of the surprise and shock of misfortune which gives impetus to the less unrelieved inevitability of *Madame Bovary*. This new dispiriting quality is typified in Flaubert's treatment of Louise Roque, the young provincial girl who passionately loves Frédéric and to whom he plays the part of a sort of chaste Rodolphe. When Louise eventually marries Deslauriers and then runs away with another man, Flaubert coldly reports the news as a kind of tawdry *fait divers*, comic and rather trivial. Yet Louise is one of the few characters in the novel who is prepared to tie her colours to the mast and try to live her life with that boldness Emma sometimes shows. Does Frédéric live his own life at all, or just the life that the novel's sense of the passage of time imposes on him? His hopeless yet successful effort to preserve intact his adolescent passion for Madame Arnoux makes his story that of a man who ages without ever growing up.

II

To put it like this is to ask whether *L'Education Sentimentale* in the end gives us only a partial sense of time. Time is a medium for creation and growth as well as aging and decay and Frédéric's time is much more a passing than a becoming. No wonder Flaubert cared little for Stendhal. Though Julien and Fabrice die young while Frédéric goes on and on 'living', they live more than Frédéric ever does. In Flaubert, the will to live which they embody is confined to an Arnoux or a Homais. The effect of this is felt in his treatment of the revolution of 1848. If it is an 'episode' in a limiting sense, as James implies, it is because Flaubert, like his hero, turns his back on what may be new and creative in the change it fights for and concentrates on what makes it seem absurd and futile. Perhaps the most deeply felt political scene in the novel is when the mob sack the treasures of the Tuileries. Frédéric turns away in disgust because they are vandalising what now belongs to them. The accursed, democratic nineteenth century is at its work of destroying beauty and civilisation. The scene corresponds to the one where Frédéric himself turns from Madame Arnoux to Rosanette: something fine is profaned but no 'terrible beauty is born'. He dabbles in politics himself in 1848 but he is, of course, too sensitive to really do anything. Flaubert has as much sympathy for his distaste for action as he ever has for him. And so, by the exquisite Fontainbleau scenes, he seems to be papering over the uncreative void he has put at the heart of his hero with beautiful descriptions of external reality. The revolution is marvellously *described* but Frédéric's own inert romanticism becomes a pretext for turning away from the developing political situation to a lyrical meditation on nature and history:

> Les résidences royales ont en elles une mélancolie particulière, qui tient sans doute à leurs dimensions trop considérables pour le petit nombre de leurs hôtes, au silence qu'on est surpris d'y trouver après tant de fanfares, à leur luxe immobile prouvant par sa vieillesse la fugacité des dynasties, l'éternelle misère de tout; cette exhalaison des siècles, engourdissante et funèbre comme un parfum de momie, se fait sentir même aux têtes naïves. Rosanette baîllait démésurément. Ils s'en retournèrent à l'hotel.[9]
>
> (The homes of royalty harbour a melancholy all their own, which no doubt derives from their over-spaciousness for their small number of occupants, from the silence that, after so many fanfares, one is surprised to find in them and from their static luxury whose age demonstrates the fleeting-ness of dynasties and the eternal wretchedness of everything: this exhalation of the centuries, numbing and funereal as the odour of a mummy, makes itself felt even in simple minds. Rosanette was yawning immoderately. They went back to the hotel.)

Style, however beautiful, has ceased to be enough. Despite the distancing irony of the last two sentences, Flaubert enjoys seconding Frédéric's meditative vacation from contemporary events. The prose becomes 'engourdissante et funèbre' itself, paralysed by its own melancholy sentiment. It has a wonderful lugubrious resonance but none of that Stendhalian agility which can make what is happening here and now happen inside a character's consciousness. Can the revolution be said to go on inside Frédéric at all? Or does he just observe it like a novelist *manqué*?

In Fontainebleau both novelist and hero turn for comfort from a contemporary anguish to the thought of the immemorial sadness of life. They need to generalise, to see 1848 as a ripple on the surface of history which, after a brief upheaval, will soon regain its calm and leave life as it has always been. *Plus ça change. . . .* This is why 1848 is presented episodically as a welter of brilliant detail. Its barricades and debates are treated just like the dinners and affairs and money-dealings that precede and follow it. That way, it seems to make no change in the consciousness of those who live through it. The naïve Dussardier becomes a figure of pathos and Sénécal a turncoat: their revolutionary passion is a measure of their impercipience; one is a dreamer, the other is ironically made to enact his own disillusion. The handful of letters Flaubert himself wrote in 1848 (like all the books he later read about it?) suggest, perhaps, that he could not really explain the failure of his generation as a consequence of the revolution but needed the revolution as a way of accounting for the failure. Could he see his own 'moral history' through an event in which he barely participated? I suspect, rather, that by writing an impassive record of 1848, at a distance from the feeling it generated, he was making the politics he had lived through into history and finding a way of talking about contemporary life without having to examine his own strange relation – part disengaged, part in complicity – with his Second Empire world. Perhaps his novelist's detachment from 1848 was a mirror of his detachment from the France of the 1860s? In a sense *L'Education* is as much an historical novel as *Salammbô* is. It is not surprising that Flaubert never wrote his long-pondered novel on life under Napoleon III.

Flaubert might be defended here on the grounds that 1848 was a revolution which failed but that would, I think, be to follow a false scent. If we look at the deeply unhappy letters he wrote during and after the Commune, only a year or two after *L'Education* was published, we see both how relatively satisfied he had been by the world created by 1848 and how he instinctively felt that the only way civilisation could change was through decline. This is why Edmund Wilson's wit rings untrue when he conjectures that James, reading *L'Education*, felt touched by Flaubert's satire on 'the pusillanimity of the bourgeois soul'.[10] In many ways James could sniff out the cant of the developing nineteenth century as well as Flaubert could: he was, after all, an American. But as an American he had both a belief in the future and a reluctance to define a human soul in terms of the characteristics of the class to which it belonged. This comes out in *The Princess Casamassima,* in the figure of Hyacinth Robinson, who may at first seem to show only James's inability to conceive of the humanity of a man 'of the people' any differently from the humanity of 'the better sort' but who also shows, more deeply, his willingness to believe in a common human spirit that could transcend class. *The Princess* shares much of the political feeling of *L'Education* (it is much concerned with the fate of culture after the revolution) but it is an entirely different kind of novel, its political events largely imaginary where Flaubert's were historical. It deals with revolutionism in the present as a means of peering into the future. It is, despite many shortcomings, a work of inquiry as well as a post-mortem on a nearly concluded era.

Hyacinth is a poor bookbinder, the illegitimate child of a French seamstress and an English lord. Like Frédéric he is trapped in his social position and like Frédéric he is sensitive, ineffectual and feels a cut above those around him. Unlike Frédéric he has appetite as well as desire for what he loves; he feels his lowly position as a mere viewpoint on the unenterable sweet-shop window of life and he is determined to enter the sweet-shop before he dies:

> He was liable to moods in which the sense of exclusion from all he would have liked most to enjoy in life settled on him like a pall. They had a bitterness, but they were not invidious – they were not moods of vengeance, of imaginary spoliation: they were simply states of paralysing melancholy, of infinite sad reflexion, in which he felt how in this world of effort and suffering life was endurable, the spirit able to expand, only in the best conditions, and how a sordid struggle in which one should go down to the grave without having tasted them was not worth the misery it would cost, the dull demoralisation it would involve.[11]

This mixture of feelings makes him sympathise both with a group of revolutionaries and with the culture of the classes they want to overthrow. The far-fetched contradiction of his parentage (complicated by the fact that the Frenchness he has inherited from his plebeian mother is felt as the source both of his artistic and his revolutionary feelings) seems to determine his sensibility. It is a contradiction which James transforms from a piece of novelistic romance into an image of the social contradiction of the world in which Hyacinth lives. He does this by doing what Flaubert never does with Emma Bovary: he lets Hyacinth live in the world of his dreams. He visits Medley, the home of the bored, dazzling Princess Casamassima, who is flirting with anarchism because she regrets her marriage, and, unlike Emma at La Vaubyessard, he is allowed to stay long enough in Medley to find out what he is really missing in life and what Medley is really like. Later, he gets a chance to visit Paris and Venice too. What these unlikely experiences do is to help Hyacinth understand better the contradiction he is living: his dilemma becomes an insight into the problems of his society. Lionel Trilling puts this insight in a nutshell:

Hyacinth recognises what very few people wish to admit, that civilisation has a price, and a high one. Civilisations differ from one another as much in what they give up as in what they acquire; but all civilisations are alike in that they renounce something for something else.[12]

What can Hyacinth renounce? His soul is divided between his sense of the injustice of society and his sense of the beauty which can come out of its unjust system. Any choice would mean giving up an essential part of himself.

That, at least, is the classic tragic predicament James tries to create in *The Princess*. The light, self-conscious Hyacinth does not in fact sustain the weight of the contradiction he is asked to live out. One always believes far more in his aesthetics than his politics and his choice between civilisation and revolution, even when he has to kill himself to prevent the anarchist outrage he is pledged to commit, is a foregone conclusion. He does not die because he feels opposite emotions with equal intensity or because he sees no answer to a tragic clash of Right with Right; he dies because his situation destines him to take one side when, by natural inclination, he takes the other.[13] Besides, we always feel James's personal affinity for his hero's artistic sensibility, which makes it hard not to feel that one Right is more right than the other. So Hyacinth's fate seems mainly a way for James to explore his consciousness, a special individual fate and not a representative and tragic one. His drift toward death, so expressive of the Jamesian fusion of the love of life with the need to renounce it, is the solo part: the larger dilemmas from which it springs are only an accompaniment. We can hardly get a sense of necessity from a novel which asks us to believe that the mere presence of French blood in Hyacinth is enough to make him instinctively responsive to a culture from which he is supposed to be deprived by birth. That responsiveness that singles him out from his class surely means that he need not be 'excluded' from culture at all, but just from wealth. And since it is so instinctive we hardly believe in his making the anarchist vow that is to doom him: he knows too well where his own heart lies. If he goes through with his revolutionary commitment until it kills him it must be because the part of his heart that doesn't lie with art lies, not with political reform, but in the blank, death-like realm his self-sacrifice takes him too. For what is distinctive in his character is that he feels his identity as a sort of deathly, will-less conundrum:

His own character? He was to cover that up as carefully as possible; he was to go through life in a mask, in a borrowed mantle; he was to be every day and every hour an actor. (I, p. 77.)

In death too he appears as 'something black, something ambiguous, something outstretched'. (II, pp. 381–2.) And James simply endorses his suicide as his only way of being himself; he is unironic and approving when he tells us how, near death, Hyacinth becomes 'more and more aware of all the superiority still left him to cling to'. (II, p, 335.) It is not, in the last resort, the contradictions of society, or the accident of Hyacinth's birth, which make this death, but something in his own sensibility.[14] Life would have been a greater tragedy to him than death is and the rigmarole of his end is really a melodramatic salvation from his initial fate of being an intelligent pauper unable to get in the sweet-shop.

What lessons, then, does *The Princess Casamassima* contain for the reader of *L'Education* and of James's critique of Flaubert?[15] In the first place, it shows us how James's need to 'communicate' with his hero could make his art factitious, how his most apparently dramatic situations are often those where he is most personal and definite about where the reader's 'sympathy' is to go. In *The Tragic Muse*, for example, a similar clash between the claims of culture and the claims of politics is again resolved by the author's pulling hard on one side of the argument: the M.P. hero, Nick Dormer, who gives up his seat to become a painter, fusses for far too long about a decision he is always bound to make because James wants him to make it. In *The Bostonians*, another novel of the eighties, Verena's decision to marry Ransom is equally rigged and equally indisputable, though James's scheming is more attractive in a comedy. We do not sense a philosophy behind *L'Education* in the same direct way that we can sense *Culture and Anarchy* behind these novels of James's. If a Hyacinth Robinson is too weak a vessel for the complex life he has to project, just as James says Frédéric is, he is weak precisely because of what makes him, in Jamesian terms, a fitter hero than Frédéric: it is too easy to 'communicate' with him because James asks for too much 'sympathy' on his behalf. Yet, in spite of this, Hyacinth's 'fine consciousness' can be an advantage to the novel. The wit of his letter from Venice, for instance, where he imagines his anarchist superior wanting to 'cut up the ceilings of the Veronese into strips, so that everyone might have a little piece' (II, p. 130), gets beyond private bitterness to confront the radical with a real dilemma about the place of art in his new order in a way that Frédéric's sardonic response to 1848 never does. Hyacinth's ability to think also makes his feelings of being lost in society more complex than an Emma's or a Frédéric's: it helps us see how his sense of exclusion from his world is what makes him belong to it, like all the other people it excludes. He can think generally enough for consciousness to be a more real social fact in *The Princess* than it is in *L'Education*.[16] To see this is to ask, as James did, whether *L'Education* is depressing in a limited way because its hero is too unimaginative to probe or fully respond to his own tragedy. Does consciousness have the vital place in Flaubert's 'moral history' that it ought to have? Can a Frédéric really feel the full disillusion of his generation?[17] More depends on this than whether or not we are willing to 'sympathise' with him.

III

Jame's 'sympathy' for Hyacinth's intelligence may be different in kind from the compassion Flaubert feels for all the characters of *L'Education Sentimentale* – the fact that it is a sympathy which aids thought still makes one uncertain about what Flaubert can offer in place of it. Is the compassion he feels for Frédéric and the rest enough to give them any real tragic life? This question has, perhaps, already been suggested by the way George Moore could seem to relish a feeling of pleasurable condescension in the 'pity' that *L'Education* made him feel. Where does this 'pity' go to?

James, I think, helps us to see the bearing of this inquiry in what he has to say about Madame Arnoux, even though he is too eager to romanticise her into an avatar of one of his own heroines:

Almost nothing that she says is repeated, almost nothing that she does is shown. She is an image none the less beautiful and vague, an image of passion cherished and abjured, renouncing all sustenance and yet persisting in life. Only she has for real distinction the extreme drawback that she is offered us quite preponderantly through Frédéric's vision of her, that we see her in practically no other light. Now Flaubert unfortunately has not been able not so to discredit Frédéric's vision, in general, his vision of everyone and everything, and is particular of his own life, that it makes a medium good enough to convey adequately a noble impression. Mme Arnoux is of course ever so much the best thing in his life – which is saying little; but his life is made up of such queer material that we find ourselves displeased at her being 'in' it on whatever terms; all the more that she seems scarcely to affect, improve or determine it. Her creator in short never had a more awkward idea than this attempt to give us the benefit of such a conception in such a way. . . . (P. 68.)

The phrase 'a noble impression' is too cold and words like 'beautiful and vague' make her too evanescent to evoke the woman who is made real to us in her frustrated love for Frédéric and her humiliating marriage. The pure etiolated renunciation James attributes to her puts us in mind more of a Fleda Vetch or the insubstantial nobility of a Milly Theale. Madame Arnoux is as much flesh and blood as 'image'. In seeing her too much through the eyes of the young Frédéric, James betrays the instinct of a novelist who always liked to isolate his 'romance' figures from the world they are blighted by – just as Madame de Cintré is isolated in a convent at the end of *The American*. James in fact treats her just as Frédéric does, which is a nice irony. When Flaubert conveys, for example, her feelings of motherhood, he conveys more than the romantic image of a maternal bosom that Frédéric sees. He must have drawn as much on his knowledge of his own mother's devotion as on the beauty of Madame Schlésinger (with whom he fell in love as an adolescent on a Trouville beach) when he described Madame Arnoux with her children.[18] We also see her through the eyes of her unfaithful husband and the jealous Rosanette. She can be both infinitely desirable and, at the same time, an ordinary, rather prudish bourgeoise who is being worn out by life. The novel is more moving if we see that Frédéric's devotion is inspired by a real woman and not just a saint. The deepest irony about her white hair when she visits him in the penultimate chapter is that it sets the seal on her humanity. He is forced to see what he has always wanted to avoid seeing: that she is not a beautiful memory but, like everyone, a subject of time which, in destroying her ideality, makes her human. No wonder the creator of Milly Theale turned away from this humanness to something more ideal.

The real beauty of Madame Arnoux depends, in fact, on the 'queer material' she is mixed up in. She belongs to the 'ground' that Frédéric cannot leave; indeed it is partly Frédéric, like her husband and children, who tie her there. She may refuse his love but she still gets sullied by the presence at her door of Rosanette, the woman Frédéric turns to in his frustration:

> La fréquentation de ces deux femmes faisait dans sa vie comme deux musiques: l'une folâtre, emportée, divertissante, l'autre grave et presque religieuse; et, vibrant à la fois, elles augmentaient toujours, et peu à peu se mêlaient; car, si Madame Arnoux venait à l'effleurer du doigt seulement, l'image de l'autre, tout de suite, se présentait à son désir, parce qu'il avait, de ce côté-là, une chance moins lointaine; et, dans la compagnie de Rosanette, quand il lui arrivait d'avoir le cœur ému, il se rappelait immédiatement son grand amour. (P. 207.)

> (The society of these two women seemed to make two kinds of music sound in his life: one frolicsome, fiery and amusing, the other grave and almost religious; and, throbbing at one and the same time, they went on growing louder and little by little

began to merge together. For, if Madame Arnoux's finger happened just to brush against him, the image of the other woman at once presented itself to his desire, because in that direction he had a less remote chance, and, at moments when his heart felt moved in the company of Rosanette, he immediately recalled his true love.)

The two musics can never be kept apart (perhaps because neither is really complete or perfect) and Frédéric's sexuality contradicts his need to spiritualise Madame Arnoux. The echo of Rosanette in her music adds both to her beauty and her pathos.

Yet, in the end, the irony of Flaubert's insight into Frédéric's love is melted away by the sheer intensity with which his longing for Madame Arnoux is evoked:

Elle ne faisait rien pour exciter son amour, perdue dans cette insouciance qui caractérise les grands bonheurs. Pendant toute la saison, elle porta une robe de chambre en soie brune, bordée de velours pareil, vêtement large convenant à la mollesse de ses attitudes et de sa physionomie sérieuse. D'ailleurs, elle touchait au mois d'août des femmes, époque toute à la fois de réflexion et de tendresse, où la maturité qui commence colore le regard d'une flamme plus profonde, quand la force du cœur se mêle à l'expérience de la vie, et que, sur la fin de ses épanouissements, l'être complet déborde de richesses dans l' harmonie de sa beauté. Jamais elle n'avait eu plus de douceur, d'indulgence. Sûre de ne pas faillir, elle s'abandonnait à un sentiment qui lui semblait un droit conquis par ses chagrins. Cela était si bon, du reste, et si nouveau! Quel abîme entre la grossièreté d'Arnoux et les adorations de Frédéric!

Il tremblait de perdre par un mot tout ce qu'il croyait avoir gagné, se disant qu'on peut ressaisir une occasion et qu'on ne rattrape jamais une sottise. Il voulait qu'elle se donnât, et non la prendre. L'assurance de son amour le délectait comme un avant-goût de la possession, et puis le charme de sa personne lui troublait le cœur plus que les sens. C'était une béatitude indéfinie, un tel enivrement, qu'il en oubliait jusqu'à la possibilité d'un bonheur absolu. Loin d'elle, des convoitises furieuses le dévoraient.

Bientôt il y eut dans leurs dialogues de grands intervalles de silence. Quelquefois, une sorte de pudeur sexuelle les faisait rougir l'un devant l'autre. (Pp. 391–2.)

(Lost in that carefree feeling that characterises great happiness, she did nothing to excite his love. Throughout the season, she wore a brown silk dressing gown, trimmed with velvet of the same colour, an ample garment that suited her soft, indolent postures and her serious countenance. Moreover, she was nearing

the high summer of womanhood, that August time when reflective-
ness and tenderness come together, when incipient maturity
colours the expression with a deeper flame, when strength of heart
fuses with experience of life, and, its full-bloom over, the whole
being overflows with riches in the harmony of its beauty. Never
had she been more soft or more indulgent. Certain of not succumbing, she was giving way to a feeling, which to her seemed
a right won by her sorrows. And besides, it was so good, so new!
What an abyss between Arnoux's grossness and Frédéric's adora-
tion!

He trembled at the thought of losing, by one word, everything
he imagined he had gained, telling himself that one may seize
another opportunity but one never makes up for a blunder. He
wanted her to give herself, not to take her. The assurance of her
love delighted him like a foretaste of its possession, and besides,
the charm of her person stirred his heart more than his senses.
It was so intoxicating, this indefinite bliss, that he came to forget
even the possibility of his happiness being made absolute. When
he was far away from her, he was eaten up by fierce longings.

Soon there were long intervals of silence in their conversations.
Sometimes, a sort of sexual modesty made them blush in each
other's presence.)

The way their voluptuous modesty both consecrates and undermines
their love is rendered by a sensuous poetry that James must have
missed when he read the novel. When he describes Madame
Arnoux's beauty as being 'otherwise than for the senses' (p. 67) he
misses out the thing in it that makes it convincing as well as ideal.
But, if he failed to see the way Flaubert enriched the impression
Frédéric himself has of her, his sense of her beauty does suggest
the way this passage prompts in us a kind of still feeling whose
stasis is akin to the feeling of 'pity'. Her beauty of character makes
her more statuesque than instinct with free life: our response to it
remains calm. 'Pity' too leaves us calm.

'Almost nothing that she says is repeated. . . .' This is where
James hits the nail on the head. The effect of Flaubert's poetry is
to make Madame Arnoux dwell in profound silence. The poignant
blend of lyricism and precision in the passage just quoted depends
on the way the prose controls the degree to which Frédéric and his
'grand amour' can 'communicate' with each other. Especially in their
moments of intimacy, they seem to love in silence. It is as if, at the
core of Flaubert's vision, lay the premise that the heart is con-
demned to remain buried in its own inner solitude and that this
premise dictates the course of their love. The feeling that human
communication is doomed from the start takes away from the tragic

effect of the book and confines its pathos to something more simply lyrical and pitying. Perhaps some such feeling accounted for James's being depressed by the novel: if its characters never have a chance of real communication, how can we 'communicate' with them? Only compassion can fill our distance from them and compassion is no longer enough.

To say this is to ask for a more, not a less, 'tragic novel' than the one George Moore describes. For it is part of the tragic experience that in it people come to recognise the truth about themselves together. It is when Lear meets Cordelia after the storm or when Electra finally recognises the returned Orestes that we can share their insight into what is tragic in their lives. At these moments of shared understanding, both irony and compassion are superseded by the strange sense of awe and elation – awe at what is seen, elation at finally seeing it as it is – that is called 'tragic joy'. It is something that *L'Education*, most of all in its conclusion, sets out to refuse us. It is also the point at which, because of death or doubt, the story of the friendship of Bouvard and Pécuchet breaks off. James, I think, whether or not he ever reached that point himself, would have set it down as the threshold of the true classic art which the ironic Flaubert never quite reached.

I want to conclude this account of *L'Education Sentimentale* by turning back to two remarks which I quoted in discussing tragedy in the fifth chapter of this book and did not fully explore there. The first is from Leavis:

> The sense of heightened life that goes with the tragic experience is conditioned by a transcending of the ego.

Do we only transcend our ego when the characters transcend theirs in tragic recognition? Is this the perception that Leavis's stress on the 'individual sentience' obscured? If it is a true perception we may feel that *L'Education* leaves us imprisoned in its author's ego – his bitterness and disillusion of *un*-heightened life – to the end. Yet, to return as well to Lawrence:

> . . . a great soul like Flaubert's has a pure satisfaction and joy in its own consciousness, even if the consciousness be only of ultimate tragedy or misery.

Did 'misery' loom larger than this 'joy' when Flaubert wrote his novel? In his final conversation with Deslauriers, Frédéric's consciousness is all of failure and it brings him not 'joy' but melancholy. Perhaps that is where the novel leaves its reader too, at what James called the 'leak in its stored sadness . . . by which its moral dignity escapes'. (P. 67.) In other words, it *is* an 'epic without air'.

I do not see how to refute such a judgement but it is not a happy conclusion to come to about a book that still seems, like only a few other novels, as if one will never have finished reading it. A more complete answer to James on *L'Education* would be one of the best things this book could hope to prompt.

IV

James's doubts about *L'Education*, like my own, boil down to a feeling that it never quite gets beyond the description of life to a sense of its drama. To create drama a writer needs some belief that, at times, people can communicate themselves to each other, can imagine what the other really feels besides just sensing his or her otherness. Ralph and Isabel are meant to communicate in this way in the unsuccessful scene at Ralph's death-bed. James believed more in communication than did Flaubert, just as he had more trust in the imagination itself, the faculty through which another's feelings can be recognised. The free, plastic quality of his imagination is given to his characters in their constant attempts to fathom and relate to each other. Santayana once said, after visiting James, that, 'Henry was calm, he liked to see things as they are, and be free afterwards to imagine how they might have been'.[19] The remark hints at both the romancer's detachment from the actual and the possibilities for ironic and idealising treatment of the characters whom he endowed with such imaginativeness. The essential Jamesian drama, whether of communication or misunderstanding, is, like *The Ambassadors*, a kind of comedy of the imagination. A good example of it is *In The Cage*, a brilliant tale he wrote in the 1890s.

The heroine of *In The Cage* is a telegraphist in a Mayfair post office. What she likes best is to study high society through the telegrams its members send each other. She is also engaged to Mr Mudge, a grocer's assistant in Chalk Farm, who is prosaic as his name. In the safety provided by her 'sounder' her lively imagination can both observe life and find a refuge from it. She proceeds to transform two of her clients, Captain Everard and Lady Bradeen, into figures in a romance of her own invention. The tale does not rely on the kind of irony Flaubert uses in *Madame Bovary*, when, for instance, we are brought down to earth by the sudden sight of the peasants at la Vaubyessard, peering through the windows at their masters and mistresses dancing. Unlike Emma, the telegraph girl is well aware of the discrepancy between the creatures of her imagination and the pack of sybarites who frequent her post office.

She is obsessed with the real people because she hates them: "They're *too* real! They're selfish brutes.'[20] Sordid reality cannot shatter her dreams because it is precisely reality's sordidnes which vindicates them. Her dream-world lies not just beyond her cage, in Mayfair, as Emma's lies in Paris or Italy, but inside her own imagination, and she knows it.

This imagination is clearly meant as an analogy to James's own gift as a novelist. The girl's snatches of dialogue with Captain Everard remind us of the way he too asks us to read between the lines, both of the page and of reality itself:

> Everything, so far as they chose to consider it so, might mean almost anything. The want of margin in the cage, when he peeped through the bars, wholly ceased to be appreciable. It was a drawback only in a superficial commerce. With Captain Everard she had simply the margin of the universe. (P. 173.)

This strangely passive pragmatism run mad turns the world into a comic phantasmagoria for which all our interpretations are only a kind of play.[21] Actuality is put in abeyance by what the imagination can glean from it: 'if nothing was more impossible than the fact, nothing was more intense than the vision.' (P. 179.) And, in a queer way, this waywardness in the girl's mind comes to enrich her world and testify to its aliveness:

> As the weeks went on there she lived more and more into the world of whiffs and glimpses, and found her divinations work faster and stretch further. It was a prodigious view as the pressure heightened, a panorama fed with facts and figures, flushed with a torrent of colour and accompanied with wondrous world-music. What it mainly came to at this period was a picture of how London could amuse itself; and that, with the running commentary of a witness so exclusively a witness, turned for the most part to a hardening of the heart. (Pp. 152–3.)

A Frédéric Moreau perhaps hears no such 'world-music', even though the reader of *L'Education* does, but he is not 'so exclusively a witness' either. The telegraph girl runs little risk of falling in love with Captain Everard herself (or, for that matter, with poor Mr Mudge). Is it the spectacle of fashionable dissipation that hardens her 'heart', or is it rather the exclusiveness of her witnessing of it? James raises questions about the 'cage' which he is only prepared to answer ambiguously. It cannot be simply a prison of self since it also symbolises a vicarious living which we are invited to share in. Yet the girl's need to know more and more about the people she

watches becomes too inhuman to be valued for itself, too like a need
for the sensation of power. It reminds one of Flaubert's temptation
to survey life as if from the top of a pyramid. When Captain Everard
comes in at the end of the story to ask the girl to trace a telegram
on which his and Lady Bradeen's future depends, she is frighten-
ingly objective:

> It came to her there, with her eyes on his face, that she held the
> whole thing in her hand, held it as she held her pencil, which
> might have broken at that instant in her tightened grip. This
> made her feel like the very fountain of fate, but the emotion was
> such a flood that she had to press it back with all her force. That
> was positively the reason, again, of her flute-like Paddington tone.
> 'You can't give us anything a little nearer?' Her 'little' and her 'us'
> came straight from Paddington. These things were no false note
> for him – his difficulty absorbed them all. The eyes with which
> he pressed her, and in the depths of which she read terror and
> rage and literal tears, were just the same he would have shown
> any other prim person. (P. 221.)

The Captain is more human than the girl, even if James only
suggests his humanness in order to manipulate it. When she finds
his telegram (she remembers them all by heart) his happiness is more
real than her exultant feeling of power. If this makes her a kind of
monster as well as a humourously seen 'prim person', what are we
to make of the way the tale has celebrated her imagination? Is
imagination itself monstrous, a pursuit of a purely private joy?
Lubbock tells us that James often spoke of himself as 'a confirmed
spectator, one who looked on from the brink instead of plunging on
his own account; but if this seemed a pale substitute for direct
contact he knew very well that it was a much richer and more
adventurous life, really, than it is given to most people to lead.'[22]
This back-handed compliment links naturally with the girl's safety
in her cage; neither she nor James is interested in what can be made
of life *in* life. That is the province of Mr Mudge. Her imagination
thrives on an immunity from experience. It is this which sustains
the ebullience of the charade-like intellectual comedy and preserves
the lightness of tone that comes from its untouched receptivity. If
a Frédéric Moreau is less imaginative he is still far more stretched
by life and far more human.

The highly-strung imagination of the telegraph girl is, to a greater
or lesser extent, given to all the characters in the much less simply
urbane comedy of *The Awkward Age*. Edmund Wilson thought
the characters of that novel were a hideous crew of ghouls all prey-
ing on each other but that is only a small part of the impression

they make. Their imaginativeness, like their talk, is also always directed to finding out how to make contact with each other. The novel has some exquisite passages of mutual understanding to set against its social satire. As well as depicting a sordidly real late Victorian London society it also has suggestions of what an ideal society might be like. It corresponds as much to Eliot's picture of James's romance of community as to Wilson's rejection:

> His romanticism implied no defective observation of the things he wanted to observe; it was not the romanticism of those who dream because they are too lazy or too fearful to face the fact; it issued rather from the imperative insistence of an ideal which tormented him. He was possessed by the vision of an ideal society; he saw (not fancied) the relations between the members of such a society. And no one in the end has ever been more aware – or with more benignity, or less bitterness – of the disparity between possibility and fact.[23]

Perhaps this 'ideal society' seems a little too like the sort of ethereal club James imagines in *The Great Good Place*, but Eliot does bring out that blithely philosophic vision – blending vivacity with wry but peaceful contemplation – that distinguishes the comedy of *The Awkward Age*. This comedy, like the novel's much-admired 'dramatic' form, depends on the way all the characters are all the time engaged in a ludicrous, sad and, sometimes, sublime effort to 'communicate'. These dramatic gifts may appear to give the book a broader scope than the unplumbed, personal art of *The Portrait of a Lady*. No one would deny that the control of dialogue gives the novel an extreme brilliance of surface, but the essential question to ask about it, here, does not take what a Congreve can offer as all that 'dramatic' means: Is *The Awkward Age* a *drama* of the kind *L'Education Sentimentale* failed to be? Or is its dramatic virtuosity rather the source to James of a safe detachment such as he needed after his failure in the theatre a few years earlier? Does it go beyond 'the cage'?

Edel, writing of James's sufferings in the 1890s, says, implying no criticism, that:

> His emotions were blocked, defended, confused, full of past and recent hurt. At this moment, therefore, James begins to use the supremacy of his intellect. He concerns himself more ultimately with 'method' than ever before. Rational form and mind were thus interposed against the chaos of feeling. . . . His best, his 'safest' identity was the artist; there he was in full possession.[24]

Is it the same thing to 'use the supremacy of the intellect' as to use the intelligence? Edel's James sounds rather like the telegraph girl exultantly fishing out the Captain's missing telegram. In the prefaces and notebooks James is always saying things about 'drama' which gell with this:

> I have been positively struck by the quantity of meaning and the number of intentions, the extent of *ground for interest*, as I may call it, that I have succeeded in working scenically, yet without loss of sharpness, clearness or 'atmosphere', into each of my illuminating Occasions. . . .[25]

Is Edel's James the real James, or is this 'working scenically' something which in fact resulted in a dramatic comedy in the sense in which those words are applicable to Molière or Shakespeare?

The *donnée* of *The Awkward Age* is the question of when a young girl can be deemed to be 'out' in modern society. Nanda Brookenham's position is 'awkward' because she is neither 'out' nor 'in'. Aggie, on the other hand, a *jeune fille* from Italy chaperoned by a vulgar Duchess aunt, begins by being too 'in' and then, after her marriage, comes 'out' with a vengeance in unabashed misconduct. Nanda, who *is* innocent, though she 'knows' more than Aggie, embarrasses Mrs Brookenham, a young, attractive, abnormally inquisitive hostess, who fears that Nanda's presence 'downstairs' will curb freedom of talk in her *salon*. The corruption of Buckingham Crescent is of an attenuated sort: apart from visits from the odd beauty gracefully lingering on the brink of adultery and the loans of French novels, it is all verbal. And it is through talk that the novel unfolds. The unquenchable talk of Mrs Brook's 'set' gives James plenty of scope to be nasty about people being nasty about each other in the kind of maliciously sympathising social comedy he excels at. Its grace and wit isn't quotable because it depends on the *frisson* of excitement generated over long periods of dialogue. The whole of Book 8 – the crucial dinner party at Tishy Grendon's before Mitchy and Aggie go on honeymoon – is a good example. Yet the novel is deeper than its brilliant Wildean surface, even if it is less assured and polished in its depths. Its essence is poured in with Mr Longdon, who brings a sane naïveté to bear on all the talk. For the depths, Mrs Brook would not be a model of an ideal reader, as she is for the surface.

Mr Longdon is a 'fresh eye, an outside mind' that Mitchy thinks the 'set' needs.[26] He finally grows almost as good at intuitive conversational leaps at half-meanings as the others are. He is like an allegory of Time Past, newly out in London himself and shockable by the changes in its 'tone', a genteel Pickwick from Beccles, Suffolk, where he inhabits a grander version of Lamb House, Rye. We can

smile at him as long as we take him very seriously too. He has unsuccessfully loved Mrs Brook's mother, Lady Julia, and still loves
her memory enough to be charmed that Nanda ressembles her.
He wants to rescue Nanda from the modern life which, alas, makes
her sound so unlike her grandmother. His own tone is impeccable,
gentlemanly like Dickens's Mr Twemlow. His first step is to try to
persuade the dazzling Vanderbank (whose mother was another of
his flames) to marry Nanda. Van, who is already reserved for Mrs
Brook, is less put off by the money Mr Longdon wants to settle on
her than by the fact that she 'knows' too much to be his wife. He
is a sort of Jamesian Eugene Wrayburn, very fussy about where his
wife comes from. Though Mr Longdon focuses a contrast in the
novel between old and new (almost good and bad), the 'set' are all
charmed by him and his pretty tales of Lady Julia. They all subscribe to the Jamesian emotion for the word 'old', for example, as
a synonym of poetry and value (see p. 179). Even Mrs Brook
cherishes him as a 'fairy godmother'. (P. 158) The novel is no clash
of generations, like *Fathers and Sons* or *The Way of all Flesh*. In it,
every age is an awkward age and its driving force is towards a comic
reconcilement of them all, as if to exorcise the whirring sense of
time and change from modern London.

Mitchy describes the 'set's' philosophy as 'share and share alike –
one beautiful intelligence'. (P. 263.) They share Mr Longdon. He
becomes a ball in their conversational rallies. This time Nanda, who
has just met him, is what starts him as a topic:

'Do you like him, Nanda?'
She showed some surprise at the question. 'How can I know
so soon?'
'*He* knows already.'
Mitchy, with his eyes on her, became radiant to interpret. 'He
knows that he's pierced to the heart!'
'The matter with him, as you call it', Vanderbank brought out,
'is one of the most beautiful things I've ever seen.' He looked
at her as with a hope that she would understand it. 'Beautiful,
beautiful, beautiful!'
'Precisely', Mitchy continued, 'the victim done for by one
glance of the goddess!'
Nanda, motionless in her chair, fixed her other friend with
clear curiosity. ' "Beautiful"? Why beautiful?'
Vanderbank, about to speak, checked himself. 'I won't spoil
it. Have it from *him*!' – and, returning to the old man, he this
time went out.
Mitchy and Nanda looked at each other. 'But isn't it rather
awful?' Mitchy demanded.

She got up without answering; she slowly came away from the table. 'I think I do know if I like him.'

'Well you may', Mitchy exclaimed, 'after his putting before you probably, on the whole, the greatest of your triumphs.'

'And I also know, I think, Mr Mitchy, that I like *you*.' (Pp. 123–4.)

If we are unsure of what is being communicated we have no doubt about the talent for communicating that this elegantly sensitive exchange shows. Mitchy and Nanda fall to talking with just as much polish of the fact that he loves her while she does not love him, then Van comes to take her to Mr Longdon. Van then tells Mitchy what Mr Longdon will do:

'Will she understand? She has everything in the world but one', he added. But that's half.'

Vanderbank, before him, lighted for himself. 'What is it?'

'A sense of humour.'

'Oh yes, she's serious.'

Mitchy smoked a little. 'She's tragic.'

His friend, at the fire, watched a moment the empty portion of the other room, then walked across to give the door a light push that all but closed it. 'It's rather odd', he remarked as he came back – 'that's quite what I just said to him. But he won't treat her to comedy.' (P. 126.)

Like all the talk in the book, this knows just where to make a perfect close with a telling hint about the future.

Mitchy and Van, moving easily to a common thought, define how we are to think of Nanda. Though there are under-currents in the thought – Mitchy loves her, she loves Van and Van loves no one, save perhaps himself – they concur to invest her with that mantle of discreetly proud pathos which is to be her theme-music. This music harmonises so well with Mr Longdon's old time courtesy and sentiment that it makes a moral and emotional touchstone against which to measure Mrs Brook's 'set'. The method may be dramatic but its deepest effect is lyric, for the moral standard is expressed lyrically. The Nanda–Mr Longdon alliance may seem saccharine (Pound was much irked by James's laments for 'the old lavender')[27] but it sharpens the contrast between the worlds of Jane Austen and Oscar Wilde. Nanda is very much of her own time, in ways even more so than her mother, and needs to be educated into older values. Mr Longdon has to explain to her the difference between the world where Mitchy can rent a country house (neither Nanda nor Van have any idea who its owner is) and the world of

Beccles, fruit of time and tradition. The living rhythm of Beccles is lost from a life of tea parties and visits to rented houses. Nanda must be saved from the emotional abyss that opens like a crevasse in the bright surface of her mother's life, when she lets her own place in the country:

'Edward, who's furious at what I've taken for it, had his idea that we should go there this year ourselves.'

'And now,' – Vanderbank took her up – 'that fond fancy has become simply the ghost of a dead thought, a ghost that, in company with a thousand predecessors, haunts the house in the twilight and pops at you out of odd corners.'

'Oh, Edward's dead thoughts are indeed a cheerful company and worthy of the perpetual mental mourning we seem to go about in. . . . The apparitions following the deaths of so many thoughts *are* particularly awful in the twilight, so that at this season, while the day drags and drags, I'm glad to have any one with me who may keep them at a distance.'

Vanderbank had not sat down; slowly, familiarly, he turned about. 'And where's Nanda?'

'Oh, *she* doesn't help – she attracts rather the worst of the bogies.' (Pp. 249–50.)

The 'set' is beginning to break up and this, not least because of the wit, is one of the most moving moments in the novel, a measure of its real dramatic ability to take sudden plunges beneath the glittering talk into the depths of what a person is feeling. There is nothing so good in the way Madame Merle is handled; Nanda does not restrict the scope of *The Awkward Age* as Isabel does the scope of *The Portrait of a Lady*.

So, having seen this, it is a shock to find that the novel is all the time preparing for itself a resolution which will keep at bay these ghosts of the past and fears of the future that afflict Mrs Brook. In Nanda the 'bogies' are made natural and sublime. She does not get Van, as Mr Longdon hopes, and she lets him off lightly. Quite why she has let him off is unclear because there is no reason why he should be obliged to love her just because she loves him – he never commits himself to a thing. In fact, the real point about her love is that its hopelessness lends pathos to her eventual renunciation. All the pure affections in the novel, like Mitchy's for Nanda and Mr Longdon's for Lady Julia, are sanctified by unsuccess. This is romantic because the thwarted feelings don't go anywhere else, as Frédéric's have to when Madame Arnoux fails to meet him in the rue Tronchet. Nanda concentrates on what makes marriage impossible for her: she could only marry the kind of man who would

mind the fact that she has come too far 'out'. Mitchy puts this to
her point-blank:

> 'Do you positively *like* to love in vain?'
> It was a question, the way she turned back to him seemed
> to say, that deserved a responsible answer. 'Yes.' (Pp. 317–8.)

Much earlier she already saw Beccles as a more plausible sanctuary
than marriage:

> 'But come down to Suffolk for sanity.'
> 'You mean then that I may come alone?'
> 'I won't receive you, I assure you, on any other terms. I want
> to show you', he continued, 'what life *can* give. Not, of course',
> he subjoined, 'of this sort of thing.'
> 'No – you've told me. Of peace.'
> 'Of peace', said Mr Longdon. 'Oh, you don't know – you
> haven't the least idea. That's just why I want to show you.'
> (P. 171.)

There is no question as to whether 'peace', so enticing to an elderly
bachelor, is what 'life' should give to a girl like Nanda or what
it is kind to offer her. Beccles radiates a poetry which can be relied
on to dissolve her tragedy. You only need to live enough to be able
to give life up. Her unrequited love for Van is itself a life – to put
behind her:

> 'It would be easier for me,' he [Mr Longdon] went on heedless,
> 'if you didn't, my poor child, so wonderfully love him.'
> 'Ah, but I don't – please believe me when I assure you I *don't*!'
> she broke out. It burst from her, flaring up, in a queer quaver
> that ended in something queerer still – in her abrupt collapse,
> on the spot, into the nearest chair, where she choked with a
> torrent of tears. Her buried face could only, after a moment, give
> way to the flood, and she sobbed in a passion as sharp and brief
> as the flurry of a wild thing for an instant uncaged. . . . (P. 479.)

It only remains for Mr Longdon to close the cage with comfort and
all is well, 'all passion spent'; Nanda can be as safe in Beccles as
the girl 'in the cage' by her 'sounder'. And this is where the drama
of the book is resolved in lyrical pity; James is quite clear as
to where he wants Nanda to be: 'in'.[28]

The Awkward Age is a novel about communication in which at
the end nothing is left for the heroine to communicate but 'peace'.
It is not the 'peace' which succeeds intense dramatic conflicts

because the novel's drama lies in an elaborate heading-off of dramatic action. The 'ideal society' that transpires is of a severely limited kind – a kind of present nostalgia flows from the quasi father/daughter relationship of Nanda and Mr Longdon. It is not unlike what James's secretary described when she said that his 'Utopia was an anarchy where nobody would be responsible for any human being but only for his own civilised character.'[20] But the pair are still human in their retreat from ordinary humanity. The wistful, elegiac moral glamour that enshrouds them is the quintessential Jamesian emotion released by the ending of this triumph of virtuosity. It has the beauty of a personal, lyric emotion of renunciation which has been exquisitely *dramatised*, not the impersonal emotion generated by meanings held in tension with each other that is experienced in true drama. Nevertheless, the emotion is there in all its purity for us to receive, not submerged by other themes, and the clarity of its bringing out justifies the book's method as the 'architecture' of *The Portrait of a Lady* fails to do. If questions about Nanda and her 'fairy godmother' stay unanswered they also stay in our minds with a touching and intriguing resonance. The impression is of a James who has fathomed his own sensibility more lucidly than he fathomed Isabel Archer's 'fear'. We at least know what we are asked to value in Nanda and our respect for her is not faked or inveigled. This gives the book the truest kind of comic peace of mind that lay within the reach of the excited imagination of Henry James.

This, perhaps, is a good place at which to end – if not conclude. It seems possible to enjoy both *L'Education Sentimentale* and *The Awkward Age*, different and, even, opposed as they are. Both point towards a kind of art in their own and in other authors that lies beyond the scope of this short study. Both suggest that an understanding of James's last novels would need, for fulness, to consider his relation to Flaubert. And both tell us a little about how difficult the nineteenth-century novelists found it to create a real tragic emotion. Beyond that, I prefer to leave the issues which the two writers raise free from the clutch of my critical judgements. As Flaubert was so fond of saying, 'L'ineptie consiste à vouloir conclure'.

Notes

For Flaubert's works I have used *Oeuvres Complètes de Gustave Flaubert* (Conard, Paris, 1926–33), 22 vols. For his letters: *Correspondance de Gustave Flaubert: Nouvelle Edition Augmentée* (Conard, 1926–33), 9 vols., and its *Supplément* in 4 vols., eds. René Dumesnil, Jean Pommier & Claude Digeon (Conard, 1954). For James's novels I refer to *The Novels and Stories of Henry James*, ed. Percy Lubbock (Macmillan, London, 1921–3), 35 vols. This edition contains some works not in the *New York Edition* but follows its text for those which are. All other titles by Flaubert and James are listed separately. Unless otherwise stated, the place of publication for books with titles in English is London and, for books with titles in French, Paris.

PREFACE

1. *Portraits of Places* (1883), pp. 75–6.
2. 'John Ruskin', *Contre Sainte-Beuve précédée de Pastiches et Mélanges et suivi de Essais et Articles*, ed. Pierre Clarac & Ives Sandre (1971), pp. 140–1. (My translation.)
3. *Marginalia to Reynolds's 'Discourses', Poetry and Prose of William Blake*, ed. Geoffrey Keynes (1948), pp. 779–80.
4. 'Les Deux Critiques', *Essais Critiques* (1964), p. 249.
5. *The Art of the Novel: Critical Prefaces by Henry James*, ed. with introd. by R. P. Blackmur (New York, 1962), p. 9.
6. Marius Bewley, *The Complex Fate* (1952), p. 6.
7. *French Poets and Novelists*, 1st ed. 1878 (1884), p. 243.
8. *Selected Letters of Henry James*, ed. Leon Edel (1956), p. 106.
9. I have argued for this view of *Little Dorrit* in 'The Poetry of *Little Dorrit*', *The Cambridge Quarterly*, IV, no. 1 (1968–9), 38–53.

CHAPTER I

1. 'Henry James', *Literary Essays of Ezra Pound*, ed. T. S. Eliot (1954), p. 332.
2. Quoted, from 'The Nation' (1872), in Edel, *Henry James: The Conquest of London, 1870–1883* (1962), p. 30.
3. *Hawthorne* (1879), p. 162.
4. Van Wyck Brooks, *New England: Indian Summer, 1865–1915* (1940), p. 200.
5. Morris Roberts, *Henry James's Criticism* (Cambridge, Mass., 1929), p. 62.
6. *W. W. Story and his Friends*, 2 vols. (1903), II, p. 209.
7. *Selected Letters*, pp. 51–2.
8. *Partial Portraits* (1888), p. 273.
9. *French Poets and Novelists*, pp. 64–5.
10. *Partial Portraits*, p. 214.
11. 'Nana', *The House of Fiction: Essays on the Novel by Henry James*, ed. Edel (1962), p. 279.

12. 'Gustave Flaubert', *Essays in London and Elsewhere* (1893), p. 158.

13. *The Letters of Henry James*, 2 vols., ed. Percy Lubbock (1920), vol. I, pp. 288–9.

14. *Notes on Novelists and Other Notes* (1914), p. 49 & p. 47.

15. *Essays in London*, p. 140.

16. Quoted in Ellen Douglass Leyburn, *Strange Alloy: The Relation of Comedy to Tragedy in the Fiction of Henry James* (Chapel Hill, 1968), p. 169.

17. *Letters*, vol. I, pp. 100–1.

18. *Correspondance de Gustave Flaubert*, vol. I, pp. 199–200.

19. *Oeuvres de Jeunesse Inédites*, 3 vols. (Conard, 1910), vol. I, p. 487.

20. Jean-Paul Sartre, 'Flaubert: Du Poète à l'Artiste', *Les Temps Modernes*, XXII (1966), 240.

21. 'Shakespeare and the Stoicism of Seneca', *Selected Essays* (1963), pp. 131–2.

22. *Flaubert: Correspondance*, ed. Jean Bruneau (Gallimard, 1973), vol. I, p. 431. (The letter is incomplete in Conard.)

23. *Par les Champs et par les Grèves* (Conard, 1910), p. 35.

24. ibid., p. 50.

25. *Chatterton, Oeuvres Complètes d'Alfred de Vigny*, ed. F. Baldensperger, 2 vols. (1948), vol. I, pp. 868–9.

26. 'Flaubert: Du Poète à l'Artiste', 461.

27. Maxime Du Camp, *Souvenirs Littéraires*, 2 vols. (1892), vol. I, p. 165.

28. Marie-Jeanne Durry, *Flaubert et ses Projets Inédits* (1950), p. 106.

29. Edmond & Jules de Goncourt, *Journal: Mémoires de la Vie Littéraire*, ed. Robert Ricatte, 4 vols. (1956), vol. III, p. 46.

30. cf. James's description of Balzac as 'a Tory of the deepest dye. How well, as a rich romancer, he knew what he was about in adopting this profession of faith, will be plain. . . .' *French Poets and Novelists*, p. 83.

31. Quoted by René Dumesnil in *La Vocation de Gustave Flaubert* (1961), p. 250.

32. Rather as Yeats sailed to Byzantium in quest of a union of thought and action.

33. Albert Cassagne, *La Théorie de l'Art pour l'Art en France* (1906), is still very helpful on this aspect of Flaubert. He enables us to see how different the English tradition has been. cf. 'A man who advocates aesthetic effort and deprecates social effort is only likely to be understood by a class to which social effort has become a stale matter.' *The Return of the Native* (1878), Book 3, chapter 2. Hardy's words describe part of what happened to the movement.

34. See Bruneau's commentary to his edition of *Le 'Conte Oriental' de Flaubert* (1973).

35. 'Tragic Philosophy', *Scrutiny*, IV, no. 4 (1936), 375.

36. 'Marbres et Plâtres', *Oeuvres Critiques*, ed. Henri Mitterand, 2 vols. (1968), vol. I, p. 208.

37. See Maurice Blanchot on this in 'Le Tour d'Ecrou', *Le Livre à Venir* (1959), pp. 155–64.

38. For James as a 'pragmatist'' see Bewley, *The Complex Fate*, p. 148 & passim.

39. *Hawthorne*, p. 66.

40. *Art of the Novel*, p. 25.

41. 'Livres d'Aujourd'hui et Demain', *Oeuvres Critiques*, vol. I, p. 919.

42. *Le Roman Naturaliste* (1892), pp. 206–7.

43. *Le Génie de Flaubert* (1913), p. 226.

44. *L'Art Romantique, Oeuvres Complètes de Baudelaire*, ed. Y.-G. Le Dantec (1954), p. 993.

45. *Correspondance: Supplément*, vol. II, pp. 91–2. Taine's questions are on p. 91.

46. 'Tragedy and the "Medium" ', *The Common Pursuit* (1962), p. 126.

47. *Souvenirs Littéraires*, vol. I, p. 238.

48. Caroline de Commanville, 'Souvenirs Intimes', *Correspondance de Gustave Flaubert*, vol. I, p. xxxix.

49. Quoted in Géorg Lukács, *The Historical Novel*, trans. Hannah & Stanley Mitchell (1969), p. 122.

50. *Adam Bede*, chapter 17. Compare Baudelaire on *Madame Bovary*: 'Let us therefore be vulgar in our choice of subject, since the choice of too great a subject is an impertinence for the nineteenth-century reader.' *L'Art Romantique, Oeuvres Complètes*, p. 1007.

51. 'Métaphysique de la Tragédie' (1908), quoted by Lucien Goldmann in *Le Dieu Caché* (1965), p. 10.

52. *The George Eliot Letters*, ed. Gordon Haight, 7 vols. (1954–6), vol. IV, pp. 300–1.

53. *Souvenirs, Notes et Pensées Intimes, 1838–1841*, avant-propos de Lucie Chevalley Sabatier (1965), pp. 71–2.

54. 'The Tragic Theatre', *Essays and Introductions* (1969), p. 243.

CHAPTER 2

1. See Georges-Paul Collet, *George Moore et la France* (1957); Walter Ferguson, *The Influence of Flaubert on George Moore* (Philadelphia, 1934); W. C. Frierson, *L'Influence du Naturalisme Français sur les Romanciers Anglais* (1925); Mary Neale, *Flaubert en Angleterre: Etude sur les Lecteurs Anglais de Flaubert* (Bordeaux, 1966).

2. *The Great Tradition: George Eliot, Henry James, Joseph Conrad* (1962), p. 17. Leavis is exceptionally combative about Flaubert: 'I would without hesitation surrender the whole œuvre of Flaubert for *Dombey and Son*, or *Little Dorrit*.' (*Spectator*, January, 1963.)

3. 'Flaubert, II', *Scrutiny*, XIII (1945–6), 291. Flaubert in fact only believed in either 'la forme' or 'le fond' as inter-dependent; see Charles Carlut, *La Correspondance de Flaubert: Etude et Répertoire Critique* (1968), pp. 390–4, for some relevant quotations.

4. *Partial Portraits*, pp. 319–20.

5. Both remarks are quoted by Edel in *Henry James: The Conquest of London, 1870–1883* (1962), p. 227.

6. For a suggestive discussion of different kinds of pity in tragic drama of the eighteenth and nineteenth centuries, see Raymond Williams, *Modern Tragedy* (1969).

7. *Madame Bovary: Mœurs de Province* (Conard, 1921), p. 94.

8. '*Madame Bovary* par M. G. F.', *Causeries du Lundi*, XVI vols. (1912), XIII, p. 362.

9. 'Count Leo Tolstoi', *Essays in Criticism: Second Series*, vol. IV, p. 203 of *The Works of Matthew Arnold*, XV vols. (1903–4).

10. For a contrast to Arnold, see Charles Du Bos: 'But it's much less of a petrification in question here than of a transfer of the heart to the head . . . and the heart develops new capacities, made all of solidity and no longer of fusion, and reacts in its turn on the mind. . . .' 'Sur le Milieu Intérieur Chez Flaubert', *Approximations* (1965), p. 176.

11. A different account of Flaubert's reading Shakespeare and of James on Flaubert is given in Jonathan Culler's *Flaubert: The Uses of Uncertainty* (1974), pp. 122–34. Culler points out that Flaubert gets the scene number from *King Lear* wrong but I don't think the mistake makes much difference to what he says.

12. *L'Education Sentimentale: Histoire d'un Jeune Homme* (Conard, 1923), p. 266.

13. *Literary Essays*, p. 300.

14. In the essay on Turgenev in *French Poets and Novelists*, James took a similar view of *Uncle Tom's Cabin.* (It is certainly not my case that James's art was 'personal' in the way Harriet Beecher Stowe's was.)

15. *The Historical Novel*, p. 230.

16. 'Gustave Flaubert', *Notes on Novelists*, p. 58. James wrote the essay while working on *The Ambassadors* and it appeared in 1902 when that novel was being serialised. It is one of the major critical pronouncements of the 'major phase'.

17. E.T., *D. H. Lawrence: A Personal Record* (1935), p. 105.

18. See *Mensonge Romantique et Vérité Romanesque* (1961), especially pp. 145–147.

19. 'Beauty out of Place: Flaubert's *Madame Bovary, Eleven Essays in the European Novel* (New York, 1964), p. 57.

20. Leavis gives a cogent defence of this paragraph in 'James as Critic', his introduction to Morris Shapira's *Henry James: Selected Literary Criticism* (1968), pp. 13–24.

21. This recalls M. Dambreuse's reaction to the speech he gets Frédéric to compose: 'He lauded its form, so as not to have to give his opinion on the meaning.' *Education*, p. 431. A critic James read who does more than he does to discuss the meaning was his friend Paul Bourget. The 1902 essay in a more extreme way develops the case of Bourget's Oxford lecture of 1897: 'A Lecture in Oxford: Gustave Flaubert', *The Westminster Review*, LXII, n.s. (1897), 152–64.

22. This arrives by a different route at ideas similar to some of Sartre's; see his fascinating comparison between an actor playing Hamlet and the way the young Flaubert sees his experience from the point of view of Another (i.e. Dr Flaubert): 'Such is Gustave: a receptacle for sentences placed in him by Another, learnt by heart, felt as alienation and therefore believed, he finds himself in a world where Truth is the Other.' *L'Idiot de la Famille*, vol. I, p. 170. The acting analogy runs from p. 166 to p. 175 and is interesting for *Hamlet* too.

23. Vernon Lee's fictional portrait of James seems to me acute on this: '. . . this shrinkingness of nature (which foolish persons call egoism) was the necessary complement to his power of intellectual analysis; and that any departure from the position of dispassionate spectator of the world's follies and miseries would mean also a departure from his real duty as a novelist.' 'Lady Tal', *Vanitas* (1892), p. 53. This is how the young James imagined Flaubert but, for example, Flaubert's letters always show him openly exploring personal emotion *at the same time* as he strives to be a detached artist, much more than James's own, more urbane letters do.

CHAPTER 3

1. Flaubert's conception of Emma crystallised when he changed his original heroine – who was exalted and refined – to a *bourgeoise* who simply wished to be exalted and refined. See the letter of 14 November 1850 to Bouilhet in Bruneau, *Correspondance*, vol. I, p. 708. (Expurgated in Conard.)

2. *Madame Bovary: Nouvelle Version Précédée des Scénarios Inédits*, ed. Jean Pommier & Gabrielle Lelveu (1949), p. 235. In quoting from this edition I follow the editors' practice of italicising everything Flaubert retained in his final text.

3. 'Balzac's Novels', *Hours in a Library*, 3 vols. (1892), vol. I, pp. 231–2.

4. Balzac's emotional facility must have counted for much in James's view of him as the 'master' novelist.

5. 'German Books: Thomas Mann', *Phoenix: The Posthumous Papers of D. H. Lawrence*, ed. Edward D. McDonald (1936, 1970), p. 312.

6. For the opposite view, see the essay on *Madame Bovary* in Michael Black, *The Literature of Fidelity* (1975). For Renan on Homais, see *Souvenirs d'Enfance et de Jeunesse* (1883), chapter 3.

7. *Phoenix*, p. 226.

8. Flaubert and Hardy are both typical of their time in the way they let a penchant for tragic plotting distract them from their own most authentic tragic feeling.

9. 'I practise literature for my own sake, like a bourgeois turning serviette rings in his attic.' (*Corr.*, VI, p. 276.)

10. I am indebted to the discussion of tragedy and impersonality in I. A. Richards, *Principles of Literary Criticism* (1960), pp. 245–53.

11. Like the landscape, the 'technique' of *style indirect libre* seems to absorb Emma's words and feelings without echoing them. By robbing her of her voice Flaubert entrenches her more deeply in her world, though this does make her voice more resonant when it is heard. The narrative perhaps deprives her of a voice so that, at moments, she may find one.

12. Though the image perhaps feels superimposed on what it describes. This is a common complaint against Flaubert's style; see the Goncourts *Journal* for 16 January 1884, Murry in *Countries of the Mind* and Proust, 'A Propos du Style de Flaubert', *Contre Sainte-Beuve etc.*, pp. 586–600.

13. See *L'Idiot de la Famille*, vol. II, pp. 1275–92 for a brilliant attack on Flaubert for dehumanising Emma and Léon in this scene. Sartre is ruthless in making the novel serve his analysis of its author. His insight and invention feel too much of a *tour de force* because of his blind spots. He is so up in arms at Flaubert's cruelty to Emma that he misses the fact that she is held at a distance as a control on his anguished sympathy for her. Sartre's own sympathy for Emma feels factitious because it is there to further his pitiless moral denunciations of her creator. He is also very liable to get irritated at Flaubert's vein of compassion and pathos.

14. Thibaudet finely observed: 'Each time that Emma is purely sensual, he speaks of her with a delicate and almost religious emotion, as Milton speaks of Eve; he drops the impassive or ironic tone and abandons himself to that music by which an author assumes his character and takes it as a substitute for himself.' *Gustave Flaubert* (1922), p. 102.

15. 'Nature, humanisme, tragédie', *Pour un Nouveau Roman* (1967), p. 66.

16. For a profound discussion of 'la stupeur' – and its relation to 'la rêverie'

– in Flaubert, see Du Bos, *Approximations*, p. 168. See also *L'Education Sentimentale*, p. 459 for a similarly pointed use of 'impassible'.

17. cf. Thibaudet, 'There can be no novel of fate or destiny save where there is an absence of will-power. And this is so in Emma's case.' *Gustave Flaubert*, p. 107. (Though this assumes that she does not want to die at the end.)

18. 'La Création de la Forme chez Flaubert', *Littérature et Sensation* (1954), p. 160.

19. Brombert is interesting on the way a sense of tragedy precedes actual tragedy in Flaubert, though he is too seduced by the 'death of tragedy' notion. See *The Novels of Gustave Flaubert* (Princeton, New Jersey, 1966).

20. This is corroborated by Flaubert's unusual method of composition in which the scenarios for the plot came before the actual writing. He was programming himself as well as Emma. The most recent text of the scenarios is in *Oeuvres Complètes de Gustave Flaubert* (Club de l'Honnête Homme, 1971), vol. I.

CHAPTER 4

1. *Le Problème du Style* (1902), p. 104.

2. The one person Emma doesn't see through is Homais who neither delights nor horrifies her as he does Flaubert. Hence Faguet's slick witticism: 'The misfortune of Mme Bovary is not to have married M. Homais.' *Flaubert* (1899), p. 90.

3. 'Daniel Deronda: A Conversation', *Partial Portraits*, p. 89.

4. A character in *Le Candidat*, Flaubert's political play, says at one point, 'the months run away, the surrounding mediocrity penetrates you, and one arrives quietly at resignation, that tranquil form of despair'. *Théâtre de Gustave Flaubert* (Conard, 1927), p. 90.

5. *Collected Letters of D. H. Lawrence*, ed. Harry T. Moore, 2 vols. (1962), vol. I, p. 150.

6. '*Mastro-Don Gesualdo*, by Giovanni Verga', *Phoenix*, pp. 225–6.

7. He surely mars his account by relating Flaubert (of all people!) to the 'emotional-democratic, treasure-of-the-humble period of the nineteenth century'. *Phoenix*, p. 226. What did he make of Homais? (*The Treasure of the Humble* is a play by Maeterlinck.)

8. *Phoenix*, p. 409.

9. See Eugene Goodheart, 'English Social Criticism and the Spirit of Reformation', *Clio*, V, no. 1 (1975), 73–95. He argues for seeing Lawrence in the protestant tradition of Carlyle, Ruskin and Arnold which he opposes (a little patly) to the more catholic tradition of Art for Art.

10. *Phoenix*, pp. 409–10.

11. 'Preface to *Touch and Go*', *Phoenix II* (1970), p. 291.

12. See Leo Bersani's *Balzac to Beckett: Centre and Circumference in French Fiction* (O.U.P., New York, 1970). He argues that Flaubert's work is essentially an attack on imagination and contrasts it both with James and Proust who give 'Imaginative versions of reality'. (p. 191.)

13. *Death in Venice*, trans. H. T. Lowe-Porter (1928, 1971), p. 32.

14. *The Great Tradition*, p. 17.

15. *Essays in London*, p. 157.

16. *The Great Tradition*, p. 181.

17. The catholic Charles Du Bos writes of James, 'I came more and more to see him as without spiritual, religious or metaphysical content, *untouched by all the inner moral dramas: his whole, his tremendous moral power belonging to the world of standards, of taste, always in fine of art.*' *Journal*, 9 vols. (1946–61), vol. I, p. 251. (Italics for Du Bos' own English.)

18. *Phoenix*, p. 415.

19. *Phoenix*, p. 419.

20. Poetry for Flaubert is less something discovered in the world, as it is for Wordsworth, than something taken out of it: 'In the past people thought sugar came only from sugar cane. Nowadays it is taken from virtually everything; the same thing applies to poetry. Let us extract it no matter where, for it lies in everything and everywhere: there is not an atom of matter which does not contain thought; and let us get used to considering the world as a work of art whose processes we must reproduce in our works.' *Corr.*, III, p. 138.

21. Like Flaubert Emma becomes a devotee of the Marquis de Sade (p. 399). See a tale like Sade's *Courval et Florville ou le Fatalisme.*

22. cf. Bersani: Flaubert 'saves his most poetic effects for the dismissal of words'. (p. 180.)

23. At Emma's only visit to Binet, at the end of the novel, he seems a parody of the impassive artist, 'lost at last in one of those complete joys that no doubt belong only to mean occupations, which amuse the intelligence by easy difficulties and satisfy it in a realisation beyond which there is nothing left to dream.' (p. 422.)

24. 'You call me "the brahmin". It is too great an honour but I would certainly like to be one.' *Corr.*, I, p. 427.

25. Emma gives Rodolphe an amulet inscribed *amor nel cor* (p. 264) which corresponds exactly to one Louise gave Flaubert. There is another parallel in the hotel meetings of both the real and the fictional lovers.

26. *Journal*, 28 January 1878, vol. II, pp. 1221–2. For Koutchouk-Hanem see Auriant, *Koutchouk-Hanem, l'Almée de Flaubert, suivis de onze essais sur la vie de Flaubert et sur son œuvre* (1943).

27. See the way Flaubert distinguishes 'pity' and 'sympathy': 'I want to have neither love, nor hate, nor pity, nor anger. As for sympathy, that is different: one never has enough of it.' *Corr.*, V, p. 397.

CHAPTER 5

1. *Tamburlaine*, part 1, act V, scene i.

2. 'Tragedy and the "Medium" ', *The Common Pursuit* (1969), p. 128 & p. 129.

3. 'One could define tragedy as a universe of agonising questions to which man has no answer.' Goldmann, *Le Dieu Caché*, p. 52 n.

4. '*The Europeans*', '*Anna Karenina*' and Other Essays (1967), p. 73.

5. *The Great Tradition*, p. 157.

6. See the essay on Daudet in *Partial Portraits*, pp. 198–9, for an example.

7. *Approximations*, p. 167.

8. But Rodolphe is just the type Emma would like, a kind of French Grandcourt. His cold arrogance promises the sort of brutal sex she would not have found with her over-kind husband or the feminine Léon. Birds of a feather? Some of Flaubert's cruder letters show the Rodolphe in himself, e.g. the im-

portant discussion of love and art sent to Louise on 30 April 1847, *Corr.*, II, pp. 19–22.

9. See *Contre Sainte-Beuve*, p. 269, for similar points.

10. At the end of *Salammbô* Flaubert says of the flayed Mâtho: 'Apart from his eyes, he no longer had a human appearance . . .' (Conard), pp. 412. See Lawrence on this scene's disgustingness, *Phoenix II*, pp. 417–17.

11. *Journal*, 26 February 1973, vol. II, p. 927.

12. From the 1845 *Education Sentimentale*, *Oeuvres de Jeunesse Inédites*, vol. III, p. 151.

13. 'Introduction to *Mastro-don Gesualdo* by Giovanni Verga', *Phoenix II*, pp. 281–2. (This is a different essay from the one with a similar title in *Phoenix*.)

14. *Bouvard et Pécuchet, œuvre posthume* (Conard, 1923), p. 294.

15. *Countries of the Mind*, 1st series (1921), p. 170.

16. *Phoenix*, p. 308.

17. 'This book, which exists only through style, has style itself as a continual danger.' *Corr.*, IV, p. 16.

18. *The Novels of Flaubert*, p. 245.

19. *Trois Contes* (Conard, 1921), p. 51.

20. In a letter to Flaubert, cited in Conard, *Trois Contes*, p. 220.

21. *Contre Sainte-Beuve*, p. 587.

22. cf. an 1875 entry in Hardy's notebooks: 'Reading the Life of Goethe. Schlegel says that "the deepest want and deficiency of all modern art lies in the fact that artists have no mythology".' *The Notebook of Thomas Hardy*, ed. Evelyn Hardy (1955), p. 51.

23. As Georg Brandes did: 'The story seems rather adapted to the public of the thirteenth century, or to polished connoisseurs, than to ordinary modern readers.' *Creative Spirits of the Nineteenth Century* (1924), p. 257. Yet the medieval world of the tale betrays no feeling of reconstruction as *Salammbô* does.

24. *La Légende de Saint Julien l'Hospitalier, Trois Contes*, p. 113.

25. The one major change Flaubert made in the legend was to turn the leper from an angel into Christ. The text of the legend, as told by Saint Antonin, is given in Marcel Schwob's *Spicilège* (1896), p. 112.

26. Baudelaire, 'La Beauté, *Les Fleurs du Mal*. (My translation.)

CHAPTER 6

1. Preface to *Roderick Hudson, The Art of the Novel*, p. 5.

2. A more cogent critique of the James 'cult' is Martin Green's 'Henry James and the Great Tradition', *Re-Appraisals: Some Commonsense Readings in American Literature* (1963), pp. 144–66.

3. See Michael Egan, *Henry James: The Ibsen Years* (1972); Philip Grover, *Henry James and the French Literary Mind* (1973); Lyall H. Powers, *Henry James and the Naturalist Movement* (Michigan State U.P., 1971). (The point made here is developed in my review of Egan in *The New Edinburgh Review*, no. 21 (1973), 30–2.)

4. *French Poets and Novelists*, p. 206.

5. *The American Henry James* (Rutgers U.P., 1957), p. 198.

6. *The Houses that James Built, and Other Literary Studies* (Michigan State U.P., 1964), p. 14. The passage in *Madame Bovary* Stallman refers to is on pp. 271–2.

7. *The Portrait of a Lady*, 2 vols., vol. I, pp. 207–8.

8. Dorothea Krook, *The Ordeal of Consciousness in Henry James* (1962), p. 13.

9. D. W. Jefferson, *Henry James* (1960), p. 36.

10. *Partial Portraits*, p. 89.

11. *Henry James: The Critical Heritage*, ed. Roger Gard (1968), p. 129. Howells is supported by James's *Notebooks*: 'The obvious criticism of course will be that it is not finished – that I have not seen the heroine to the end of her situation – that I have left her *en l'air*. This is both true and false. The *whole* of anything is never told; you can only take what groups together. What I have done has that unity – it groups together.' p. 18.

12. *Critical Heritage*, p. 93.

13. *The Great Tradition*, p. 125.

14. Reprinted in *The House of Fiction*, pp. 77–8.

15. The novel was much revised for the New York edition and it is that text which is quoted here. Important changes, from my point of view, were that Isabel's 'fear' was made clearer and James's affection for her deepened. A good essay on the revisions is F. O. Mattheissen's in *Henry James: The Major Phase* (New York, 1963), pp. 152–86.

16. On one occasion Osmond sees her as an 'apparition' (I, p. 348).

17. For an account of the term *ficelle* see the remarks on Henrietta and Maria Gostrey (in *The Ambassadors*) in *The Art of the Novel*: 'Each of these persons is but wheels to the coach; neither belongs to the body of that vehicle, or is for a moment accommodated with a seat inside. There the subject alone is ensconced. . . .' (p. 54.) This subordination gives James less light to shed on his 'subject'. Strether's relation to Maria becomes more functional than dramatic.

18. I owe the idea of this comparison to an excellent article by J. M. Newton, 'Isabel Archer's Spiritual Disease and Henry James's', *The Cambridge Quarterly*, II, no. 1 (1966), 3–22. I have a large general debt to this article. My own case is in many ways similar to it, though I think Newton is perhaps too close to the task of arguing against Leavis to be charitable enough to James or Isabel or to avoid making the novel more amenable to his objections than it always is.

19. *Middlemarch*, chapter 29.

20. *The Major Phase*, p. 183.

21. *The Eccentric Design: Form in the Classic American Novel* (New York, 1963), p. 238.

22. Later (II, p. 116), Isabel also tells Warburton that he ought to marry and then bites her lip as she does here.

23. I cannot agree to the odd compliment Leavis pays Ralph: 'He has a central position, and can place everyone.' *The Great Tradition*, p. 166. He can't 'place' himself. James never explains why his relations with Madame Merle become strained nor why Osmond dislikes him so much. Perhaps this is because he is central though it makes him seem like a *ficelle*.

24. *The Opposing Self: Nine Essays in Criticism* (1955), p. 90.

25. 'The Fearful Self: Henry James's *The Portrait of a Lady*', *The Critical Quarterly*, VII (1965), 212–14.

26. One sign that this use of Henrietta as a mouthpiece for common-sense is exceptional is that the Henrietta of this passage is far too acute to have pressed Goodwood's claims on Isabel as the Henrietta of the rest of the novel does.

CHAPTER 7

1. *Modern Painters, vol. IV, The Works of John Ruskin*, ed. E. T. Cook and Alexander Wedderburn, 39 vols. (1903–12), vol. VI, pp. 19–22.
2. ibid., p. 23.
3. 'Italy Revisited', *Portraits of Places*, p. 68.
4. *Tragedy is Not Enough*, trans. Harald A. T. Reiche, Harry T. Moore and Karl W. Deutsch (1953), p. 75.
5. James gratuitously mentions that the Countess Gemini has had three children who have all died young (I, p. 356).
6. His coldness, odious in marriage, is an attraction in courtship: 'Contentment, on his part, took no vulgar form; excitement in the most self-conscious of men, was a kind of ecstasy of self-control. This disposition, however, made him an admirable lover. . . .' (II, p. 68.)
7. 'Maule's Well or Henry James and the relation of morals to manners', *In Defense of Reason* (Denver U.P., 1947), p. 332.
8. All we know about Osmond and Madame Merle as lovers comes from the Countess in chapter 51. Isabel pities Madame Merle when she finds out that she is Pansy's mother but James takes care not to let the pity get out of hand: it is made clear that Pansy loves Isabel and dislikes Madame Merle. (II, pp. 337–8.)
9. *The Novelist's Responsibility* (1967), pp. 121–2.
10. Virginia Woolf has a good description of this kind of pathos; she speaks of James's 'gesture as of one shrinking from the sight of distress, combined with an irresistible instinct of pity drawing him again and again to its presence. . . .' *The Death of the Moth, and Other Essays* (1943), p. 85.
11. *Tragedy is Not Enough*, p. 88.
12. *Oeuvres Complètes de Montaigne*, ed. Albert Thibaudet & Maurice Rat (1962), p. 16. (My translation.)
13. For an interesting discussion of this passage, see Q. D. Leavis, 'A Note on Literary Indebtedness: Dickens, George Eliot, Henry James', *Hudson Review*, VIII (1955), 423–8.
14. *The Lion and the Honeycomb: Essays in Solicitude and Critique* (1956), p. 276.
15. Quoted by Edel, *Henry James: The Treacherous Years, 1895–1900* (1969), p. 304.
16. ibid., p. 331.
17. 'Lettre à Charles Du Bos', *Nouvelle Revue Française*, XXXIII (1929), 762.

CHAPTER 8

1. *Literary Essays*, p. 289.
2. *Notes on Novelists*, p. 66.
3. 'The Ambiguity of Henry James', *The Triple Thinkers* (1962), p. 117.
4. 'Préface', *Lettres de Gustave Flaubert à George Sand* (1884), p. xxi.
5. 'Flaubert et la Bêtise Humaine', *Promenades Littéraires*, 7 vols. (1912–29), vol. IV, p. 206. For a good discussion of Gourmont on Flaubert, see G. R. Strickland, 'Flaubert, Pound and Eliot', *The Cambridge Quarterly*, II, no. 3 (1967), 242–63.

6. Du Bos called the novel, 'A book of which a first reading is by definition a let-down but which, once one has begun to give oneself up to its movement, never ceases to deepen its hold on us.' *Approximations*, p. 181.

7. 'A Tragic Novel', *Cosmopolis*, VII (1897), 55.

8. ibid., p. 46.

9. *L'Education Sentimentale*, p. 462.

10. 'The Politics of Flaubert', *The Triple Thinkers*, p. 95.

11. *The Princess Casamassima*, 2 vols. (first published 1886), vol. I, p. 149.

12. 'The Princess Casamassima', *The Liberal Imagination: Essays on Literature and Society* (1951), p. 83.

13. Trilling tries to see Hyacinth as the hero of an Hegelian type of tragedy but he seems to foist the theory onto the novel. Hyacinth is much more the sort of unrepresentative individual hero that Williams sees as typical of nineteenth-century 'liberal tragedy' in his *Modern Tragedy*.

14. Lyall H. Powers, in *Henry James and the Naturalist Movement*, sees the novel's clash of character and environment as deriving from James's interest in Zola and his group in the 1880s. This makes Hyacinth simpler than he really is.

15. Grover, op. cit., compares the two novels, to James's advantage, on pp. 92–107.

16. Williams elaborates this idea in his discussion of James in *The English Novel from Dickens to Lawrence* (1974).

17. Flaubert's preoccupation with failure is interestingly treated by Paul Bourget in the essay on Turgenev in *Essais de Psychologie Contemporaine* (1884). Bourget was a great admirer of Stendhal.

18. The story of Flaubert's love for Madame Schlésinger is told, rather romantically, by Gérard-Gailly in *Le Grand Amour de Flaubert* (1944).

19. Quoted by Edel, *Henry James: The Master* (1972), p. 367.

20. *The Complete Tales of Henry James*, ed. Edel, 12 vols. (1961–4), vol. X, p. 139.

21. cf. a James letter of 1899: 'Thank God, however, I've no *opinions* –not even on the Dreyfus case. I'm more and more only aware of things as a more or less mad panorama, phantasmagoria, and dime museum.' *Letters*, vol. I, p. 318.

22. *Letters*, vol. II, p. 437.

23. From *Vanity Fair* for 1924, quoted by Krook, op. cit., p. 2.

24. Edel, *The Treacherous Years*, p. 101. Note how much this view confirms the James of Vernon Lee in *Lady Tal*.

25. *The Art of the Novel*, p. 116.

26. *The Awkward Age* (1922), p. 110.

27. *Literary Essays*, p. 325.

28. A useful contrast to *The Awkward Age* is Henry Green's *Party Going* (1939). This apparently Jamesian comedy of high life, also a dialogue novel, does not let its own brand of mannered brio soften its darker insights. The equivalent of Mr Longdon, Miss Fellowes, falls ill just as the party is due to begin. She is less comfortingly elderly and reminds us of a death that is to come, not a past that has faded without decay.

29. Theodora Bosanquet, *Henry James at Work* (1924), p. 33.

Index

Works are included under their respective authors